Lumber Baron of the Comstock Lode

Other Books by Jack Harpster

The Curious Life of Nevada's LaVere Redfield: The Silver Dollar King
Captive! The Story of David Ogden and the Iroquois (With Ken Stalter)
King of the Slots: William "Si" Redd
The Railroad Tycoon Who Built Chicago: A Biography of William B. Ogden
100 Years in the Nevada Governor's Mansion
Helping Hands, Helping Hearts: The Story of Opportunity Village
John Ogden, the Pilgrim (1609-1682): A Man of More Than Ordinary Mark

LUMBER BARON
OF THE COMSTOCK LODE

The Life & Times of Duane L. Bliss

Jack Harpster

AHP
American History Press

Copyright © 2015 Jack Harpster

All rights reserved. No part of this book may be transmitted in any form by any means electronic, mechanical or otherwise using devices now existing or yet to be invented without prior written permission from the publisher and copyright holder.

American History Press

Staunton, Virginia
(888) 521-1789
Visit us on the Internet at:
www.Americanhistorypress.com

ISBN 13: 978-1-939995-10-0

Library of Congress Control Number: 2015934032

Manufactured in the United States of America on acid-free paper. This book meets all ANSI standards for archival quality.

Table of Contents

List of Illustrations	ix
Acknowledgments	xi
Foreword by Ronald M. James	xiii
Chapter 1. A Voyage of Self Discovery	1
Chapter 2. The Isthmus Over	7
Chapter 3. Gold! The California Years	13
Chapter 4. The Comstock Lode	27
Chapter 5. The Banker's Wife	45
Chapter 6. The Bank Ring	57
Chapter 7. The Virginia & Truckee Railroad	67
Chapter 8. The Carson & Tahoe Lumber & Fluming Company	81
Chapter 9. Boom and Bust	93
Chapter 10. Building a Lumbering Monolith	101
Chapter 11. The End of an Era	121
Chapter 12. Becoming a Conservationist	133
Chapter 13. The Grand Old Man of Lake Tahoe	149
Chapter 14. Innkeepers to the World	159
Chapter 15. A Life Well Lived	167
Afterword	177
Notes	179
Bibliography	199
Index	209
About the Author	221

List of Illustrations

Early nineteenth century Berkshire County mill	2
"The Way to California" drawing	9
San Francisco Bay, 1850	16
Woodside Store, Woodside, CA	21
Virginia City, Utah Territory, 1860	28
Gold Hill, Utah Territory, 1860	30
Duane L. Bliss, c. 1865	35
Deidesheimer square-set timbering system	41
Alamarin B. Paul & Company Bankers advertisement, 1863	47
Devils Gate on the Comstock, 1860	53
Quartz mills at Gold Hill, 1865	64
Freight wagons on the Comstock, 1868	71
Engine #4, Virginia & Truckee Railroad, crossing a trestle	87
Lumber mill #1, Carson & Tahoe Lumber & Fluming Company, Glenbrook, NV	90
Summit Logging Camp, 1883	94
Lake Tahoe map of D. L. Bliss's business interests, 1870-1907	96
Wicked Slaughterhouse Canyon switchback	102
Lake Tahoe Railroad hauls lumber up the western slope of the Sierra	111
Carson & Tahoe Lumber & Fluming Company's steamer Meteor	113
Carson & Tahoe Lumber & Fluming Company lumber storage yard, Carson City, NV	114
Bliss Mansion, Carson City, NV	117
Lake Valley Railroad, Bijou, CA	123
Bliss summer home, Glenbrook, NV, early 1890s	127

Duane L. Bliss and daughter Hope at Comstock mine, 1890s	128
Stagecoach on new road at Point of Rocks, Lake Tahoe, 1863	130
Hetch Hetchy Valley, California	134
Duane and Elizabeth Bliss, 1890s	151
Steamship SS *Tahoe*, "The Queen of the Lake"	153
Lake Tahoe Railway, Truckee, CA, late 1890s	156
Wharf at the Tahoe Tavern resort	160
Tahoe Tavern, 1911	162
Glenbrook Inn & Ranch, Glenbrook, NV, early 1900s	166
Duane L. Bliss, 1906	168
Three generations of Bliss men, 1920s	173

Acknowledgments

There are always a large number of people and organizations that assist in making a book come alive. The author gets all the credit, but he never does it alone.

First and foremost, I'd like to thank William "Bill" Bliss, the great grandson of Duane Leroy Bliss, without whom this book would still be just a loose pile of half-written pages. Bill co-authored a book about the Bliss family that was published by the University of Nevada Press in 1992, so he was no stranger to the process. But this earlier book delved more into the later generations of the Bliss family, particularly their deep involvement in the Lake Tahoe community. So Bill was as interested as I was in learning about the many adventures of his famous great-grandfather that had not been covered adequately or accurately in that previous work. Over the years Bill has also contributed the family's business records—dating back to Nevada's pre-statehood days—to the University of Nevada's Special Collections Department, and without those voluminous manuscripts, photos, maps, ledgers and ephemera, this story could not have been told.

A special thanks also goes out to the helpful staff at the Special Collections Department, University of Nevada Mathewson-IGT Knowledge Center, headed by the capable Donnelyn Curtis, whose expertise in finding just what I needed every time was invaluable. With their help, and with the broad and diverse works held in this wonderful library, my task was eased considerably. The professionals at our Nevada Historical Society library, headed by Michael Maher, also came through for me, as they always have. The collections at the Society are unbelievably broad and deep, and the experienced staff doesn't just help when asked, they ask to help. They are wonderful folks to work with.

So many individuals also came through for me, but a few deserve special recognition. Ronald M. James—academic, historian, preservationist, author—and one of the country's foremost experts on the Comstock and its people, kindly agreed to write the Foreword for this work, for which I

Acknowledgements

am most appreciative. Ellen St. Sure, a great granddaughter of D. L. Bliss, provided valuable assistance as I tried to put the Bliss family genealogy in order, and Gwenda Elin Gustafson, an expert on the family's early roots, was also a great help. Thank you, ladies.

Finally, I must recognize the diverse help and support of a most unusual group of men and women that I've been fortunate enough to become part of. The "Never Sweats" are a jovial, fun-loving group of top-notch Nevada historians, writers, editors, scholars, hale-fellows-well-met, and merry pontificators who, individually and as a group, have pointed me in the right direction many times—and occasionally, in the wrong direction—as I've slaved over this manuscript. The Never Sweats' spiritual inspiration comes from Nevada's most famous—or infamous, he would claim—citizen—a young Samuel Clements—who once said something that could serve as the unofficial credo of the group: "Good friends, good books and a sleepy conscience: this is the ideal life."

Jack Harpster
Reno, Nevada
April 2015

Foreword

The great Comstock Lode, discovered in 1859, became famous in the annals of history for its wealth and for the invention or early use of many examples of new technologies. What is often forgotten is that the mining district also became the prototype for how to build an infrastructure to support a remote mining community. Whether in Colorado, South Africa, or Australia, underground excavations looked like those of the Comstock for the next half-century. But the strategies to import needed materials also gained a great deal from approaches developed in Nevada.

It's easy to focus on mines and wealth, but supplies are critical – indeed some are essential – to the success of an isolated excavation. Lumber was one of those materials. Without millions of feet of lumber to construct the newly developed square-set timbering, mining on the Comstock would not have been possible. It was vital that entrepreneurs arrived at a means to harvest the ancient forests of the Sierra, mill the logs, and bring the wood east to the mines.

D. L. Bliss was one those critical players who made the success of the Comstock possible. His role—and the part played by others like him—allowed for the installation of square-sets needed to excavate roughly seven hundred miles of underground tunneling beneath the Comstock communities. Jack Harpster describes the three indispensable industries—mining, milling, and lumbering—that depended on one another in a symbiotic relationship. Indeed, that was the case. Many types of supplies were needed for mining and to feed and clothe a community, but wood was at the heart of the mines.

History remembers the names of John Mackay, James Fair, William Sharon, and William Ralston as the silver barons and financiers who brought today's equivalent of billions of dollars in precious metals to the

Foreword

world. But D. L. Bliss was no less important. Without his lumber, none of the fame and fortune enjoyed by others would have been possible.

Ronald M. James

Mr. James is the executive director of the Comstock Foundation for History and Culture and serves as adjunct faculty in historic preservation at the University of Nevada, Reno. He was the administrator of Nevada's State Historic Preservation Office for three decades. He has written, co-written and edited twelve books on history, folklore, and archaeology, including The Roar and the Silence: A History of Virginia City and the Comstock Lode; Comstock Women: The Making of a Mining Community; *and* The Gold Rush Letters of E. Allen Grosh *and* Hosea B. Grosh.

CHAPTER 1

A Voyage of Self Discovery

Duane Leroy Bliss was born on June 10, 1833 in Savoy, a small town nestled in the Berkshire Hills of western Massachusetts. He was the first and only child of William Bliss and Lucia Mary (Barney) Bliss, also Savoy natives. Duane represented the ninth generation of the Bliss family in America. His great (7) grandfather, Thomas Bliss (1588-1647), a blacksmith, had arrived in the New World in about 1638 from the hamlet of Preston Parva in Northamptonshire, England. The Bliss family and its many branches is one of the oldest and most enduring family lines in the United States, and they were pioneers during the founding of Savoy.[1]

The area that encompassed the Berkshire Hills was a beautiful land, covered in groves of forests. Small streams meandered through the hilly terrain and fed into three rivers that flowed through the surrounding valleys. By the 1830s the Berkshire Hills town of Savoy had evolved into a collection of six small villages: The Brier, Spruce Corner, New State, Savoy Center, The Tannery, and Savoy Hollow. The latter—located in the southern end of the town—had developed into the commercial center, with two hotels, two stores, two churches and a number of small businesses, all surrounded by homes and small farms. It had also become a logging center, with six sawmills in operation in addition to a number of Savoy stills busy distilling hemlock spruce oil that was used in salves and linaments.[2]

One description of the town of Savoy in the early nineteenth century noted that in order to get by, a man had to have many talents. Savoy historian Jane Benedict Phinney's description of Duane's father, William Bliss, paints a perfect word portrait of such a versatile Berkshire Hills man: "William Bliss was a cabinet maker, a carpenter, a sleigh and wagon builder, a wheelwright, a glazier, a knife sharpener, a clock man, a livery man, a merchant and a coffin maker. He was a 'jack of all trades', and a very good one. From 1830 to 1874, he kept precise records of his work and the people he did business with."[3]

The Yale-Duryea mill in the bucolic Berkshire Hills of western Massachusetts, shown here, was built in 1823, a decade before Duane Bliss was born in nearby Savoy. Duane was a member of the ninth generation of the Bliss family in America. (Library of Congress)

William operated a small mercantile with an adjoining workshop on Main Road in Savoy Hollow, where most of Savoy's commercial district congregated. The Bowker Hotel was the most important building in the

Chapter 1. A Voyage of Self Discovery

village, and it had many stalls or small stores both inside the building or just outside on its perimeter. One of those was William Bliss's store and workshop.[4] William was a hard-working man, and his meticulous records of sales and activities provide a unique look into mid-nineteenth century small town America. During any average period, William's jobs may have looked like this:

> *...turning one set of bedstead posts; working on...a washing machine; varnishing stands; killing a calf; mending a wagon; patching and plastering; setting glass in school house; mending and painting butter box; caseing window; fixing [a] yoke; [making] coffin for child; making a barn door; fixing stable floor; filing a saw; fixing 2 compasses; killing and butchering a sheep.*[5]

Duane was raised as an only child, unusual in the day, probably a result of his mother's poor health. All of his forebears on both sides of the family had been intelligent, honest, hard working and self-reliant people; and all of those positive attributes were passed on to the young boy.

It is likely that Duane began his education at one of the public schools in Savoy, which had been established in 1797 with an $80 budget granted by the town council. In 1843, when Duane was ten years old, Drury Academy, a private school, was founded in the nearby town of North Adams with a $3,000 grant from the estate of local farmer Nathan Drury. Recognizing their son's potential, Duane's parents enrolled him in the new co-ed academy. There were seventy-five male students and fifty-five female students enrolled in the school's first term, and classes were offered in English, grammar, arithmetic, algebra, French, drawing, and piano, among other subjects. Duane would complete his formal education at Drury Academy three years later, at age thirteen, by which time the bright youngster had learned all that the local schools had to teach him.[6] This was evidenced by the fact that he would be hired only a few years later, while still a teenager, to teach in one of the Savoy public schools.

Hope Bliss, Duane's daughter, wrote a brief biographical sketch about her father following his death. In it she documented his education and his strong attachment to his mother: "...with the careful teaching of his very intellectual...mother, he progressed rapidly into boyhood and he was able with unusual intelligence to absorb his daily difficult tasks; and, this partly because he was inspired by the constant companionship of this mother, whom he so adored." Hope also noted of her father's studies that "...he was almost a prodigy in mathematics."[7]

The primary reason why young Duane left school at the young age of thirteen was that he suffered a great emotional loss at that time. Savoy historian Phinney noted that the town was inexplicably hit by a series of devastating illnesses and plagues during the second quarter of the nineteenth century: "Dysentery, Small Pox, Consumption, Influenza, all killers," she noted in her town history. Duane's father, the town coffin maker, was kept inordinately busy during this period, according to his meticulously-kept business records. "Over a period of thirteen years, the records of William Bliss show a total of one hundred and six coffins made by him," Phinney wrote.[8]

Bliss likely constructed one of those coffins for his own wife, and Duane's beloved mother, Lucia Mary Bliss, who passed away on April 6, 1846 at only thirty-six years of age. Perhaps inured by all the death surrounding him, William Bliss recovered rather quickly, re-marrying less than one-and-one-half years later. His second wife was Eliza S. (Bates) Bliss, forty years old and daughter of Savoy resident and War of 1812 veteran Dexter B. Bates.[9]

We can only imagine the impact his mother's death had on young Duane. He was "grief-stricken," according to his daughter Hope's biographical sketch. To make matters worse, his father's hasty romance and re-marriage caused Duane to feel unwanted at home. Ignoring his father, he visited with an aunt, probably his mother's sister, Deborah Barney. He asked her permission to "run away" to New York to stay with an uncle, his father's younger brother Newell Bliss. Newell's wife had died in 1848 while he was running a dry goods shop in the Berkshire County village of Pittsfield. He had subsequently sold the store and moved to New York City, where he had entered the clothing business.[10]

Gaining permission from his aunt, Duane set out for New York City. Despite the young teenager's grief, he seems to have inherited his ancestors' lust for adventure and discovery, enflamed, perhaps, by the exciting times in which he was growing up. The second quarter of the nineteenth century was an exceptional period in world history, particularly in America. It was an age of scientific discovery, a time when scientists and naturalists were reaching far beyond their own borders to learn more about the world around them. Included in this movement were Englishman Charles Darwin and his HMS Beagle expeditions that spent years studying the biology, geology and anthropology of South America and the South Pacific; American explorer and writer John Lloyd Stephens and his discoveries and writings about the

Chapter 1. A Voyage of Self Discovery

Mayan civilization in Mesoamerica; and U.S. Navy Lieutenant Charles Wilkes and his United States Exploring Expedition of the South Seas (now known as the Pacific Ocean). Then there were the newly published works by the dean of tropical field exploration, German naturalist and explorer Baron Alexander von Humboldt, whose earlier voyages of discovery in Central and South America had first suggested the possibility of building a canal to connect the Atlantic and Pacific Oceans.

Many adventuresome young men were also drawn to the works of Herman Melville, an independent-minded New Englander with a roving disposition of his own. As a youth, Melville had signed on as a cabin boy on a ship sailing to Liverpool. In his early books published in the mid-1840s he described and expanded on that adventure, as well as his shipboard exploits in the South Seas. In 1850, about the time young Duane Bliss would leave home permanently to follow his own wanderlust, Melville moved to the nearby Berkshire town of Pittsfield. His early writings would be a catalyst for many young men in that area to take to the high seas. We can only speculate that Duane Bliss may have been among that number who had been influenced by Melville's writings.

One day, after arriving in New York City, Duane wandered down to the city's busy wharves. Hundreds of majestic sailing ships, smoke-belching steamers, and ungainly fishing skiffs bobbed in the swells or bustled from place to place in New York Harbor. Duane was instantly and thoroughly captivated. He approached a kindly-looking captain whose sailing ship was being loaded with supplies, and asked if he needed a cabin boy. Something in the demeanor of the young boy must have impressed the captain, and he told Duane that with the proper adult permissions—which Duane quickly obtained from his uncle, Newell Bliss—he could join the crew for their upcoming six-month voyage to South America.[11]

The captain—whose name and exact seagoing destination were never revealed in the Bliss family papers—got more than he had bargained for in his young cabin boy. With his superb mathematical skills, Duane was able to assist the captain in navigating by longitude and latitude, rather than celestially, and in return the captain taught Duane the rudiments of astronomy. The trip was so beneficial to both parties that Duane was offered a second six-month voyage to South America once the ship returned to New York which he gladly accepted.[12]

After his second voyage of self-discovery—because that's what his two adventures had turned out to be—Duane returned to Savoy. With his

5

new emotional growth and maturity he was able to mend fences with his father. Despite his young age—he was only sixteen by this time—Duane obtained a job teaching at the Savoy School. He also continued with his own mathematical studies under "an unusually good master," Hope Bliss wrote.[13]

Obviously, Duane was no longer a boy; he had become a young man. And what a time it was to be a young man with the spirit of adventure coursing through your veins. Just a decade later, speaking of his older brother Orion, who had just been appointed Secretary of Nevada Territory, and reflecting perhaps for an entire generation of young men like himself and Duane Bliss, Samuel Clemens wrote in Roughing It: "I coveted...the long, strange journey he [his brother, Orion] was going to make, and the curious new world he was going to explore.... He would...be able to talk as calmly about San Francisco and the ocean, and 'the isthmus' as if nothing was of any consequence to have seen these miracles face to face."[14]

Duane Leroy Bliss, like Mark Twain a decade later, was standing at the threshold of his next grand adventure, and he couldn't wait to get started.

CHAPTER 2

The Isthmus Over

For any adventuresome young New Englander during the mid-century, California was the place to be. When word finally trickled east eight months after gold had been discovered at Sutter's Mill in Coloma, California in January, 1848, it sparked a frenzy of excitement across the entire North American continent. Hundreds, then thousands, of fortune-seekers from every corner of the continent joined a flood of immigrants from around the world, all heading for this new El Dorado, the fabled city of gold of the Spanish Conquistadors. But getting there was not an easy task.

Historian and author David McCullough, citing an earlier historical account, noted there were only three ways to get from the Atlantic coastal states to California: "The Plains across, the Horn around, or the Isthmus over."[1]

The first route—the Plains across—was overland, nearly 3,000 grueling miles of difficult and at times dangerous travel. It usually began by taking a steamship up the known waterways, then continued by wagon train or afoot. Two years earlier, the Mormons, under Brigham Young, had proven that such a journey was possible, although even these highly motivated pioneers had stopped short of having to cross the fearsome Sierra Nevada. It would be nearly a decade before John Butterfield and his famed stagecoach line would traverse the vast expanse of the American West, and two decades before the transcontinental railroad would permanently tie East to West in 1869.

The second route—the Horn around— was the arduous 13,000-mile trip by sea around stormy Cape Horn at the southern tip of South America. In the earliest days of the California Gold Rush, this was the favored method by most Eastern dreamers because of its speed. But once the third route developed, interest in the Cape Horn route quickly diminished.

The third route—the Isthmus Over—was the combination sea-and-overland travel by way of Central or South America. The Isthmus of Panama quickly became the overwhelming favorite from among the many Central and South America choices to cross from the Atlantic to the Pacific Ocean.

Although he had a good position with the Savoy School, with perhaps a number of other splendid opportunities knocking at his door, young Bliss's two ocean voyages had opened his eyes to the world around him. When the news of the California gold strike finally reached Savoy, it spurred the young man into action. He had saved most of the money he had earned on his two earlier working cruises, his teaching salary and a small inheritance from his mother. In addition, he had read everything he could find on California upon hearing the astonishing news of the gold strike in that faraway place. In late 1850 Bliss was finally able to book passage on one of the crowded ships heading from New York City to Panama.

Two years earlier, before the discovery of gold in California, only 335 hearty souls had crossed the Isthmus of Panama on their way from New York to San Francisco. But in 1850 Bliss would be one of 13,809 intrepid travelers making the journey.[2] One of the voyagers on the *Crescent City*, probably not too different from Bliss's ship, recorded, "The decks of our steamer were crowded to suffocation with departing adventurers and their friends—our ribs were in danger of fracture from pressure of the crowd—our shins from contusion against the gold machines, forcing pumps, crowbars, shovels, axes, picks, pocket-pistols, and pickpockets...."[3]

Few details are known about this first leg of Bliss's journey to California except that he likely departed from New York and arrived in Panama nine or ten days later. It was on this segment of his journey that Duane Bliss would make the acquaintance of a stranger who would watch over him during the remainder of the trip. It has been speculated that this man's surname may have been Diston, but nowhere is it recorded who this man was, where he was from, or even his full name. In their biographical sketches both William and Hope Bliss stated that he was a professional gambler, but that was apparently the only description ever passed down to them by their father. Whether Diston really existed, or was just an invention of Bliss's two children intended to inflate his legacy, we cannot be certain.[4]

The final destination for all of the ships heading from New York to the Isthmus of Panama was the mouth of the *Rio Chagres*, or Chagres River, in the Caribbean Sea on Panama's north central coast. Upon arrival, ships had to anchor about a mile from the mouth of the river, since a sandbar blocked

Chapter 2. The Isthmus Over

"The Way They Go to California" is an 1849 Currier & Ives cartoon that humorously shows the frenetic way would-be-49ers headed for California and its gold. Of the three real-world choices of travel, Duane Bliss would choose what historian David McCullough described as "The Isthmus Over" route. (Library of Congress)

the entrance. From there, local natives ferried passengers to the small village of Chagres, located on the south side of the river, employing dugout canoes with low palmetto-thatched roofs, called *bongos*, normally used to transport bananas. One early traveler described this humid, sticky little village as "a low, miserable town, of thirty thatched huts" while another said "The houses are only hovels that in the States, would not even do for...a respectable cow house."[5] In spite of this, those voyagers who were astute or curious enough to look past the grime and poverty of the village were rewarded with the sight of the picturesque and romantic old Spanish castle of San Lorenzo, where dark and ruined battlements kept watch over the Chagres villagers from a nearby hilltop. Still, most travelers spent as little time as absolutely necessary in Chagres. In addition to the exorbitant prices charged by the natives, the filthy village was also known as an incubator for contagious tropical diseases and fevers.

For hundreds of years the Rio Chagres had carried people and cargo from the Caribbean Sea deep into the jungle, where overland trails would

9

then lead them to Panama City on the Pacific Ocean. The most notable early traveler on this route was Welsh pirate Captain Henry Morgan, who used the crossing in 1671 to sack and burn Panama City, at the time the richest city in New Spain. The dangerous and difficult trip across the Isthmus would be made easier in 1855, when construction of the Panama Railroad was completed, but for earlier travelers like Captain Morgan and Massachusetts teenager Duane Bliss, there was no easy crossing.

The next leg of the journey, an overnight boat trip, would carry Bliss and his fellow travelers up the Rio Chagres to a small village called Gorgona, where the next challenge—the overland journey through the mountainous jungle by foot or by mule—would begin.

In these earliest days of the human stampede across the Isthmus, travel from Chagres to Panama City was very decentralized and disorganized. It could take anywhere from three days to two weeks to make the journey, depending upon the availability of transportation, the weather, the number of travelers seeking services, and other factors. You could not buy one ticket to make the entire crossing; each leg of the trip was negotiated separately with the local natives.[6]

The trip up the Rio Chagres gave Duane Bliss his first real taste of the jungle. The torrid heat, the biting insects, and the heavy green slime lying blanket-like on the surface of the river were all hard to forget, and even more difficult to ignore. But the luxuriant green foliage, the birds of every color and stripe flitting about in the overhead canopy, and the swarms of majestic blue butterflies seemed to partially counter the ugliness, at least for a sensitive young man like Bliss.

"The river itself [was] a beautiful limpid stream about fifty yards wide," wrote one traveler. "The shores, at first low and marshy, soon became more elevated, and are crowned with the most exuberant and abundant vegetation...the banana and plantain, the palmetto, the graceful cocoanut and cabbage trees, the papaya and mango, bearing their delicious fruit, the pine apple, the orange and lime, were seen in all directions...."[7]

The deforesting and road grading for the trans-Panama railroad had just begun, and Bliss probably caught occasional glimpses through the foliage that revealed teams of native laborers hard bent to the task.

The next afternoon Bliss reached Gorgona. The small village in the interior was not unlike Chagres; it was smaller, and much more crowded, but not as begrimed and feculent as the nasty little village at the mouth of the river. One 1849 goldfield aspirant described the physical beauty of the

Chapter 2. The Isthmus Over

village: "The scenery here partakes of a bolder and more varied character. From the high table-land on which the town is built, mountains rise in every direction, forming a complete amphitheatre perpetually reflected from the sparkling streamlet in their midst."[8]

Because Gorgona was smaller, there were not as many native entrepreneurs set up to separate travelers from their money. As a result, fewer suppliers of services made the town a bottleneck for those crossing the Isthmus, and the high demand for the services that did exist drove prices up to an exorbitant level. For instance, hiring a mule for the remainder of the trip could cost up to $20, a month's pay for most men. Bliss likely obtained accommodations for the night in one of the few hotels in Gorgona. Conversation in the small, sticky inn may have centered on the bandits who, it was rumored, might attack travelers along the trail.

The next morning Bliss would have boarded a skiff for the final few miles upriver to the tiny village of Las Cruces, where the river ends. From there he joined a mule train for the final twenty-two mile overland journey to Panama City. This leg followed the *Camino de Cruces*, or Cruces Trail, a muddy, three-foot wide, rock-strewn path that was more trough than trail. During the wet season this swampy route was nearly impassable, but somehow the resilient, sure-footed mules kept slogging along, one hoof-step at a time. Sarah Merrian Brooks, a right proper young lady from Boston with a spirit of adventure, duplicated Bliss's journey only a year or so after he had made the trip. Of this final leg from Las Cruces to Panama City, she wrote of the hearty pack animals that would carry them over the mountains to the sea:

> *Kicks and oaths were delivered indiscriminately, pack-saddles were cinched, and every mule [is] waiting for his load. And what a sight they were! Such broken-down, miserable beasts! Hundreds of them, lame, halt, and blind, ringboned and spavined, big and little, mostly little—everything that could be gathered up in all the country—were brought into requisition to carry the army of people who...had to cross that mountain.*

Once on the trail, she described the sights and sounds that the argonauts all shared:

> *The gentle breeze of the mountain, so different from the sluggish and humid air which had oppressed us on the river, seemed to make all nature revive. Even the birds attempted a feeble song, each with its bit of bright flower, carried like a little sail*

on its back.... Our trail lay over a spur, or high peak, and as we gradually ascended we frequently came in sight of the Chagres River far below us, bordered with huge trees, which were garlanded and festooned with brilliant flowers.

Our descent of the mountain was much more rapid than the ascent had been...[and] we began to see signs of living.... Children swarmed around, entirely naked, and the paroquets [small, slender parrots] seemed as numerous and as much at home as the children. They hopped on the children's heads, crawled up their legs, pecked at their food, and made themselves quite happy in any way which suited them.[9]

Once Bliss and his fellow travelers reached Panama City, most would have checked into one of many hostelries haphazardly spruced up to take advantage of the burgeoning goldfield traffic. "The old ruined houses have been patched up with whitewash," one traveler noted, adding, "The main street is composed almost entirely of hotels, eating houses and 'hells' [bars]."[10]

Within the next few days Duane Bliss signed onto a clipper ship headed for San Francisco. It is doubtful that he ever read the regretful words of a fellow isthmus traveler—another Massachusetts native—that appeared in the *Providence* [RI] *Journal*. But given the difficult nature of the trip, Bliss might have wholeheartedly agreed with the man's words:

I have not time to give my reasons for what I am about to say, but in saying it I utter the united sentiment of every passenger whom I have heard speak upon the subject. It is this—and I say it in the fear of God and love of man, to one and all—by no means, for any consideration, attempt to come this route. I had rather risk the doubling of Cape Horn a dozen times, or all the dangers and toils of the overland route for a year, than repeat this journey.[11]

Despite the terrible rigors of the trip, young Duane Bliss couldn't have been happier. He was about to embark on another grand adventure, one that would put him the eventual path to fame and fortune beyond his wildest dreams.

CHAPTER 3

Gold! The California Years

Early California was populated by an infinite number of fascinating men and women. Few were more interesting than bibliophile and amateur historian Hubert Howe Bancroft.

Born in Ohio in 1832, as a young man Bancroft had worked for a brother-in-law in his bookstore in Buffalo, New York before heading to California in 1852 to open a West Coast branch of the store. Within a few years, under Bancroft's guidance, the firm had grown into a successful bookstore and publishing house in San Francisco.

Within a decade of his arrival, Bancroft had begun collecting historical research materials and regional writings for the publication of a Pacific Coast handbook. During that time his collection had swelled to a monumental 16,000 volumes, covering everything from Alaska south through Mexico and Central America, but always focusing primarily on California and the Pacific Coast states and territories. His collection covered the period from early native Indian cultures through the Spanish Colonial era and beyond, and consisted of books, manuscripts, pamphlets, maps, newspapers and periodicals. He and his staff augmented the research with oral history interviews with early pioneers and those who helped to build the great Pacific West. The end result of Bancroft's life work was a massive thirty-nine volume history of western North America that he either wrote, edited or supervised. Although Bancroft has not always been recognized as a first-rate historian—he had no formal training in the field and many of his practices were questionable by today's standards—still, his work is so extensive that it cannot be overlooked as a valuable resource in the study of western United States history. In 1905—and prior to his death in 1918—the University of California purchased his book and manuscript collections, which formed the nucleus for the world renown Bancroft Library at the University of California, Berkeley.[1]

In 1887 Bancroft, or one of his assistants, interviewed Duane L. Bliss about his background, his decade in California, and his more recent years in Nevada, particularly his work with the Virginia & Truckee Railroad. This interview manuscript consists of only nine leaves in the massive Bancroft Collection, so it is not a comprehensive biography of Bliss's life. However, it is the most dependable source of information on the man, and can be relied upon for its accuracy, since the information came from Bliss himself.

Bliss had departed Massachusetts for California "in the latter part of 1850," according to the Bancroft interview, and he arrived in San Francisco on January 16, 1851.[2] Extant records make it impossible to confirm Bliss's arrival date as recorded in the interview. The best extant source is Louis J. Rasmussen's three-volume San Francisco Passenger Lists that reconstructs many, but not all, of ship arrival passenger lists that were lost in a 1940 San Francisco fire. However, Duane, or D. L., Bliss does not show up on any of Rasmussen's lists. San Francisco's tri-weekly Alta California newspaper did carry ship arrival information, but did not publish passenger lists until later in 1851. However, the newspaper does show one ship arrival on January 16, 1851 from Panama, the date Bliss stated that he had arrived. It was the clipper ship *Sarah & Eliza*.[3] She was a British ship built in the early 1830s that had often made the run from her home port on Prince Edward Island, Canada to the British Isles and back. Lacking any further confirmation, there is no reason to question Bliss's arrival date, since he personally provided it to Bancroft, so we can assume its authenticity.

When the *Sarah & Eliza* hove into the port of San Francisco on January 16 it anchored well out from the shoreline, since docking facilities were scarce. The California Gold Rush was in full swing, and literally hundreds of sailing ships and steamers bobbed in the calm waters of the bay, all competing for space. Duane Bliss must have been ecstatic—although somewhat surprised—when he caught his first glimpse of the ragtag city he had come so far to see. A fellow traveler who had disembarked from his steamer just a short time earlier aptly described the scene:

> *Rising abruptly from the water, an amphitheatre of three or four ugly round-topped barren hills, with their intervening holes, form the site of the notorious town of San Francisco.*
>
> *Threading our way in a small boat among some fifty sails of vessels lying at anchor in the cove . . . we landed among the slippery rocks underneath a high bank, up which we scrambled some fifty feet, perpendicular. Here was a strange scene. Vessels from nearly every quarter of the globe had brought the denizens of every clime . . . we were in the Cosmopolis of the world.*

Chapter 3. Gold! The California Years

About the burgeoning city of about 30,000 people when Bliss arrived, the traveler noted:

About three hundred houses, stores, shanties and sheds, with a great many tents, composed the town at that period. The houses were mostly built of rough boards and unpainted; brown cotton or calico nailed against the beams and joists answered for wall and ceiling of the better class of tenements. With the exception of the brick warehouses of Howard & Mellers, the establishments of the commercial houses of which we had heard so much, were inferior to the outhouses of the country seats on the Hudson . . . .[4]

Like so many travelers before him, Bliss would have been amazed by the differences between San Francisco and New York City or Boston, but how excited the young adventurer must have been at that moment. Bliss was still a teenager when he arrived in California, and he would not become a prominent citizen of the West until a decade after his later move to western Utah Territory in 1860. His unremarkable career during his California years earned him scant attention in newspapers and early historical accounts of the areas where he lived and worked. California had only gained statehood in late 1850, and official records were few in the state's first decade. Thus, what follows in this chapter is the author's reconstruction of Duane Bliss's life from his landing in California in early 1851 until 1860 when he left the state, based upon the scant credible information that does exist.

The young man had arrived at a precarious time. San Francisco was rocked with a series of earthquakes and damaged by a series of devastating fires throughout 1850 and 1851. Thus the city was usually in a state of chaos and confusion, and was continually cleaning up and rebuilding. One of the worst of the fires occurred on May 4, 1851, and it is possible that young Duane Bliss was still in the city at that time. San Francisco resident William Smith Jewett, in a letter to his family in the East, provides a little comic relief to the chaos that followed each calamity: "[I am] one of the sufferers by the late awful conflagration of claptraps, paper houses, hencoops, &c . . . . It was really amusing to see us all scampering half dressed with our lumber on our backs, running about like ants when their nest is disturbed, each with a precious egg."[5] Jewett's comment about the lumber being so valuable that it was one of the first things a person sought to save from fire—"a precious egg" he called it—was prescient for young Bliss, who in later years would

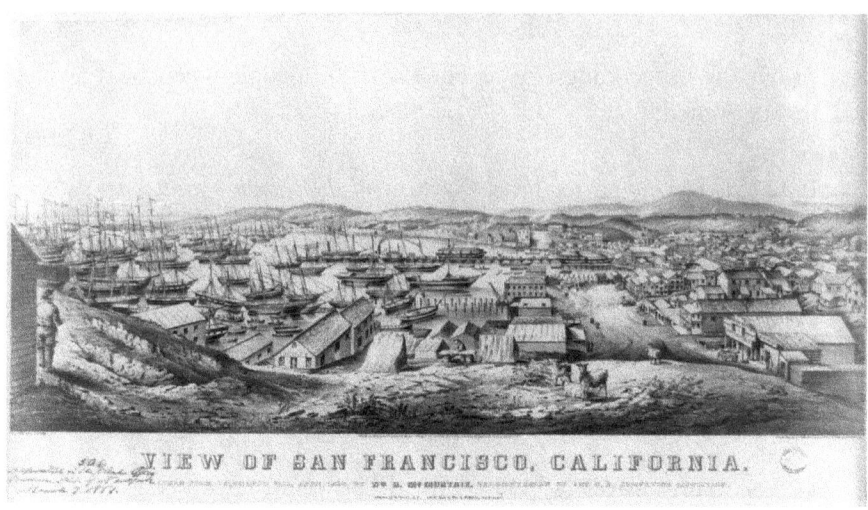

A view of San Francisco and its busy harbor in 1850, taken from Telegraph Hill, shows the burgeoning city as Duane Bliss would have seen it upon arriving from Panama. Population at the time was about 25,000, but most residents were transitory, heading for the gold country, so an exact count was impossible. (Library of Congress)

make his fortune producing lumber and timber from the forests in the Lake Tahoe Basin of Nevada and California.

Bliss probably spent some time in the city, as it was a fascinating and alluring place peopled by fellow gold seekers from around the globe: ". . . mostly men, young or of middle age, very few women, fewer children," wrote Mary Hill, quoting from an 1892 *Century Magazine* article. "Here were British subjects, Frenchmen, Germans, and Dutch, Italians, Spaniards, Norwegians, Swedes and Swiss, Jews, Turks, Chinese, Kanakas [Hawaiian Islanders], New Zealanders, Malays, and Negroes . . . and the dwellers . . . in Boston and New Orleans, Chicago and Peoria, Hoboken and Hackensack."[6]

San Francisco was a good place for Bliss to temporarily hang his hat while he explored his mining options, learned a little about the trade, and discovered where the "hot" digging and placer sites were located. He may have started with a small book entitled *California as it is & as it May be: A Guide to the Gold Region*, the first English language book printed in California. Published in 1849, about a year before statehood, it was authored by Polish refugee and gold prospector Felix Paul Wierzbicki. The book became a valuable guide for would-be miners and other early English-speaking settlers who wanted to learn about California. Bliss may have seen the book, because

Chapter 3. Gold! The California Years

he followed the advice Wierzbicki proffered: "We may say in general terms, that further south from the Tuolomy [sic] [River] ... the diggers were not so numerous as elsewhere, consequently there is yet a better chance there than in other points."[7]

Once he had decided to begin his serious search for gold in Tuolumne County, Bliss would have outfitted himself in San Francisco with the clothing, food, bedding and tools he would need, which would have been expensive for a young fellow with a limited poke. Then he would have set out for the Tuolumne County Gold Rush town of Columbia—dubbed the "Gem of the Southern Mines"—as Wierzbicki had advised his readers to do.[8]

Bliss spent at least a year-and-a-half working the streams in the vicinity of Columbia. We know this from the only official state record of his whereabouts in the early 1850s—an 1852 California State Census conducted in November of that year. It listed "D. L. Bliss, 19 years old, from Massachusetts" living by himself in the county. Although there is no profession, trade or occupation listed on that record for Bliss, the majority of the men identified themselves as miners, so it is a safe guess that Bliss was still busy seeking his fortune in the streams and rivers of Tuolumne County.[9] Columbia's population during Bliss's stay in the area had swelled to over 5,000 by 1852. There were eight hotels, four banks, two firehouses, two bookstores, one newspaper, three churches and seventeen general stores. For entertainment, there were over forty drinking and gambling establishments, and a local community brass band to entertain citizens. There were, however, few women, a similar situation to that which existed in most of the Gold Rush mining towns. Darius Ogden Mills, with whom Bliss would partner in a number of Nevada ventures in later years, had an assay office and bank in town, but whether he and Bliss were acquainted during the latter's Columbia years is not known.

Despite his hard work, it is doubtful whether young Bliss made much of a living for himself. By the time he had arrived, most of the easy gold was gone, already picked up or panned by the thousands who had come before him. Late in 1852 or early in 1853 Bliss decided to give up on mining in Tuolumne County, and try to improve his luck elsewhere. Loose talk in the towns and mining camps often centered on the latest areas where gold was being found. A boy of only fourteen, it was said, had found $3,467 worth of gold in less than two months on the Mokelumne River, to the north in Calaveras County, while a woman from Sonora had panned $2,125 worth in forty-six days working the same streams.[10] Perhaps Bliss had heard those stories, because that's where the young man headed next.[11]

The first gold discovered along the wild Mokelumne River was found in the spring of 1848. It was one of the richest ore-bearing rivers in the southern end of the Gold Rush region. Through the late 1840s and the early 1850s eager miners swarmed up and down the creeks and dry creek beds fanning from the river. Here, at times seemingly overnight, they built mining camps along the rich sand and gravel banks, or "bars," as the miners called them. Spanish-speaking miners called these gold-bearing banks *placers*, from the Spanish word meaning shoal or alluvial sand deposit. Big Bar was one of the most prominent of the early placer deposits located near Mokelumne Hill, which at the time was only a trading post.

After Big Bar had been depleted, miners headed downstream to establish themselves at Middle Bar, Poverty Bar, Oregon Bar and finally Winter's Bar, where Duane Bliss headed next to try to improve his luck.[12] We do not know how much time Bliss spent working the streams of Calaveras County, but it was probably not too long. The Bancroft interview said, ". . . in 1852 [he] entered a store near Redwood City," but that date is arguable. He was still in Tuolumne County in November 1852 when the State Census was taken, and he did some mining in Calaveras County after that, so it is unlikely that he went to the store in Woodside [near Redwood City] until some time in 1853.

*

South of San Francisco, the area that divides the bay from the Pacific Ocean was a verdant, stream-filled paradise in the 1850s, where towering, old growth redwood trees (*Sequoia sempervirens*) seemed to almost touch the sky. Known as the Peninsula, this was not the gold country of eastern California, but rather the lumbering country of western California. It was here that Duane Bliss lived and worked from sometime in 1853 until his departure for Utah Territory in January 1860.

In 1849, twenty-year-old Massachusetts native Matthias Alfred Parkhurst had arrived in the San Andreas Valley on the Peninsula and leased or purchased a rectangular 127-acre parcel of land. He named his new property "Woodside." Parkhurst and a partner set about making heavy wooden shingles taken from the old-growth forest on his land, shipping them to San Francisco or San Jose. After a short time Parkhurst's partner decided to return to the goldfields, so Parkhurst bought him out.[13]

Meanwhile, two other men, also from Massachusetts, settled in the same area, and they are credited with rafting the first big shipment of lumber

Chapter 3. Gold! The California Years

from the redwood forests to San Francisco. Dr. R. O. (Robert Orville) Tripp was an amiable, ambitious ex-dentist, one of the earliest to set up a practice in San Francisco in his small ramshackle house at the corner of Vallejo and Stockton streets. His partner in the lumbering trade was a rough-and-tumble frontiersman named James "Grizzly" Ryder. It was said that Ryder had earned his moniker after being severely mauled by a grizzly bear, an incident that caused him to abandon his lumbering career, leaving Tripp, like Parkhurst, without a partner. Soon these two men got together, and in early 1850 they established a new enterprise. The following year they went into the mercantile business, opening a small store in a cabin on their property in Woodside.[14]

Lumbering the Peninsula's redwood forests can be traced back to Spanish Colonial times. The resulting timber had been used in the construction of the Presidio, the missions of San Francisco and Santa Clara, and the Pueblo San Jose. The Gold Rush and the attendant explosive growth of San Francisco created a new market for forest products, and more than a dozen sawmills sprung up in and around Woodside to meet the growing demand. Pacific tidewaters reached all the way to nearby Redwood City, creating a slough where a crude but workable port was built for shipping lumber both north and south. It became known as the Redwood Embarcadero, and soon it also supported a small shipbuilding operation for use in the lumber trade. All of the men involved in these new industries needed a place to shop, and Tripp and Parkhurst were ready to serve them in their small store.

Operating a general store in conjunction with one's home was not an unusual practice on the Western frontier, and many shrewd businessmen found there was more money to be made selling goods to the lumbering community than actually joining them in their dangerous and seasonal work. The store became known as the Woodside Store. In 1851 Tripp was elected to serve a term as a San Francisco County supervisor—San Mateo County, in which Woodside is presently located, did not become a political entity until 1856—and he went to San Francisco every Sunday to fulfill his political duties and purchase inventory for the store, returning on Tuesday. During Tripp's absences Parkhurst ran the store and kept the books. In 1853 the San Francisco County Assessor put a value on the store and its contents at $2,500, a handsome sum in its day.[15]

Somehow Duane Bliss had learned of the Woodside Store, and having grown weary of his futile search for gold, he decided to make the trip down the San Francisco Peninsula to interview for a position. He must have hit it off with the voluble Dr. Tripp, who was later in his life described as, "a tall, thin old fellow with a kindly word for everyone, and whenever he talked he had a habit of peering over the top of his spectacles . . . ."[16] Although Tripp would eventually live to be ninety-three years old, and was said to be known by almost every resident of the county, he was only thirty-eight years old when Bliss first met him.

Mathias Parkhurst was much more reserved than his partner. A quiet, well-educated man, he enjoyed the solitude of a good book, which probably endeared him to Bliss, who was also a serious reader. Parkhurst, however, was a sickly man, and he would pass away at only thirty-four years of age in 1863. Parkhurst's infirmities, on top of Tripp's political duties, may have been the reasons the partners decided to hire a fulltime clerk to help in the store.

Duane's father, William, had run a very similar store in Savoy Hollow while Duane was growing up, since it was a tradition that male children would begin helping out in their father's business as soon as they were old enough. As a result Duane had plenty of experience in all aspects of operating a mercantile, and Dr. Tripp and Mr. Parkhurst hired Duane on the spot. The *Redwood City Democrat* described D. L. Bliss as the "first clerk of the Woodside store," which would indicate that the two owners had managed their commercial affairs alone up to the time of Bliss's employment.[17]

The following year, with a steady job and a regular income to depend upon, Bliss made a big change in his life. On June 14, 1854, just two weeks after his twenty-first birthday, he married twenty-year old Mary Elizabeth Healy. Miss Healy, who was born on July 4, 1833, was the daughter of Irish immigrants, and had been brought up in the working class Irish Catholic neighborhood of South Boston.[18] It is not clear if Bliss met the young woman in California, or if he had known her earlier in Massachusetts. The 1850 U.S. Census for Massachusetts does show a Mary Elizabeth Healey (note different spelling) of the correct age, living with her family in Worcester, a city about midway between Boston and Savoy, but we cannot know with any certainty if this is the same woman. It is more likely that Miss Healy was living in California when the young couple met and courted.

Later that year, Dr. Tripp and Mr. Parkhurst decided to expand into a larger store. A daily stagecoach run between San Francisco and Woodside had been established by this time, and it made regular mail delivery routine. The partners added a postal station to their new two-story building, "hurriedly built of rough redwood slabs" according to one source. The

Chapter 3. Gold! The California Years

The Woodside store was the hub of the lumbering community on the San Francisco Peninsula when Duane Bliss joined proprietor, Dr. R.O. Tripp (far left, with the white beard) as a clerk at his mercantile in 1853. Today, the store still exists as the San Mateo County Woodside Store Museum. (San Mateo County Historical Association)

store was completed by fall. A local newspaper correspondent described the little Woodside community during the 1850s: "Woodside, about six miles from Redwood City, though it makes no pretensions to the title of town of village, is nevertheless somewhat of a public place. Situated at the foot of the mountains, in the immediate vicinity of several [lumber] mills, it is the center of quite a trade. It has one store in which is the post-office."[19]

Lumbermen and teamsters would often stop by the Woodside Store on their way to the Redwood Embarcadero, and soon a small commercial district grew up around it. Although this provided food, lodgings, supplies and even entertainment for the travelers, the store itself was always the community's focal point. [20] A newspaper advertisement indicated the wide assortment of goods that were offered on its shelves:

WOODSIDE STORE
Tripp & Parkhurst ... Proprietors
At the Woodside Store consumers can be sure of finding all the goods usually to be obtained at a country store suitable for farmers and others.
Agricultural Implements
Dry Goods, Clothing
Groceries, Provisions
Hardware, Cutlery
Stable & Fancy Goods of all kinds
Wines
Liquors
Tobacco etc.
can be purchased at the most reasonable prices.
The Post Office is in this store.[21]

The store's sales records, neatly recorded in Parkhurst's flowing cursive, delineated every transaction by customer name, items purchased, and whether paid by cash or credit. A typical entry might include: "1 pr. boots, 2 shirts, 4 lb. pork, Rum, 1 bx. Pills, 1 axe, sugar, rope, 1 draw knife, 1 can flea powder" with similar entries to follow. The store's fragile, yellowing sales records have been carefully preserved, and are available for study by serious researchers at the San Mateo County Historical Association in Redwood City.[22]

Duane Bliss was a diligent worker, and he thrived in his job at the store. On July 4, 1855 he and Mary Elizabeth had a baby daughter. They named her Lucia Mary, after Duane's mother. On the child's first birthday, Woodside had a big celebration, not in Lucia Mary's honor but in celebration of Independence Day. The store had become the unofficial gathering place in the community, and the whole town assembled there for the festivities. A large new American flag was unfurled by young Lucas Greer and hoisted up a tall pole built and installed for the occasion by local lumberjacks. A fife and drum corps led a small parade down the dusty King's Mountain Road, playing "The Girl I Left Behind Me," followed by a rousing version of "The Star Spangled Banner." It was a festive day for the entire community.[23]

Dr. Tripp still occasionally practiced dentistry, and a humorous Bliss family story described an incident which occurred during one session. Dr. Tripp's dental chair was located inside the store. One night Mr. Parkhurst had a terrible toothache, and Dr. Tripp decided the offending tooth had to come out. Bliss was given the task of holding the lantern high above Parkhurst's

Chapter 3. Gold! The California Years

head while Dr. Tripp tried to extract the stubborn tooth. He pulled and he pulled while Parkhurst groaned and shrieked with pain, finally slipping off the chair onto the floor. But Dr. Tripp never loosened his iron grip on the forceps, tumbling to the floor with Parkhurst; and the two men rolled over and over one another on the hard-packed earthen floor. Eventually they rolled over a large drip pan positioned under a molasses keg; and shortly thereafter Dr. Tripp's arm came up, triumphantly holding the tooth in his forceps, both men dripping in molasses.[24]

In addition to selling bottles of liquor, the Woodside Store also freely served it, although the enterprise was never officially licensed as a tavern. Dr. Tripp was a founding member of the Woodside Dell Temperance Society; but, according to Woodside historian Dorothy Regnery, ". . . his conscience must not have been bothered when financial principles were applied to business." A large barrel of Continental Whiskey sat on the counter, ostensibly to ease the pain for Dr. Tripp's dental patients. The first drink was free, but additional rounds required a contribution. It was amazing the number of lumbermen and farmers around Woodside who seemed to have a toothache at any given time.[25]

On June 30, 1857 Mary Elizabeth Bliss gave birth to the couple's second daughter, who they named Belle Matilda. Unfortunately, the child only survived for two months. The California Mortuary and Cemetery Records show a "Bellzora M. Bliss," also a two-month old infant, dying on the same date in Sacramento, so this could have been Duane and Mary Elizabeth's child. If so, why the death is reported as having occurred in Sacramento is not known. This infant was initially interred in Sacramento, but she was reinterred in San Francisco in June, 1861. This adds further credence to the assumption that this was Duane and Mary Elizabeth's daughter who, records indicate, was indeed reinterred in San Francisco.[26]

At about the same time Tripp and Parkhurst had hired Bliss as the store's clerk, they also hired a thirty-one-year-old Massachusetts spinster, Emaline Skelton, as a housekeeper. In less than a year she and bachelor Tripp were married in San Francisco. Soon they built a new house right across the road from the store on the same property where the original store had been located. They also planted a number of fruit trees and melon vines on the property, which within a few years would become a wonderful orchard, its fresh bounty selling quickly from the store's shelves.[27]

On July 30, 1859, Mary Elizabeth, Duane's wife of only five years, died of unknown causes just a few weeks after her twenty-sixth birthday. There was no church building to hold a service in Woodside, or a formal cemetery for her interment. A wooded knoll north of the store, often called "God's Acre of Woodside," was occasionally used as a burial site for Woodside pioneers, and there were small cemeteries in nearby Searsville and Redwood City, but Bliss chose to bury his wife in San Francisco. Her death was also recorded in that city, so it is possible that Duane had taken her there for medical treatment. She was interred in one of the city's earliest cemeteries, Lone Mountain, which sat high atop one of the fabled "Seven Hills of San Francisco." In 1867 the name of the cemetery was changed to Laurel Hill, and in 1941 the bodies were re-interred in Cypress Lawn Memorial Park in Colma, California. The heartbroken Bliss was left caring for four-year old Lucia Mary by himself.[28]

At the end of 1859 Bliss decided to leave California and head for northern Nevada, known as Washoe, then part of Utah Territory. There were a number of factors that may have influenced his decision. First, there were rumors that the Tripp and Parkhurst partnership was going to be dissolved. This did not turn out to be true, but it did spur a decision by the partners that Parkhurst would be the sole operator of the store, even though his health was failing.[29] Also, Bliss may have simply felt that he needed a change of scenery, a chance to put some distance for he and Lucia Mary from the state where they had experienced so much emotional pain over their recent losses. Finally, it could have been the pull of the recently discovered Comstock Lode that attracted Bliss, another opportunity to improve the financial future for him and his daughter.

Whatever the reasons, in early 1860 father and daughter left California and ventured to the mining boomtown of Virginia City. Years later, while relating his life for H. H. Bancroft, Bliss wrote that he had arrived in Virginia City on January 16, 1860, exactly nine years to the day after he had arrived in San Francisco from Panama.[30]

Forty-three years after he had left California for Utah Territory, where he achieved fame and fortune, Duane Bliss returned to the small general store in Woodside to visit his old friend and employer, Dr. Tripp. An article in the *Redwood City Democrat*, dated January 8, 1903, summarized his visit:

> D. L. Bliss, who will be remembered by old residents as the first clerk of the Woodside store, but now a hotel keeper at Lake Tahoe, and also one of the foremost mining men of the State, paid a visit to his old employer, R. O. Tripp, last Saturday.

Chapter 3. Gold! The California Years

Mr. Bliss was much pleased to find his estimable friend so hale and hearty after an absence of forty years.

The store where Duane Bliss had worked so long and had experienced so much grief and pain at the passing of his young wife and daughter still stood on that day in 1903. It still stands today, at the same spot on King's Mountain Road, but now as the Woodside Store Museum, providing twenty-first century visitors with a time capsule look at Bliss's Woodside of a half-century ago.

CHAPTER 4

The Comstock Lode

On January 16, 1860 Duane Bliss arrived in Virginia City, in western Utah Territory, with his four-year old daughter Lucia Mary.[1] Their first home was probably a tent in Virginia City, but enterprising men were already throwing up wooden stores and lodging houses. There were few women in Virginia City at the time—a mining boomtown was not the place for young ladies—but Bliss would not have had a problem finding one of them to care for Lucia Mary while he sought work.

In the Bancroft interview Bliss stated that after arriving on the Comstock, he had prospected "for awhile," and the 1860 Federal Census concurs, listing him as a "miner." But these were difficult times for miners—the thousands who had abruptly descended on the mountains and streams of western Utah Territory soon exceeded the number of Paiute Indians who had occupied the land for centuries, and the limited food supply and vital resources in the region were severely strained. Skirmishes between the white prospectors and the band of Paiutes increased, and in May it erupted into the greatest confrontation between the races in the region's history.

There was no formal government in the area, so a contingent of 105 white settlers banded together as vigilantes and set out to teach the Paiute a lesson. But they underestimated their enemy and were baited into a trap, and three-quarters of the men were killed on the bank of the Truckee River above Pyramid Lake. Virginia City, Gold Hill and Silver City residents quickly began to fortify their makeshift little villages, fearing marauding Indians would arrive at any minute. The miners' rump government closed down all the mining claims, and passed a resolution that none of the claims would be forfeited due to the inactivity. Reinforcements from California and troopers from the U.S. Army arrived, and a second battle with the Paiute was fought to a draw in early June, an encounter that put an end to what is known in western history as the Pyramid Lake War.[2]

Early Virginia City on Sun Mountain as Duane Bliss would have seen it upon his arrival in 1860. (From a drawing by J. Ross Browne for his 1860 book, *A Peep at Washoe*)

Duane Bliss had little time to celebrate the peace that now descended on the Comstock. In late June, just weeks shy of her fifth birthday, little Lucia Mary Bliss passed away. The young man had now lost his entire family. Bliss delivered the body of his young daughter to San Francisco, where she would

Chapter 4. The Comstock Lode

join her mother and sister at Lone Mountain Cemetery. Perhaps Lucia Mary had been gravely ill and her death anticipated, because shortly before she died, on June 11, Duane had had the remains of his other daughter, Belle Matilda, disinterred in Sacramento and reburied in San Francisco's Lone Mountain Cemetery beside her mother.[3]

When Bliss returned to Virginia City, he must have realized that prospecting was not for him. He had enjoyed little success as a prospector in California, and even less in Utah Territory. Thousands of the men he had met and worked beside in the gold fields were either uneducated or ignorant, or both, and their futures would be bleak if Lady Luck didn't smile on them. Not Bliss. He was blessed with a solid education and a keen mind, and he just needed to find his niche out here on the frontier. He relocated to nearby Gold Hill, probably to one of the many boarding houses that had sprung up, and began searching for the right opportunity.

Unlike most mountain ranges in western Utah Territory—the area would become Nevada Territory in 1861, and the state of Nevada in 1864—the Virginia Range follows a northeast-to-southwest trend, lying between the Truckee and Carson Rivers. Located directly east of the Washoe Valley and the Truckee Meadows, it is not as steep and abrupt as the eastern face of the Sierra Nevada that lies about twenty miles west of it. Rather, its topography consists of rolling sagebrush-covered hills, dotted with an occasional pinon tree, separated by shallow canyons. The region's rivers, even the two aforementioned, are more streams than rivers, and as one early historian pointed out, western Utah did not have a single river that was navigable for steamboats.

Sun Mountain, soon to be renamed Mount Davidson [but still called Sun Mountain to this day by many locals and throughout this book] was the Virginia Range's highest peak at 7,864 feet. Sprawled across the eastern face of Sun Mountain's hills and canyons, roughly 1,600 feet below the summit, was a great vein of silver-bearing quartz that extended for almost four miles. The huge vein, which would soon become known as the Comstock Lode, had lain undisturbed for eons, silently mocking the hoard of gold seekers who had unknowingly trampled over its hidden riches on their way to California's gold fields. Oh yes, there was gold, too, on Sun Mountain, but for a decade it would serve primarily to keep the miners' eyes off the real prize—that huge vein of silver.

As early as 1849, en route to the California gold fields, a company of Mormons crossing Utah Territory's fearsome Great Basin had found placer

When Duane Bliss moved to neighboring Gold Hill in 1860, the settlement was little more than a rowdy gold mining camp with 638 men (but no women) sharing wooden shanties, tents and other crude dwellings. Naturally, there was also a saloon. (From a drawing by J. Ross Browne for his 1860 book, *A Peep at Washoe*)

gold in the streams coursing down one of Sun Mountain's canyons, often taking out $5 to $8 worth of the precious gold flakes in a day's labor. But Sun Mountain's treasures paled in comparison to California's gold—or so the prospectors had believed—so they trekked on. But, as miners tend to do, they freely shared the news of their Utah Territory diggings around the campfires of the Mother Lode gold camps.[4]

Later in the decade, as the pickings became slim in California's rivers and streams, prospectors began re-thinking their dreams of striking it rich. Perhaps the stories they had heard over the years about western Utah were

Chapter 4. The Comstock Lode

true. It was just good old common horse sense that if gold had leeched out of the mountains and been washed down the streams and gullies on the western slopes of the Sierra Nevada, that the same thing must have happened on the eastern slopes, or perhaps in the smaller ranges east of that. It was an intriguing idea. Thus a few of these disgruntled California prospectors began trekking back over the mountains to ply their trade in the streams on the eastern slopes of the Sierra Nevada. A few of the heartiest ventured even further east and began prospecting in the alluvial plains below Sun Mountain. Most of these latter efforts were concentrated at the base of Gold Canyon, where the Mormons had made their find, or four miles north in Six Mile Canyon, and a small settlement called Johntown soon appeared at the foot of Gold Canyon. Here the miners congregated at the end of the day's work and spent their nights in tents or thatch-covered holes in the side of a nearby hill. Here they also whiled away the winter months when they were unable to work, and began building crude wooden shanties to replace their caves and tents.

Mining on Sun Mountain was very different than mining in the Sierra Nevada. Still, it was gold, not silver, that was on the minds of the early Sun Mountain prospectors. As Comstock historian Ronald James observed of these miners, ". . . the California experience had shaped their expectations. They understood gold. They knew how to acquire it, and they preferred to work alone or in small teams."[5] And so through the latter half of the 1850s they labored on at the lower reaches of Gold Canyon and Six Mile Canyon, looking only for gold and ignoring the blue-black sludge that clogged their rocker boxes. As it became more and more difficult to find virgin creek beds that had not been exhausted by earlier placer miners, many prospectors returned to California or to their hometowns with empty pokes.

In January 1859 four prospectors began working their way up Gold Canyon, and in a little hill near the head of the canyon they discovered a richer deposit of gold than had henceforth been found on Sun Mountain. Comstock historian William Wright wrote, "The gold was in a deposit of decomposed quartz mingled with soil, and the miners were really delving in a part of the Comstock Lode without at first knowing that they were at work on any quartz vein." These rich new diggings yielded gold by the pound at times, Wright added. This was where the town of Gold Hill soon sprung up, replacing Johntown as the miners' chief gathering place. The four men who made this find were James Finney, known in Comstock lore as "Old Virginny," "Big French John" Bishop, Aleck Henderson, and Jack Yount.[6]

In the spring of 1859 another group of prospectors returned to some diggings they had worked earlier in Six Mile Canyon. When they found that other miners had claimed all the good ground, two of the men, Patrick McLaughlin and Peter O'Riley, proceeded all the way up to the head of Six Mile Canyon and began working their rockers in a small stream. The diggings were poor, and the two Irishmen were about to give up when they happened to peer into a small pit they had dug to collect water for their rockers. They noticed a different looking material at the bottom of the hole, and decided to wash it through their rockers. By the time they were finished, the aprons in the rockers were covered with a bright, glittering layer of gold. When their exuberance subsided, the two miners noticed the heavy blue-black sludge on the apron. Unlike every miner before them, on some whim the two men set some of the sludge aside to be assayed along with the gold.[7]

It was about this time that a lazy, uneducated, but extremely clever self-promoter, Henry "Old Pancake" Comstock, happened upon the two miners. Comstock was a tall, gaunt Canadian who had failed at trapping, fur trading, and—up until he stumbled on O'Riley and McLaughlin—gold mining. But to his credit he instantly recognized the value of their gold discovery, and he lied and bullied his way into a partnership for himself and a buddy, Immanuel Penrod, with the two meeker Irishmen. Thus, through sheer audacity, Comstock became the undeserved namesake of the famous Comstock Lode.[8] The four partners' ore was sent to Nevada City in California to be assayed. What they had assumed to be gold was indeed gold, assayed at a handsome value of $876 per ton of ore. But what surprised everyone, including the assayer, Melville Atwood, was that the blue-black sludge was almost pure silver, worth $3,000 per ton.[9] The men named their mine the Ophir, and for a while the settlement that grew up around it was called "Ophir Diggings;" but by the end of 1859 it had become known as Virginia City, after James "Old Virginny" Finney.[10]

A small news item announcing the silver find appeared in San Francisco's *Alta California* newspaper on July 7, 1859. It gave no clue to the fact that this strike would change the face of the West, and turn San Francisco into one of the young nation's premier cities:

RICH SILVER MINES ON THE EASTERN SLOPE OF THE SIERRA NEVADAS.—J. F. Scott of Alpha in this county, now a resident of Truckee Meadows, has just arrived from the other side of the mountains, and reports the discovery of a vein of ore of extraordinary richness at the head of Six Mile Can[y]

Chapter 4. The Comstock Lode

> *on, about ten miles from the Truckee Meadows, between the sink of the Humboldt and Carson Valley. The vein is over four feet in thickness, and has already been traced a distance of six miles, and prospected three miles and a half. The ore is decomposed and easily worked. An assay of the ore by J. J. Ott of this city, gives a result warranting $840 to the ton, worked in an ordinary mill, leaving $130 in the tailings to be collected by the process. The metal obtained is composed of one-third silver . . . . The news of the discovery has created quite an excitement in our hitherto quiet burg.*

The headline had inaccurately described the vein as being on the eastern slope of the Sierra Nevada, while it was actually on the eastern slope of the Virginia Range. But once the word got out prospectors found it anyway, arriving on Sun Mountain from California in droves, up to 10,000 of them by one count. As one early historian noted, ". . . [they] were flocking over the mountains on horseback, on foot, with teams, and in any way that offered. Many men packed donkeys with tools and provisions, and going on foot themselves trudged over the Sierra at the best speed they were able to make."[11] Once there, these men hastily threw up tent camps at Virginia City, Gold Hill and nearby Silver City.

The rush to the Comstock was on!

When Duane Bliss relocated to Gold Hill, shortly after all of the foregoing had taken place, he became one of the town's early pioneers. J. Ross Browne, one of the first journalists to write about the Comstock, arrived just two months after Bliss, and he spoke of what both men would have seen upon arriving in Virginia City and Gold Hill:

> *Framed shanties, pitched together as if by accident; tents of canvas, of blankets, of brush, of potato-sacks and old shirts, with empty whiskey-barrels for chimneys; smoky hovels of mud and stone; coyote holes in the mountain side forcibly seized and held by men; pits and shafts with smoke issuing from every crevice . . . . The intervals of space, which may or may not have been streets, were dotted over with human beings of such sort, variety, and numbers that the famous ant-hills of Africa were as nothing in the comparison . . . . To say that they were rough, muddy, unkempt and unwashed, would be but fairly expressive of their actual appearance . . . . Here and there, to be sure, a San Francisco dandy of the "boiled shirt" and "stove-pipe" pattern loomed up in proud consciousness of the triumphs of art under adverse circumstances, but they were merely peacocks in the barn-yard.*[12]

When Bliss arrived, Gold Hill boasted 638 residents living in 179 dwellings. Less than three percent of the town's citizens were women. There were nineteen boarding houses and three hotels, three restaurants of the most basic kind, four saloons, and tradesmen of all stripes. Nearby Silver City had a near-identical population, but Virginia City—the metropolis of Sun Mountain—had nearly twice the population of the other two combined. Most of the men on the Comstock were between twenty and thirty—mining was a young man's game—and about fifteen percent were in their teens. Most of the Irish miners had settled in Virginia City, whereas Gold Hill was home to the Cornish miners. But both towns were a multilingual mishmash of Germans, English, Chinese, Scottish, Swiss, Canadians, Italians, Mexicans, Portuguese and Native Americans.[13]

Another newcomer to the Comstock added her discouraging description of the area's flora: "Nothing will grow . . . except it is irrigated. You Eastern people, with your splendid yards and flower-gardens . . . would laugh to see the Nevadans nursing pig-weeds and every blade of grass that chance produces in their yards. They will sow . . . anything that will cover the dust, and water it with as much care as you would a bed of geraniums. A very few scrub cedars and pines remain, [and] the mountains are covered with sage-brush . . . . There are no wild flowers, save a few wild daisies and thistles."[14]

About the town's mineral resources, however, The *Nevada Territorial Enterprise* newspaper wrote, "At Gold Hill, there is more gold taken out than at any other portion of the country . . . . The town is improving very fast."[15]

The fact that the Comstock vein contained both silver and gold was not the only difference between prospecting on Sun Mountain and prospecting in the western Sierra Nevada. There were other distinctions, and they were significant. First, the vast majority of Sun Mountain's gold and silver was tightly locked up in a matrix of quartz, the earth's most common mineral. Quartz is very stable, and has a strong resistance to weathering. Thus, with the exception of the small amount that eons of wind and rain had unlocked and sent down the streams, gullies and canyons, most of the gold and silver on Sun Mountain remained tightly bound up within its quartz host. This meant that once the loose gold had been placered and claimed, extraction would have to begin on the quartz vein itself, a process known as "hard rock mining." Some of the vein was at ground level, exposed in outcroppings and ledges, but most of it was buried deep underground.

Hard rock mining, unlike placer mining, was a two-step process. First the ore had to be extracted from the earth. Then it had to be processed to

Chapter 4. The Comstock Lode

The earliest known picture of Duane L. Bliss, taken in the early to mid-1860s. Bliss would have been about thirty years old at the time of this portrait, and on the cusp of beginning his banking career on the Comstock. (Courtesy of the Bliss Family)

separate the precious metals from the waste. To separate the gold and silver from the quartz in the surface outcroppings and ledges, early miners hacked chunks of the ore out with pickaxes and hammers, and then crushed it in a Mexican *arrastra*, a crude mule- or horse-powered device that pulverized the ore between harder rocks. The fine gravel that resulted was then treated in a large pan with water, salt and copper sulfates, or quicksilver. The resulting paste was then mixed with mercury, which bonded with the gold and silver and sunk to the bottom of the pan. Once heated, this material burned off the mercury, leaving only the valuable gold and silver residue.[16]

Once the placer deposits had disappeared, and the surface and sub-surface ore had been mined, the rest of the Comstock vein was much more difficult to reach. Underground mining was expensive, and beyond the reach of average prospectors, so most gave up, sold their claims to others for whatever cash they could get, and moved on. A new era in mining was about to begin—corporatized mining—and two new industries were about to be introduced to the western edge of Utah Territory: quartz milling and lumbering. Duane Bliss, the twenty-seven year old Massachusetts native who was still trying to find his way in the West, would become heavily involved in all three of these vital industries.

*

By the early 1860s all the quartz ore was being extracted from deep shafts and tunnels that honeycombed Sun Mountain, but the gold and silver still had to be separated from the quartz. Quartz milling was about to become big business on the Comstock. Between its mining and its milling, Virginia City earned the unofficial designation as the first industrial city in the West, an honor that rightfully belonged to all of the Comstock's towns and settlements.

By a stroke of good fortune, Duane Bliss made the acquaintance of an extraordinary man, ten years his senior, who was also a newcomer to the mountain. Almarin B. Paul was originally from New Jersey, and had gone to California as a '49er after gaining experience in the copper mines of Lake Superior. During the decade of the 1850s the multi-talented Paul was a merchant, a mill owner, a real estate investor, a journalist and a newspaper publisher, and he had succeeded quite nicely at most of those endeavors. By the late 1850s he was again running his own mill, the Oriental Quartz Mill in California's Nevada County, when news of the Comstock Lode erupted. In addition to his other talents, Paul was also blessed with the calculating

Chapter 4. The Comstock Lode

mind of an engineer. He was one of the first men to understand that quartz milling was the answer to unlocking the treasures of the Comstock Lode.[17]

Crushing ore in a quartz mill uses the same basic principle as the mortar and pestle used by primitive people thousands of years ago, and the device would quickly replace the Mexican *arrastras*. The process had been used for centuries, and made its debut in California during the Gold Rush era. Quartz (or stamp) mills used heavy piston-like hammers, or stamps, that were lifted by steam power then released to drop repeatedly on the ore, pulverizing it. All early quartz mills, including those on the Comstock, used this same process to crush ore. Although this method employed basic engineering, the equipment necessary to crush the ore was expensive. Machinery costs of $50,000 to $100,000 were not unusual, and as the Comstock's quartz mills grew bigger and bigger, the costs went up accordingly. Getting the necessary lumber and machinery transported up the mountain was also very expensive, especially before the first roads were built in the early 1860s.

The difference in Almarin Paul's process was in how he separated the precious metals from the quartz after it had been pulverized. He developed a new and better method that became known as the "Washoe pan process," and he decided to take this new method to the Comstock by opening a quartz mill there. He rounded up some friends with capital, and in March 1860 they formed the Washoe Gold and Silver Mining Company No. 1. Paul began scouting for the best place to build his mill, the first quartz mill on the Comstock. Water was necessary for the process, but he found most of the streams already claimed by other miners. Finally, four miles south of Virginia City, he found a small basin in Gold Canyon, just below Silver City, where the water from a number of small streams converged, a perfect place for his mill .[18]

Grading the hilly land where the mill was to be located was the first step, and in June 1860, Paul hired Duane Bliss to either assist in grading the site or to manage the task. Bliss's description of that job, from his Bancroft interview, does not clearly state exactly what his role was.[19]

Paul also began lining up customers for his mill. Two of the largest mines, the Ophir and the Mexican, refused to do business with him, and the leading assayers in San Francisco predicted failure for Paul's undertaking. But he persevered by securing contracts from the owners of many of the smaller mining claims on Gold Hill, and soon collected orders to crush and reduce 9,000 tons of ore at between $25 and $30 a ton. To get these contracts, however, he had to promise that the mill would be operational in two months, by August 12. Paul's plant engineer, William H. Baker, and the mill's builder ramped up their efforts. Machinery was ordered from Messrs. Howland, Angell and King of the Miners' Foundry in San Francisco, lumber—always a challenge to find—was ordered from the nearest sawmill, and the work went on. To everyone's surprise, on August 9 engineer Baker pulled a lever and sent the first shrill scream of a steam whistle echoing through the canyons of the Comstock, announcing the completion of the task. Two days later, and one day ahead of the deadline, the mill's twenty-four steam-propelled stamps began pulverizing rock. They had done it![20]

The mill had contracts with Holmes & Logan Company and the Alford Company, among others. It had the capacity to crush thirty tons of ore a day, and employed fifteen men. The role that Duane Bliss played in the construction of the Washoe Mill is not recorded, other than assisting in the initial site grading, but his participation must have been substantial. Only thirty days after the startup of the mill, the superintendent, C. W. Knox, resigned. Almarin Paul had seen something he liked in Bliss because he appointed the young man to be the new mill superintendent.[21] At the same time, or shortly thereafter, Bliss was also given the opportunity to buy into the new mill, which he did. This would turn out to be the beginning of a long and storied career for the young man from Massachusetts.

Paul's Washoe pan process proved to be more effective at separating gold from its quartz host than silver. Since Gold Hill's ledges were richer in gold, the mill was very successful. Within months Paul decided to build a larger mill, a sixty-four stamp mill that he would locate even closer to Gold Hill. By January 1861 this new mill was also in operation.[22] The *1st Directory of Nevada Territory* described the new mill: "This building . . . is one hundred and ten feet long and seventy-five wide, containing one hundred thousand feet of lumber. The engine is of sixty horse power, drives eight Howland batteries—eight stamps each—in all sixty-four, being the largest number in any mill in the Territory. The machinery comes from the Miners' Foundry, San Francisco, and is very massive . . . . [The mill] runs day and night, Sundays excepted, as do the mills throughout the country."[23]

Two months after the new mill went into operation, Almarin Paul and Duane Bliss entered into a contract with the former superintendent, C. W. Knox, to sell him the original mill and its attendant water privileges for $800. The deed does not stipulate which equipment was included in the sale, but given the cost of milling equipment, it's doubtful if it was part of the agreement. Most or all of it was probably moved to the new mill.[24]

Chapter 4. The Comstock Lode

For the next year-and-a-half Bliss oversaw the operation of the new mill, the largest quartz mill in the Territory. It employed fifty men, and it used more than fifty amalgamating pans to filter out the gold and silver.[25] Underground mining was one of the most dangerous jobs in the nineteenth century. Comstock historian Lord wrote that 111 miners lost their lives between 1863 and 1871.[26] And milling, like mining, could be dangerous work. In April 1861—under Bliss's watch—a worker was killed after being caught up on one of the stamps' flywheels and crushed.[27]

It was about this time, on April 12, 1861—one month after the establishment of Nevada Territory—that the Army of the Confederacy fired on the Union Army at Fort Sumter in South Carolina, nearly 2,700 miles east of Virginia City. The Civil War had begun. It had little impact on Nevada Territory, but about 1,200 local men did elect to return east and fight for the cause. Most fought on the Union side, but a handful also fought for the Confederacy.

Back on the Comstock, and because of the success Paul and other early mill operators enjoyed, competition soon became intense. By 1862, seventy-four other mills were operating on or near the Comstock, and twenty more were under construction or planned. Most of the mills crushed ore for their own mines, as the Washoe did, but also did the crushing for smaller mining operations that could not afford to build and operate their own mill.[28]

In early 1862 Bliss informed Almarin Paul that he was resigning his position. He told his employer that he planned to return to his boyhood home in Savoy, which he had not visited since leaving more than a dozen years earlier. William, his father, was still living, and perhaps it was a family visit that called him East. Or Bliss's decision may have had something to do with the Civil War, then raging in the eastern and southern states. We cannot know for sure. Perhaps he would even stay back east permanently, he told Paul. The two men had previously had a conversation that made this announcement even more surprising to Paul. In that earlier conversation, Paul had told Bliss that he and his plant engineer and friend, William H. Baker, planned to open a bank in Gold Hill, and he invited Bliss to join them as a partner in the venture. Now, Bliss had announced he was leaving. However, he told Paul that if he did decide to return to Nevada Territory, and if the generous offer still stood, he would be honored to join Paul and Baker in the banking enterprise.[29]

*

As the Comstock's mines and the quartz mills were rapidly expanding in both numbers and production output, large-scale lumbering, another new industry, was also taking hold in Nevada Territory; and it would be as vital to the success of mining the Comstock Lode's treasures as the ore itself.

Lumbering in the Tahoe-Truckee Basin—the trough separating the western face of the Carson Range, an outlier of the Sierra Nevada, and the eastern face of the main Sierra Nevada—had been initiated by settlers in the Washoe and Carson valleys in the early 1850s. These were farmers who harvested just enough timber to build their barns, houses and corrals, and to use for winter firewood. Members of the Mormon settlement at Franktown in the Washoe Valley built the first sawmill in the Nevada portion of the basin in 1856. It was a water-powered mill that ran two saws—an upright and a circular.[30]

But the 1859 frenzy of mining on the Comstock changed everything. The two Irishmen, McLaughlin and O'Riley, and their two uninvited partners, Henry Comstock and Manny Penrod, had sold one-third of their 1,400-foot Ophir Mine claim in mid-1859 to two other men in return for the men agreeing to build a couple of *arrastas* on site to grind the ore.[31] Then, in the fall of 1859, they sold the remaining portion to Judge James Walsh of Nevada City. Walsh had begun his mining operation through a shaft in the side of Sun Mountain. Miners were lowered into the shaft by a windlass that also brought the ore back to the surface in buckets. Soon the windlass was replaced by a horse pulling a winch, a device known as a "whim." As the shaft went deeper, the miners encountered water, and Walsh added a fifteen-horsepower steam engine to pump the water out and to replace the whim in hoisting the ore and miners out of the shaft. But as the miners continued deeper into the earth, the ore body widened and grew softer. The only system of mine timbering then known to mining science was to sheathe the sides of the shaft with upright pine pillars, then shore up the ceiling with poles that stretched atop these side pillars.[32]

In past mining ventures, this system had been sufficient to support the overhanging mass of rock. However, the Comstock ore body was much wider and went deeper than any vein that had been mined before, and this feeble support system was not strong enough to hold back the crushing force of the weight upon it. Cave-ins began to occur, killing or maiming a few unfortunate miners. When the Ophir shaft had reached a depth of 215 feet, the ore body was sixty-five feet wide, and miners refused to go back into the shaft for fear of being crushed to death. Work at the Ophir mine was suspended, and

Chapter 4. The Comstock Lode

one of the Ophir's directors—some sources suggest it was George Hearst, founder of the vast Hearst fortune—put the problem to a young German mining engineer, Philip Deidesheimer. He visited the Comstock, and at the end of a month's study he had developed the square-set timbering system.33 It is said that Deidesheimer's inspiration for the system was a honeybee's comb that he spotted in one of the mine shafts.

A "square-set" is a crib-like box made up of four to six-foot long timbers, interlocked at the ends by mortises and tenons. Individual cribs can be added inside a mine, set by set, in any direction and to any height, width or length, creating an endless number of configurations. Think of it as a set of toddler's wooden blocks, but hollow inside, being stacked one atop the other in an endless array of patterns. Once a square-set was placed in a shaft, the open sides in a crib could be covered with wooden slats and the crib filled with waste rock or dirt, making the whole as firm as the original mountain.

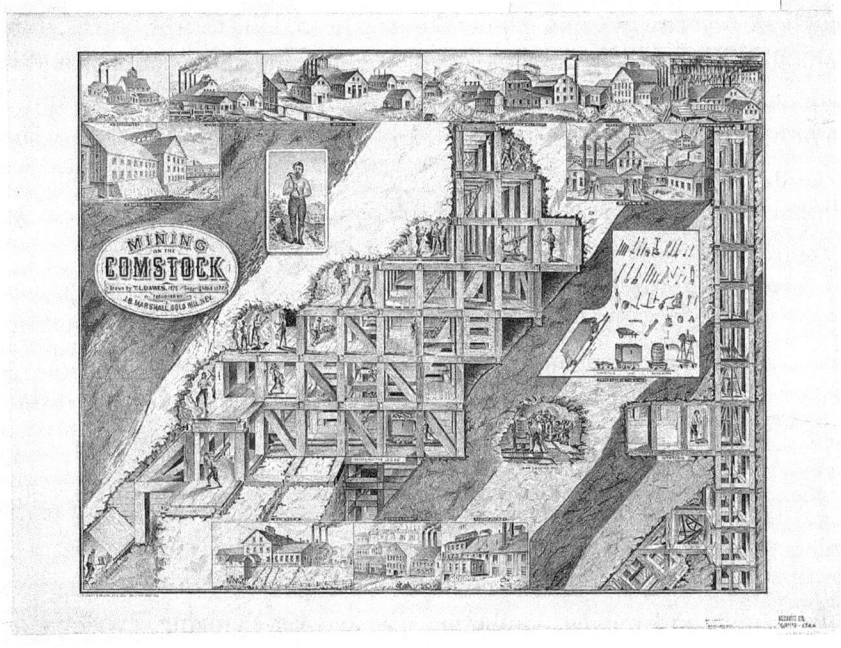

A cutaway drawing of a typical mine on the Comstock graphically illustrates the versatility of the Deidesheimer square-set timbering system that supported the silver mines as they plunged deeper and deeper—up to 3200 feet according to one estimate—into Sun Mountain, These elaborate structures, often described as being like buried cathedrals, had a voracious appetite for thick timbers and would spur the success of Duane Bliss's Carson & Tahoe Lumber & Fluming Company. (Library of Congress)

One Comstock historian described a typical square-set system as a gigantic wooden skyscraper plunging into the earth.[34]

The square-set timbering system would eventually be employed all over the world, but unfortunately for Deidesheimer he never got around to patenting the idea. He did remain at the Ophir as superintendent of the mine, and years later managed mines for John Mackay and his partners, discoverers of "The Big Bonanza."

Once Deidesheimer had solved the Comstock's biggest problem, a huge new market for timbers developed overnight. Historian Eliot Lord called the Comstock mines "the tombs of the Sierran forests," for all the lumber they devoured. He estimated that as of 1880 fully 600 million board feet of lumber had been buried in the mines, enough to build a town of six-room houses for 150,000 people. There was also a simultaneous demand for lumber to build all the mills, stores and houses on and around Sun Mountain, as well as a voracious need for the cordwood that fueled the steam engines that performed many mining functions, and heated the nearby homes, stores and offices. Because of the difficulty of transporting all this lumber up Sun Mountain from the valleys below—remember, the slopes of Sun Mountain were barren of trees—prices were exorbitant. Lumbering historian Dick Wilson, quoting the *Sacramento Union* from 1860, said the prices of lumber in Virginia City had skyrocketed from $100 per thousand board feet to $300 in just one month's time, reflecting the growing demand.[35]

Very soon dozens of sawmills, contiguous to adjoining timberland, appeared all along the eastern border of the Carson Range, serving the booming new Comstock market. The *San Francisco Bulletin* of April 23, 1860 reported on the activity at just one of the many sawmills, the Gregory-Riddle mill: "Were the capacity of the mill four times as great [as 15,000 board feet a day] . . . it could not supply the demand."[36]

Most of the sawmills were concentrated along the main streams of the valley in order to provide flotation for moving the logs from the stands of timber to the mill, and to harness the stream's energy to drive the big saws. Like mining and milling, lumbering was an ever-changing, ever-evolving industry.

The demand for lumber accelerated even more in the late 1860s as the Central Pacific Railroad was being built through the Truckee Basin. Rail ties, locomotive fuel, and housing in the towns that sprung up along the railroad created a heavy demand for building materials. *The San Francisco Call* reported in 1878, long after the fact, that 300 million board feet of lumber

Chapter 4. The Comstock Lode

was required just to build the forty miles of snow sheds that sheltered the Central Pacific's tracks crossing the Sierra Nevada summit.[37]

Mining, milling and lumbering—these three industries went hand-in-hand on the Comstock, and each was dependent on the others for its success. It was truly a symbiotic relationship. It was also a relationship that would eventually make a multi-millionaire of young Duane Bliss when he returned to the Comstock. But first, another relationship—a romantic one—would offer the young man a totally different kind of riches.

CHAPTER 5

The Banker's Wife

As planned, upon leaving his position as manager of the Washoe Quartz Mill in 1862, Duane Bliss returned to Massachusetts for a visit. During his stay, while visiting some old friends in eastern Massachusetts, he met a young lady named Elizabeth Tobey. Elizabeth was twenty-two, and lived in South Wareham, near Cape Cod. Her parents, Seth and Lucinda Tobey, were a well-to-do family with American roots dating back to early colonial days. After a brief courtship, Duane and Elizabeth became engaged. In June, missing the excitement of the West and finding no better offer than Paul's, Bliss decided to return to Nevada Territory. He and Elizabeth made plans for his return to Massachusetts in two years time, at which point they would marry. His future decided, Duane returned to Gold Hill.[1]

Almarin Paul told Bliss that the bank deal was still on, but that it would be another year before they were ready to launch the enterprise. Bliss's old job at the Washoe mill had been filled, so Paul recommended him for a position managing Lindauer & Hirschman's quartz mill in Dayton, a small community on the Carson River at the foot of Sun Mountain.[2] Because of the water from the nearby river, Dayton—originally called Chinatown—had become the hub for milling Comstock ore.

The 1863 *Second Directory of Nevada Territory* described the small mill where Bliss spent his next year: "Lindauer & Hirschman's mill—situated on the west side of the river . . . is sixty by seventy-five feet in extent; runs fifteen stamps, and crush[es] about fifteen tons of ore per day. This company own[s] in the celebrated Gold Hill Proper, and keeps their mill continually running on their own rock. . . . Employ[s] eight hands, and work[s] the ore for both gold and silver."[3] From Bliss's lodging in Gold Hill, it was a seven-mile trip down a Gold Canyon toll road to Dayton, a rough, crowded road over which most of the quartz passed in heavily laden, mule-drawn wagons.[4] Thus it's likely that Bliss took lodgings in Dayton during the year in which he worked in that town.

By 1862 mining on the Comstock had become big business. Most of the early prospectors had sold out as soon as their claims fetched a decent price. A new breed—the professional investor—had appeared on the scene. J. Ross Browne, the journalist, had referred to this type as the "San Francisco dandy of the 'boiled shirt' and 'stove-pipe' pattern."[5] These were the men with plenty of money—or in some cases, with no money at all, save for a sufficient amount to make a good appearance—and they were there with one purpose in mind: to prospect the prospectors.

The Comstock was no longer a grubbing-in-the-gravel type of mining operation. Other professionals—more skilled and often more ethical—also showed up on the Comstock. These were the bankers, the engineers, the assayers, the deep-rock miners, the equipment mechanics, and others of their ilk. The mountain had quickly become industrialized and corporatized, with expensive equipment and knowledgeable experts required to unearth and refine the Comstock's treasure. As historian Ronald James noted, "The Comstock matured . . . and as corporate structure solidified the area, the hallmarks of the freewheeling early days vanished."[6]

In 1860 the Comstock had yielded $1 million in bullion, and just two years later that figure had swelled to $6.2 million. However, in spite of the Comstock's promise, the area became mired in a deep recession. Still, bullion figures would keep climbing through 1866, then begin to drop until 1871 when it began to show signs of recovery. In 1873 John Mackay and three partners discovered a huge underground mountain of silver and gold—the "Big Bonanza" of Nevada mining lore—that propelled earnings skyward for another five years until the boom finally ended.[7]

Success in this milieu required more than a small dose of optimism. It also required money, big money, and big money meant banks and bankers. The Comstock's first bank, the Wells Fargo & Co. Express and Banking Company, opened in 1860 in Virginia City. By 1863 there were six banks on Sun Mountain.

Although Wells Fargo & Co. initially eschewed making loans, they did provide most of the other basic services that a bank provides today. Other banks that followed did provide loans, as mining and milling required capital outlays that exceeded what most mine owners could procure on their own. Ten percent interest a month, with appropriate security, became the going rate at all banks in the early years. In mid-1863, Almarin B. Paul & Co., Bankers, finally opened their doors in Gold Hill. The bank was located on Main Street, on the ground floor of the Odd Fellows Building. The remainder

Chapter 5. The Banker's Wife

In 1863 the firm of Almarin B. Paul & Company, Bankers, opened in Gold Hill. Duane Bliss was one of the partners in the enterprise. This advertisement appeared in the *Directory of Nevada Territory 1863*.

of the floor was taken up by other stores and offices, while the upper floor was occupied by the Odd Fellows Hall. The three partners in the enterprise were Almarin Paul, D. L. Bliss and William H. Baker.[8] Although there were a number of banks operating out of Virginia City, only one other one was located in Gold Hill at the time, operated by H. G. Maynard, a former Wells Fargo express agent. Later in the year Maynard was joined by a partner, and the bank became known as Maynard & Flood.[9]

While some Sun Mountain banks foundered, the Almarin B. Paul Bank prospered. It would be joined by other new banks over the next few years as everyone on the West Coast, it seemed, wanted to get a slice of the Comstock's fabulous wealth. As the solid reputation of the bank grew, so did the reputation of one of its partners, Duane Bliss. A notice in the *Gold Hill News* in January 1864 announced that the trustees of the Confidence Gold and Silver Mining Company—one of the bank's customers—had called for an assessment on their shareholders. The notice was signed, "D. L. Bliss, Secretary, Confidence G. & S. M. Com'y." The Confidence owned 100 feet on the ledge of the Comstock vein—the amount of space on the vein was the most commonly used factor in determining a mining company's potential—and it mined through a shaft at a depth of 450 feet.[10] That Bliss had been selected as a trustee and an officer of the mining company—and perhaps also as an investor—reflected his growing stature on the Comstock.

*

In early 1864 Duane Bliss took a leave from the bank and returned to his Massachusetts home to marry the young lady to whom he had become engaged two years earlier. Elizabeth Thatcher Tobey was waiting, and on April 6 the couple exchanged their vows in Wareham. The Tobeys could trace their New World roots back eight generations to Thomas Tobey's arrival in the 1640s from Wales. Elizabeth's father, Seth Fish Tobey, had inherited a sizable amount of land from his father, Curtis E. Tobey, and was, while not among the super-rich, still quite well off. Elizabeth had one living sister and two brothers, both of who would eventually re-settle in the West. One of her brothers, Walter Danforth Tobey, would live in Carson City and eventually go into business with Duane Bliss.[11]

After completing his visit with family and friends, Bliss returned to Nevada Territory with his new bride. From Carson City, Duane and Elizabeth Bliss took the only road from the territorial capital to the Comstock, the Washoe Road, on the way to their new home. At about the same time, roving writer and artist J. Ross Browne was making his second trip up the mountain for his second book, *Washoe Revisited*, which would be published in 1865. What Browne saw out of the window of his stagecoach, and penned for his book, was exactly what Elizabeth Bliss would have seen, and it was nothing like Massachusetts:

> At Empire City [near Dayton] I was quite bewildered with the busy scenes of life and industry. Quartz-mills and saw-mills had completely usurped the valley along the head of the Carson River; and now the hammering of stamps, the hissing of

Chapter 5. The Banker's Wife

steam, the whirling clouds of smoke from tall chimneys and the confused clamor of voices . . . reminded one of a manufacturing city.

. . . at Silver City, there were similar evidences of prosperity. From the descent into the canyon through Devil's Gate, and up the grade to Gold Hill, it is almost a continuous line of quartz-mills, tunnels, dumps, sluices, water-wheels, frame shanties, and grog-shops.

Gold Hill itself has swelled into the proportions of a city. It is now practically a continuation of Virginia [City]. . . . The whole hill is riddled and honey-combed with shafts and tunnels. Engine-houses for hoisting are perched on points apparently inaccessible; quartz-mills of various capacities line the sides of the canon; the main street is well flanked by brick houses, hotels, express-offices, saloons, restaurants, groggeries, and all those attractive places of resort which go to make up a flourishing mining town.[12]

Shortly after her arrival in Gold Hill, Elizabeth Bliss recorded her own observations, in a letter written to an aunt back East.

June 30, 1864
My Dear Aunt:
I remember you telling me to be sure to give you my impressions of this place. They certainly are more favorable than I expected them to be when on board the steamer. There were two gentlemen who had been there three years ago when it was but a year old, and they told me I could never live here, it was a god-forsaken place, etc., etc. Duane did not take pains to correct their statements, not caring how poor an idea I had of the place, thinking it was always better to be happily surprised than otherwise. I left the coach, after traveling in it all day and night, at Carson some seventeen miles from here with as dirty a face as I ever remember since I got to be over twenty years old. [Duane and Elizabeth had taken a steamship to San Francisco, then the stagecoach to Gold Hill] After trying a half hour to make myself decent to see strangers, [I] was presented to a young friend of Duane's who had come with Mr. Paul's team to take us to our place of destination. I saw very little of note—excepting now and then a shaft sunk in the mountain by means of which the mill was supplied with ore—until we got to Silver City which is a place about the size of Rochester, but the houses are smaller.

Elizabeth Bliss was obviously an intelligent and observant woman, due in part to her eastern upbringing and excellent schooling. But she was obviously a sensitive and optimistic person as well. Where most early Comstock women

49

saw Sun Mountain and its towns as ugly, parched places, Mrs. Bliss noticed some beauty in them:

> *The land is barren, producing only sagebrush except, occasionally, as handsome flowers as I ever saw. They were really beautiful. There was a species resembling portulaca [moss rose] very much being white and pink blossoms on one stalk; then there was a blue flower that looked precisely like larkspur, beside a variety of others. It seemed quite strange to me that they could be contented to grow where not a spear of grass showed itself. After leaving Silver City we soon found ourselves in Gold Hill, the entrance to which place is called the Devil's Gate and it truly looks as though he had a hand in building it. It is a mountainous pass, on either side of which are many huge rocks 120 feet high and in the most rugged shape you can imagine. Great boulders that are sticking out all over it looked as though they were just ready to fall. It is frightful but yet so grand. I have heard there are photographs of it and if I can find one will send it home so you will be able to form some idea of it. It did not take long to get through the pass and we had entered the most humble of all humble places, as I supposed, with my eyes as wide open as the dust and sleepless night would allow, to take in all the drawbacks at once. But instead [of] finding brown hills with enormous holes dug into them where the ore was taken out and with them a miner's hut with now and then a frame building, I found a large village with the houses, most of them small cottages, just as close at the foot of the mountain on either side of the street as they could stand. Then there are streets out into the mountain and houses are built there also. For people to get up to them from the main street there are stairs in some places and in others you have to climb on paths.*[13]

Elizabeth Bliss would have found a more civilized and sophisticated Gold Hill than her husband had first encountered four-and-a-half years earlier. Nearly one in five residents were now women, and there were many services available for them in Gold Hill and Virginia City. There were seventeen dress makers and milliners, thirteen boot and shoe makers, eighteen clothing stores and two tailors, with more arriving every month.[14] As J. Ross Browne had noted, Gold Hill had become a full-fledged city. Elizabeth Bliss was impressed—and somewhat surprised—at what she found:

> *The houses are furnished well and there is much more dress displayed here than on Beacon Street when the ladies make calls. They seldom walk out for pleasure. Their houses are too small to entertain company for any length of*

Chapter 5. The Banker's Wife

time so visiting is seldom thought of, but they call often. I have had a quantity of callers and I like them very much with but one or two exceptions. And such a display of dress I never expected to see here. They never think of wearing anything but point and thread lace. A Mrs. Winters came with her carriage to call on me yesterday and Mrs. Vesey [wife of Gold Hill Hotel proprietor, G. H. Vesey[15]*] said that her collar and sleeves must have cost one hundred dollars and the rest of her dress in comparison. She had on a thread lace cape, blue bands of silk. Cheap dress goods are not kept in the stores. And in Virginia, which is but a half a mile from here, there are better stores than in New Bedford, and I do not believe as nice silk can be found in Boston . . . .*[16]

Still, first and foremost, the Comstock was mining territory. Elizabeth's husband Duane had spent years in and around the mining and milling business before becoming a banker, and most of his friends and business associates were involved with the mines or the mills. To understand mining better, Elizabeth was certainly not above getting her hands dirty. Her letter continued:

The mines, instead of being dug in from the side, are worked by means of a shaft being sunk in them. I went down into one called the Imperial mine a distance of 450 feet. We were given one of those two specimens that Duane sent with his collection to Uncle. He put mine in with his but the specimens are all his but two. A man came into the office just after he got the collection packed and offered him $100 for it.

The mine was very dark and close. The miners were working by the light of candles and Duane and Mr. Cory had one to light Katie, a lady who went with me, and myself around. They begin at the bottom of a mine and work up. When they dig out the ore some six feet or more, they put in huge timbers six feet high and work from this [level] until they get another space the same size and then they put in timber the same size as the other on top of them, and this is the way they keep on working, up instead of down. The mountains around here are just like a honeycomb being worked in the same way, but on the outside you can see but one opening from the [hillside] through which the ore is brought to the surface. I saw one place in the Imperial that had been built up in the way I have described—six stories and they were still going up at the time. The timbers are used to keep the mine from falling in after having taken the ore out. . . .[17]

The remainder of Elizabeth's original letter has been lost, but in it she has given us a rare look at the Comstock from the untrained eye of a newcomer. The Imperial Mine Elizabeth referred to was Almarin Paul's old Washoe Gold and Silver Mining Company No. 1. Her description of the huge timber framework she saw when visiting the mine was one of the most important developments on the Comstock: Philip Deidesheimer's square-set mining system.

*

The authors of "The Advantages of Ladies' Society," one of the essays in the groundbreaking book, *Comstock Women*, pointed out that residents of Virginia City, Gold Hill and Silver City had more in common with residents of Philadelphia and San Francisco than with those of an isolated Nebraska homesteader. ". . . the Comstock's communities embodied urban culture and expectations," they wrote. Most especially, middle- and upper-class women of the Comstock made a civilized life for themselves and their families on their isolated mountainside.[18]

Mrs. Minerva Morris was a resident of Gold Hill. In October 1863, when a new newspaper, the *Gold Hill News*, was launched, Mrs. Morris, through a letter to the editor, took the opportunity to speak up for the growing importance of women in the town: "People elsewhere now only know that this is some sort of place more natural than artificial, more rough than elegant, more rich than refined. They don't know that this is a town nearly as large as the largest towns of California, and that we abound in wives, maidens and children."

She went on to speak up for the hundreds of forgotten community members—its women: " . . . I believe that the growing moral excellence of our Territory is very fully due to family and female influence, an influence which is increasing every day."[19]

Life on the Comstock for women like Elizabeth Bliss and Minerva Morris was not one-dimensional. Opportunities abounded for women to be part of the social fabric of their communities. Elizabeth's father, Seth Fish Tobey, was a farmer, but a very well-to-do land-owning farmer. She was well schooled, and used to life as an upper-middle class New England lady. But her attitudes, as reflected in her letter home, showed her to be a strong-willed, optimistic woman who would fit into her husband's world with ease, wherever that might be.

Chapter 5. The Banker's Wife

The Devil's Gate, south of Gold Hill, as it would have been observed by new bride Elizabeth Bliss on her arrival at her new home on the Comstock. From a drawing by J. Ross Browne for his 1860 book, A Peep at Washoe.

For women who wished it, there could be an active social life. There were also numerous opportunities to participate in charitable work, which of course had a strong social aspect as well. Balls, fairs, bazaars and other types of fund-raisers were a constant in Virginia City, Gold Hill and Silver City. Other activities centered about the mountain's many churches. There were three at the time in Gold Hill: St. John's Episcopal Church, St. Patrick's Catholic Church, and a Presbyterian congregation that lacked a church building. Church activities could keep a woman as busy, involved and fulfilled as she wished to be.[20]

Historian Grant Smith summed up the attitude and the spirit of the men and women who settled on the Comstock in the 1860s and 1870s: "Of course, all were going to get rich and retire to California, but in the meantime, they lived for the day. Humor was still the prevailing spirit.... A more self-reliant, independent, brave, and generous community of men and women did not exist. The world was young and they thought themselves fortunate to be living at such a time."[21]

In spite of all these opportunities available to Comstock women, the majority of their daily activities still centered around their homes and families. Duane and Elizabeth Bliss would have three of their five children while living in Gold Hill, prior to their move to Carson City in 1872.[22]

It is not known where in Gold Hill the Bliss family initially lived, since town directories in the decade of the 1860s did not provide addresses. There weren't a lot of houses for rent on the mountain, so the couple may have lodged with another family. There are no deeds in the Storey County recorders office reflecting that they purchased a house in the town.

On October 31, 1864 President Abraham Lincoln signed legislation admitting Nevada to the Union. The big event occurred only eight days prior to the 1864 presidential election, which was probably not a coincidence. Making Nevada the thirty-sixth state was a political move guaranteed to help ensure President Lincoln's reelection. However, to the folks on the Comstock it was a joyous time regardless of the reason and in spite of the Civil War that raged on in the East and South. "We got the telegram this morning announcing that the President has issued proclamation making us a *State*. Hurrah for the new state of Nevada," Alf Doten wrote. The journalist joined hundreds of other Comstock revelers the following Saturday for the official statehood celebration. "[A] Grand torchlight demonstration.... I counted procession ... and made about 3,000 all told," he wrote.[23]

Chapter 5. The Banker's Wife

Duane Bliss and a few of his Gold Hill friends and business associates also got together in the mid-1860s to found the Silver Star Lodge No. 165 of the Freemasons Society. The fraternal lodge eventually rose to a membership zenith of 194 members in 1877 when mining activity reached its peak. Nearby Virginia City also had a lodge, and the two would often hold joint gatherings, or work together on charitable projects for the benefit of their communities.[24]

Once all the statehood celebrations ended life returned to normal in Gold Hill and Virginia City. Little did all the miners and mill workers, the barbers and bootmakers, the wives and mothers, and the politicians and peddlers on the Comstock realize that very soon the entire nation would be eulogizing the very same man they had just recently been exalting.

CHAPTER 6

The Bank Ring

On April 14, 1865 all the Christian churches on the Comstock were filled, as men and their families observed Good Friday. There was a lot to celebrate and to give thanks for. Only five days earlier Robert E. Lee's Army of Northern Virginia had surrendered to Ulysses S. Grant's Army of the Potomac, virtually ending the Civil War that had ravaged the nation for the past four years. "Papers all got out an extra," wrote *Gold Hill News* editor Alf Doten, of Lee's surrender. ". . . [I]n less than 3 hours everybody was crazy drunk . . . Provost Guard came up with 2 pieces of cannon & fired in streets—flags flying everywhere—anvils, guns, pistols, everything that could made a noise did so."[1]

However, the revelry was cut short when on the very next day came the stunning news that President Abraham Lincoln had been assassinated. Three days later the *Gold Hill News* announced, "On the day the remains of the lamented President Lincoln are interred, the citizens of Gold Hill will also unite in celebration . . . by procession, prayer and funeral address." The chief marshall of the event named a number of community leaders to serve as his aides, including banker D. L. Bliss. Throughout the town flags were flown at half-mast, all the mines, mills and shops were closed, and the Catholic and Episcopal Church bells tolled from 10 a.m. until four o'clock in the afternoon. A procession of over 2,000 citizens walked solemnly through Gold Hill to Fort Homestead, a knoll overlooking the town where public observances were often held. There, a prayer and funeral address were offered in memory of the fallen president.[2]

It was a time of great sadness for Duane and Elizabeth Bliss and their neighbors. Yet little did the banker realize that in less than a month he would be standing at the threshold of amazing new opportunities, and rubbing shoulders with some of the Pacific West's most prominent and successful men.

The events that would change Duane Bliss's life had been set in motion less than a year earlier, in the late summer of 1864. William Chapman Ralston, who in later years would be credited with turning San Francisco into the leading city of the West, was sitting in his office in an ornate stone building at the corner of Sansome and California streets that housed the Bank of California. A visitor's knock on the door interrupted his work. William Sharon—"A small, though compactly formed person, quiet in manner, and reserved to the point of coldness"—had been bamboozled out of his entire fortune in a mining stock swindle, and he had gone with hat in hand to see Ralston and ask for a loan to bail him out. Ralston was a friendly, compassionate man, and he hated to see a man like Sharon, who had a wife and several children, groveling for help. So he arranged for the bank—actually, it was his bank, despite his modest title of cashier—to loan Sharon some money against his property. Then Ralston, in characteristic fashion, handed Sharon $500 out of his own pocket for his immediate needs.[3]

Despite falling victim to that mining swindle, Bill Sharon was not a gullible man. Ambitious and avaricious perhaps, but he was certainly not stupid. He was well educated, and before asking Ralston for help he had been involved in a number of different business ventures, most with some degree of success. He had been a stockbroker, a real estate salesman, a politician, an advocate for beleaguered immigrants, a land owner and a city alderman. He was also a respected orator who often quoted Shakespeare, an expert poker player, and a talented fiddler. "[Sharon] could fiddle the shirt off a man," one wag said of him.[4]

Physically, Sharon was a small man, weighing perhaps 135 pounds soaking wet. His eyes were his most discernible feature: "Detractors said they were black and beady, sly and devious; to friends they were searching, projecting intelligence," his biographer, Michael Makley, wrote. His unorthodox dress made him stand out. He wore black broadcloth, making him appear to be a minister, and a broad-brimmed slouch hat.[5]

Sharon was grateful to Ralston for the loans, but what he really needed was a job, and the timing of his visit to Ralston's office was perfect. Stateler & Arrington, a bank in Virginia City, Nevada, had gotten into financial trouble and owed the Bank of California $40,000. So Ralston hired Sharon, a man with no banking experience but with a shrewd mind, to go to the Comstock and straighten out the Stateler & Arrington mess. Ralston and Sharon were described by some historians as friends and confidants when Ralston assigned Sharon to this task, yet other historians claim that they hardly knew

Chapter 6. The Bank Ring

each other. The former is more likely the truth. Regardless, Ralston's faith in Sharon did seem to have its limits. He appointed his brother James to go along with Sharon, a role James filled for only a short time before passing away in 1866.[6]

C.C. "Charlie" Goodwin was one of those talented newspaper journalists and authors who worked alongside Mark Twain, Dan DeQuille, Alf Doten and others who left us such a magnificent legacy with their colorful descriptions of the people, places and events that made the Comstock the extraordinary place it is in American history. As a probate judge on the Comstock, and a district court judge following Nevada statehood, Goodwin later became the editor of the *Territorial Enterprise*, the *Washoe Times* and the *Salt Lake Tribune*. As a newsman, Goodwin had a unique talent for putting things in perspective. His description of the business climate that so excited Bill Sharon when he came on the scene goes a long way toward explaining why Sharon was able to manipulate the Comstock to his advantage, and earn him the enviable mantle of "King of the Comstock." As Goodwin wrote:

> *[Bill] Sharon . . . found a strange state of affairs. A good many crude quartz mills had been built, generally on insufficient capital; the cream of the croppings of the great lode had been skinned; most of the mines were in litigation; the little banks there had loaned all their money on mills and mines at a regular interest of five percent per month, but could collect neither principal nor interest, nor could run the mines nor mills; there were no pay days for miners, and Sharon found a community of several thousand people standing over immeasurable treasures, but unable to utilize them. . . . It was a case of oceans in sight but not a drop to drink.*[7]

Bill Sharon quivered with excitement at what he found. There was a situation,—an opportunity really—that Sharon knew in his bones was ripe for picking. He realized that the one raw material that was essential for developing the Comstock's riches was capital. Money would be needed to sink deep shafts into the mountainside, to shore them up with hundreds of thousands of board feet of timber, to buy expensive hoists, pumps, and other equipment, and to build costly quartz mills to crush the ore. Then there were staggering transportation costs to bring the supplies up the mountain and haul the ore down the mountain to the quartz mills. Money was the answer to all of these problems, Sharon knew. Big money.

All of the leading Comstock mining companies had their general offices in San Francisco, and banked at the Bank of California. Sharon wired

Ralston and told him they needed to open a bank on the Comstock; they had to move the money closer to where it was needed. Ralston wired back, "Come down, and we'll talk it over."[8]

Sharon easily won Ralston over with his vision. A few days later the Bank of California purchased the bank of Arnold & Blauvelt in Virginia City, a local bank with a handsome building and a profitable customer base. Thus, in late October 1864, just prior to the announcement that Nevada had been granted statehood, the Bank of California opened its agency in Virginia City. Sharon would be the general agent and James Ralston, William's brother, would assume the role of cashier. W. H. Blauvelt, who had been the junior partner in Arnold & Blauvelt, was the assistant cashier, later promoted to cashier after James Ralston passed away. Blauvelt was not unknown to the Bank of California men, since he had held a responsible position in the D. O. Mills' banking house in Sacramento before partnering in his own bank in Virginia City.[9]

So convinced was Sharon that his bank would wildly succeed that he moved into the second story of the bank building and made it his home, the better to keep a sharp eye on every aspect of the business. Having the powerful Bank of California on the Comstock set Almarin Paul, Duane Bliss and William Baker thinking about their Gold Hill bank's future. A number of small Comstock banks had already failed, and having the powerful new bank nearby could only spell trouble. W. H. Blauvelt explained why he and his partner had sold out to Ralston's bank, and the same rationale obviously applied to the Almarin B. Paul bank. In a nutshell, Blauvelt wrote, "Arnold & Blauvelt believed that [Bank of California] when established, would render business of other banks to be unprofitable . . . ."[10]

It isn't known when Almarin Paul, Duane Bliss and William Baker began discussing their bank with William Sharon. However, on May 1, 1865 a small notice appeared in the *Gold Hill News:* "BANK OF CALIFORNIA—By our advertising columns of to-day, it will be seen that Gold Hill is graced with a Branch of the Bank of California. This institution came into our State when our monetary pressure was very great, and with its extended capital relieved, materially, the wants of many of our mining companies . . . ."[11]

Immediately following the notice was a second one that reported that the Bank of California had taken over the bank of Almarin B. Paul. Paul, it said, was returning to his previous occupation as a mill operator.[12] The advertisement referred to in the first notice added that William Sharon was general agent of the new agency, and W. H. Blauvelt would be the cashier.

Chapter 6. The Bank Ring

Writing in Davis's *History of Nevada*, Blauvelt made it clear that he was the cashier in charge of the Gold Hill branch, indicating that he would manage the operation while Sharon and James Ralston concentrated on the Virginia City branch. The terms of the buyout of the Paul bank were not disclosed, but another advertisement stated that the partnership of Paul, Bliss and Baker was being dissolved with the closure of their bank.[13]

William Sharon was still a novice at banking, and his cashier, W. H. Blauvelt, held down responsibilities at both Comstock branches. An experienced banker was needed to fill out the management team, and Sharon immediately hired D. L. Bliss as assistant cashier.[14]

Bliss, along with his partners at the bank of Almarin B. Paul prior to its sale, had been active in the real estate market, buying and selling various pieces of property in and around Gold Hill. A number of their transactions involved small mining claims: Silver Vale Mining Co., Wallers Defeat Co., and Hawk Eye Mining Co. among others.[15] Bliss alone, for his personal portfolio, was involved in another transaction that indicated how shrewd a businessman he had become. In June 1865 he purchased a piece of property called the Barnes Hotel on Main Street in Gold Hill for $75. One month later he resold the same property for $2,000, a huge return on his investment.[16]

*

Who and what was this powerful new financial institution, the Bank of California, which was changing the lives of so many people, and altering forever the way business would be done on the Comstock? Prior to the 1860s, most commercial ventures were conducted by sole proprietors or partnerships. But the costs associated with mining on the Comstock were so immense that an old financial tool, incorporation, became a sudden fad. This allowed companies to accumulate capital by selling stock to the public, which allowed them to expand. Early stock shares had been sold on the streets of San Francisco by street brokers, but this process proved to be inefficient as the demand for stocks quickly accelerated. As a result, the San Francisco Mining Exchange was founded in September 1862, and it was soon followed by two other exchanges in the city and another one in Sacramento. Incorporation activity increased now that there were efficient markets in which it could operate. Historian David Lavender wrote that more than 4,000 incorporations followed in 1863, of which 2,933 were for mining companies.[17]

Over the next few years, fortunes were made and lost daily by those playing the market in mining stocks. "Overnight, chambermaids and courtesans had been converted into courted heiresses. In the twinkling of an eye, bartenders, hostlers, and watch-peddlers had become plutocrats, and had built incredible gingerbread houses on the ramparts of the city," George Lyman observed.[18] Modern-day stock market investors, or simply market watchers who remember the Internet stock trading frenzy of the late 1990s, can well understand what was happening in San Francisco in the 1860s. Manic buying . . . wildly fluctuating prices . . . huge profits and staggering losses . . . these were everyday occurrences during both periods.

By the beginning of 1864, the Comstock had yielded more than $22 million in silver and gold bullion.[19] The success of the mines on the Comstock, and the belief that its flow of wealth was endless, had wrought huge changes in San Francisco. The once-maritime capital of the West had now become the financial capital of the West. Many men saw opportunity in this new environment, and seized it. One man would rise above all the others.

William Chapman Ralston had been born in Plymouth, Ohio in 1826. For at least two generations before him, his ancestors had been riverboat people, and young Ralston initially gravitated, reluctantly, in that direction. But when gold was discovered in California in 1849 Ralston joined the thousands of other young men who headed for the goldfields.[20] While in Panama, en route to California, he was conscripted to captain the steamship *New Orleans* to San Francisco when the regular captain became ill. A brief fling as a partner in a shipping company followed, but Ralston found his real future when he opened a bank in San Francisco in 1856 with some associates. The bank had morphed into Donohoe, Ralston & Company by 1864, when Ralston dissolved the partnership while simultaneously opening a new bank, the Bank of California, the West's first solely commercial bank.

Prior to the new bank's founding, but with a specific plan of action in mind, Ralston had visited many of the city's leading businessmen touting the advantages of such an enterprise. He convinced twenty-two of his fellow leading men to invest with him for a total of $2 million, a princely sum in 1864. These men became known—not positively—as the Bank Ring. Ralston's most important recruit was Darius Ogden Mills, a wealthy ex-banker in Sacramento, and the West's most prominent and trusted financier. Mills was a reluctant partner; his plate was already full, and he already had plenty of money. But Ralston persisted, and Mills finally signed on. He would be the president of the Bank of California, but in name only. Ralston

Chapter 6. The Bank Ring

assured him that he, Ralston, would carry the more modest title of cashier, but in fact he would run the operation.[21]

On July 5, 1864 the Bank of California opened its doors in San Francisco. Beforehand the incorporators had secured over 500 accounts, totaling more than $1.6 million in deposits. Many of these new accounts were Comstock mining companies. It was an auspicious beginning.[22]

When the Bank of California opened their Virginia City branch, followed less than six months later with the branch in Gold Hill, it was obvious that William Sharon, William Ralston and the other members of the Bank Ring had a lot of faith in the Comstock. Their faith would be sorely tested throughout the latter half of the 1860s. Bill Sharon had enjoyed instant success with the Comstock branches. The local banks had formed a loose confederation in the early days agreeing that the interest on loans to mines and mills would be standardized at five per cent per month, surely a staggering rate today, but not so in the 1860s mining environment. But when Sharon opened his banks, he eschewed membership in the bankers' trade association, and he offered money at only two percent per month, and even lower when necessary. When bullion output at the mines began to slip dramatically in 1865, the mills were the first to suffer, and they began lining up at Sharon's two branches for loans to carry them through the tough times. Within a short span of time he had loaned $3.5 million to the struggling mills.[23]

But the tough times would soon be tougher than anyone imagined. *Borrasca* is a Spanish word, one of its definitions being "an exhausted mine." From the peak year of output in 1864 of $15.8 million, the Comstock mines' output slipped to $15.2 million in 1865, $14.2 million in 1866, $13.7 million in 1867, $8.5 million in 1868, and $7.5 in 1869.[24] That certainly spelled *borrasca* in anyone's book. Thousands of men began abandoning the Comstock, certain that its halcyon days were over. A few men, however— including Ralston and Sharon—were confident that there were more rich ore chambers lying undiscovered at deeper depths. Since neither man was a geologist or metallurgist, their confidence was more wishful thinking than anything else, but many experienced mining men felt the same way. Ralston had served as treasurer for several of the Comstock companies, including the Ophir, the Gould and the Curry; and he was still bullish on the Comstock.

As ore production dropped precipitously at the mines, expensive quartz milling machinery slowed down, then stopped, gathering cobwebs. What did not stop were the monthly interest payments due on the equipment at

Sharon's two Comstock banks. The first to fall was the Swansea Mill, on Gold Canyon, built in 1862 for $45,000. With its huge stamps silent, the Swansea was unable to make its payments, and it fell into foreclosure to the Bank of California. Over the next twelve months, six other quartz mills joined the Swansea in foreclosure. Mill owners pleaded with Sharon for more time, but business was business, and the hard-nosed banker showed no sympathy.[25]

Historian and journalist Sam P. Davis pointed out that this had likely been Sharon's plan all along: "If the scheme had not been thought of before, the acquisition of these mills suggested a plan by which the whole Comstock Lode could be squeezed like a lemon. The operation was not to be for the benefit of the stockholders in general, but only for those who became familiarly known as the Bank Ring."[26]

Controlling the mills, however, was only part of Sharon's grand plan. He wanted to control the mines too. By mid-1864 he had purchased fourteen shares of the Yellow Jacket Mining Company. A few other Yellow Jacket owners, principally Alvinza Hayward, were won over to his plan, and became members of the Bank Ring. The Yellow Jacket had an indebtedness

Quartz Mines at Gold Hill, about 1865. Bliss began his Comstock career managing quartz mills that crushed the mines' ore and refined it into precious metal. Later most of the mills relocated down the mountainside to the Carson River. (Special Collections Department, University of Nevada, Reno Library)

Chapter 6. The Bank Ring

of $114,716, which made it a prime takeover target. Under Sharon's direction the Yellow Jacket sank a new shaft of 360 feet, then deeper, and discovered rich ore that resulted in $6 million of paydirt over the next three years, confirming the optimistic opinions of him and Ralston that it was too early to declare *borrasca* on the Comstock. However, only $320,000 of the rich new discovery was ever distributed as dividends to shareholders. Worse, shareholders were assessed over $300,000 in order to make capital improvements to the mine. Ralston biographer Lavender pointed his finger directly at Sharon, writing, "Sharon was bulling the market, declaring a small dividend or imposing an assessment according to how he wanted prices to move. He benefitted enormously. Probably Ralston did too, but most of the investors who bought and sold according to the rigged rise and fall of prices merely filled the pockets of the manipulators."[27]

Using the same tactics, Sharon soon had control of the Chollar-Potosi mine as well. Ralston, too, had some leverage with the mines, since he was the treasurer of most of the important mines that were still bringing ore to the surface. Between the two men, and with the clout of the Bank of California behind them, they insured that the most promising ore was sent to the bank's mills, leaving the other mills, most of which were teetering on the brink of insolvency, out in the cold. It was truly a battle of survival, and Ralston and Sharon planned on surviving.[28]

Comstock historian Ronald James called the Bank Ring's strategy "the most cynical of hostile corporate takeovers."[29] By 1867 all of the leading Comstock mines and seventeen of the mills had fallen to the monopoly. William Sharon formed the Union Mill and Mining Company to manage the numerous properties. Owners of the new corporation, chartered in June 1867, were D. O. Mills, William Sharon, William Ralston and five other members of their clique.[30]

With the Bank Ring controlling the source of money that funded all Comstock activities, the mines that produced the ore, and the mills that turned it into bullion, we see the beginnings, not only of a monopoly—or a "combine" as it was called in the day—but also of a brand new style of business management control called "vertical integration." So everything was going according to William Sharon's craftily executed plan. He had truly become, as his biographer Michael Makley dubbed him, "The King of the Comstock."

Although Duane Bliss was never an "insider"—that is, a member of the Bank Ring—circumstances would evolve that would allow him too to become successful beyond his wildest dreams.

CHAPTER 7

The Virginia & Truckee Railroad

Bank Ring members' chicanery in manipulating the Comstock to their advantage was not an aberration during the period following the Civil War. Historian and academic Hal Bridges, writing in Harvard University's *Business History Review*, noted: "Widespread in American historical writing is the idea that business leaders in the United States from about 1865 to 1900 were, on the whole, a set of avaricious rascals who habitually cheated and robbed investors and consumers . . . and in general carried on predatory activities comparable to those of the robber barons of medieval Europe."[1]

The Comstock era occurred at the beginning of a new cycle that was marked by loose business ethics, and widespread use of the business tool—incorporation—was new as well. Bridges points out that the term "robber baron" may be too strong a word for the period in some cases, and that it is perhaps better explained by the concurrent growth of capitalistic enterprise and its philosophy that all motives in capitalistic success become subordinate to profit making. Either interpretation could accurately be applied to the Bank Ring and its manipulation of the Comstock.

No records exist that describe the specific duties Duane Bliss performed for Sharon, Ralston and the Bank of California during mid 1860s. He was simply an employee, although a trusted member of the bank's management, and his activities warranted no special attention in the newspapers of the day or in the jottings of the historians who recorded the events on the Comstock in later years. In fact, Bliss's job title with the bank is never mentioned. His daughter Hope, in her rambling biographical sketch, stated that her father was the assistant cashier. Since W. H. Blauvelt was the cashier, Hope Bliss's statement is reasonable. Unlike Sharon and Blauvelt, however, Bliss was an experienced Comstock quartz mill operator; so it is logical to assume that Sharon used Bliss's experience with the mills as the bank foreclosed and took them over. It would have been unsavory work, but work that had to be performed to carry out Sharon's scheme. In July 1866, Sharon also installed employee D. L. Bliss as a trustee of the Yellow Jacket Mine, to keep his eyes on things and "grease the skids" when things needed to be accomplished.[2]

During his time with the bank, Duane Bliss was not a member of the Bank Ring. He had neither the money nor the clout at this point in his career to participate at that level, so it's unlikely he was cut in on the deals that were carried out to enrich the participants. However, given his management position with the bank, and his closeness to Sharon and Ralston, he had to have been privy to inside information. He knew what was going on. The degree to which he used that information to make personal mining investment decisions is not clear. However, he did have personal investments in various Comstock mines from time to time, so to assume he did not make buy and sell decisions based upon whatever bank information he was privy to would be naïve. In spite of this, he never became wealthy through his Comstock investments.

Bliss's work at the bank, regardless of what his specific duties may have been, must have been exemplary, because he did not go unnoticed by his superiors on the Comstock or in San Francisco, as his future endeavors proved. Although he may have missed out on the big money that Bank Ring members were extracting from the Comstock, these same men offered Bliss future business opportunities that would enrich him beyond his imagination.

In attempting to assess Duane Bliss's culpability, or his lack of it, in the Bank Ring's schemes, it's helpful to read what highly respected Comstock journalist C. C. "Charlie" Goodwin, cited earlier, wrote about the leading Comstock bankers. His no-nonsense appraisal of the key men within the Bank of California provides a sound comparison of the central characters. Of banker, investor, and titular president of the Bank of California, D. O. Mills, Goodwin wrote, "Mr. Mills was an honest man, often a coldly honest man . . . he was a far-sighted business man and . . . high-minder banker . . . he never permitted his wealth to cause his nature to harden or his native instincts to wane."[3] When Mills learned of Bill Sharon's shenanigans on the Comstock, he demanded the business be closed down and Sharon fired. However, Ralston and a majority of the bank's board members disagreed—business was too good—and they overrode Mills' demand.[4] Mills' distaste for what Sharon was doing, however, did not cause him to withdraw from the enterprise.

Goodwin also admired William Ralston, although he disagreed with the man's faith in Sharon. ". . . he [Ralston] was more to San Francisco than any other man," Goodwin wrote. "He had a masterful brain [and] an

Chapter 7. The Virginia & Truckee Railroad

unquenchable public spirit . . . [and he was] a shrewd, capable, careful and honest banker."[5]

Goodwin admired the wily business genius of Bill Sharon too. "He was . . . by nature shrewd and far-seeing and could reason from cause to effect on a business proposition with the quickness of intuition." However, Goodwin did not gauge the same positive qualities of conscience, goodness, and charity in Sharon that he saw in the other two men.[6]

During the mid- to late-1860s, Duane Bliss was an employee of Mills, Ralston and Sharon. Never an equal, he was always their subordinate. He learned much from these men, as he had from his first business mentor, Almarin B. Paul. He served them all capably, and in return he was rewarded by their future patronage. Of the whole lot of them, Charlie Goodwin saved his highest praise for Bliss, published in his Salt Lake City weekly newspaper upon Bliss's death: "He has been one of the foremost men of Nevada for quite forty years . . . he was one of the most thorough men and one of the most perfect gentlemen. There was no worthier man on the west coast than Duane L. Bliss."[7]

*

Duane and Elizabeth's first child, William Seth, was born during this period, on August 25, 1865. On May 8, 1867, just a month before the couple's second child, Charles Tobey, was to be born, Duane purchased a house in Gold Hill for his growing family. It is not known where they had previously lived. For $300, he bought a house from William A. White, probably on High Street, which runs parallel to Main Street a little further up the mountainside. High Street was primarily residential, and included the large homes of some of the town's leading families. Although the deed does not specify anything about the house itself, it does state the legal description of the property as Lot 78, Block 5, Range A on the official town map. It adjoined the property of J.J Denney.[8]

A newcomer to the mountain described the challenging topography of Gold Hill:

> *Gold Hill . . . like Virginia City, [is] in a ravine, the main street being in the center of the ravine, and the streets climbing the mountain-sides on either sides of it. It is very compact, having but little room to build. The top streets [which included High Street] are three and four hundred feet above Main Street . . . . Main Street gets all*

the drainage from the hill-sides . . . and is certainly the filthiest street for a city I ever saw. Persons always have to hold their nose while passing through there on a warm day . . . yet the Gold Hill people do not seem to mind it.[9]

In only three-and-one-half years on the Comstock, Bill Sharon had accomplished amazing things for himself and his Bank Ring cronies. He had begun to amass a large personal fortune, and with each passing year he was becoming more powerful in Nevada. By the dawning of 1868, however, there were a number of disquieting things occurring that certainly would have furrowed the brow of a man as inherently anxious as Bill Sharon.

The bank's Comstock profits were good, but not spectacular. A rich silver strike across the state at Treasure Hill had drained a lot of the labor pool from the Comstock. Also, the mines had begun to exhaust the rich ore at deeper depths, and many men—but not including Bill Sharon—were talking *borrasca* once again. Finally, a former cigar salesman and successful mill operator, Adolph Sutro, had put forth the bold idea of building a gigantic tunnel under the Comstock mines leading to the Carson River that would provide drainage, ventilation and ore transport for the mines. Initially, the Bank of California supported the idea, until Ralston and Sharon realized it could jeopardize their monopoly.[10] All in all, it looked like another mining depression could be looming.

A healthy, producing Comstock was vital to the success of the Bank of California and its investors, for the city of San Francisco, and even for the state of California. Billy Ralston's bank had also become involved in a myriad of other business activities that fed the city and the state: a real estate firm, woolen mills, a carriage building company, a sugar refinery, a watch-making company, a winery, a tobacco factory, and many other ventures, all financed by Comstock money. As one of Ralston's biographers put it, "Whatever else it was accomplishing, Comstock wealth had taken California industry out of its swaddling clothes and put San Francisco commercially on its feet."[11] The Bank of California had become much more than just a financial institution; it had become a city builder and a state builder, all accomplished with Comstock funds.

Sharon and Ralston realized it was important to control and contain costs at such a time, until still deeper mining explorations struck new ore-producing veins. One of the largest and most unmanageable costs they faced was transportation, and they began to think seriously about it before Adolph Sutro and his tunnel could trump them.

Chapter 7. The Virginia & Truckee Railroad

Ponderous ore wagons, pulled tortuously up and down rough mountain roads by long strings of mules or oxen, had to endure steep, muddy trails and nearly impassable roads during their journeys. Snow in winter, followed by spring floods, only exacerbated an already intolerable situation. It was a two-way problem. Carrying tons of unprocessed ore down these roads to the Union Mill and Mining Company's seventeen Carson River mills was half of the problem. Carrying heavy timbers from the Sierra Nevada back up to the Comstock for stoking the boilers and shoring up the subterranean mines, and for hauling heavy steam hoists, donkey engines, pumps and blowers was the other half.[12]

A constant train of freight wagons pulled by horses, mules, and oxen carried necessary supplies and equipment up Sun Mountain to Virginia City, Gold Hill, and other communities on narrow, crowded dirt roads. Laden with raw ore from the mills, they returned down the mountainside to the Carson Valley quartz mills where the silver was extracted. (Special Collections Department, University of Nevada, Reno Library)

A capable corps of teamsters did all this hard work, and they were augmented by bull-whackers, mule-skinners and stage drivers, all siphoning off money that Ralston and Sharon believed they should have. The monopoly these teamsters enjoyed allowed them to charge what Ralston and Sharon considered exorbitant prices for their services.

There was an additional issue, too. There were tons and tons of sub-standard ore—ore that did not assay at a high enough precious metal content—that was piling up outside the entrance of every working mine. The mines were simply throwing aside this ore as not valuable enough to warrant the high transport rates down to the mills on the Carson River. But if it could be delivered to the mills cheaply enough, there was a great deal of untapped profit to be realized in these "worthless" ore pilings, or *tailings*.

In the 1860s, when the word "transportation" was used in any conversation, it meant only one thing: railroads. Construction on the Central Pacific Railroad, the western leg of the nation's first transcontinental railroad, had spiked the first rail to its ties in late 1863 in Sacramento. By June 1868, only months away, the first train was expected to rumble into Lake's Crossing, which had just taken on the name *Reno*. Sharon and Ralston knew it was time to act.

The Nevada Legislature had granted a railroad charter to a group of promoters in 1865—which included William Sharon—but it had never been acted upon. As a matter of fact, there had been four failed railroad franchises on Sun Mountain since 1861. On May 8, 1867, the 1865 charter was re-issued and incorporated as the Virginia & Truckee River Rail Road Company [earlier, it had briefly been referred to as the Virginia City & Carson River Railroad]. Again, William Sharon was one of the incorporators. One year later, on March 5, 1868, it was re-chartered as the Virginia & Truckee Rail Road Company, or the V&T as it was commonly called. There were initially nine directors: Alexander Baldwin, William E. Barron, Charles Bonner, John Fry, William Ralston, William Sharon, Thomas Sunderland, Thomas Bell, and Frederick Tritle.[13]

Thomas Sunderland was appointed president of the new enterprise, serving for only ten months before Sharon replaced him. Not surprisingly, Sharon was initially the largest stockholder, with 5,634 of the 30,000 outstanding shares. All of the other large shareholders were Bank Ring members. Holding 3,500 shares each were Alvinza Hayward, D. O. Mills, William Ralston and Thomas Sunderland. Twelve other men held smaller blocks of shares. Over the next five years there would be an inordinate amount

Chapter 7. The Virginia & Truckee Railroad

of buying, selling and swapping of shares among the original seventeen investors, as Ralston, Sharon and Mills manipulated the ownership of the V&T. At the end of that time, these three men owned the entire company in equal shares.[14]

To kick-start the project Sharon had called for the most talented and trustworthy mine surveyor and engineer on the Comstock, Isaac E. James, who was also the superintendent of one of the mines in the bank's portfolio. As the legend goes, with no preamble whatsoever Sharon asked James if he could survey a road from Virginia City to the Carson River. Just as curtly James answered "Yes" and Sharon replied "Do it then, at once."[15] James was well aware of the problems he faced, but he immediately set to work. By June 1869 he had accomplished the task. The railroad would be only twenty-one miles long; but, as Comstock historian Lord pointed out, ". . . the aggregate curves of the road would make 17 full coils of the track in the space of 13-1/2 miles."[16]

While James was at work on the project, Sharon arranged the financing for the railroad, making sure to keep as much of the expense as possible off the backs of participating Bank Ring members. He successfully arranged for $500,000 in public bonds from Storey and Ormsby counties, where most of the track would run, and he signed fourteen pre-paid subscriptions with most non-bank owned mines for discounts on future transportation services. Even Sharon, Ralston, and Mills, uncharacteristically, put some of their own money into the enterprise.[17]

Duane Bliss had left the employ of the Bank of California in late 1866 or early 1867. A cryptic passage in his Bancroft interview explains: "His health became impaired by indoor confinement, and he left the Bank, and engaged for a couple of years in the stock business."[18] A career change from banking, where he had made an enviable name for himself, to the livestock business was an odd choice for the thirty-four year old Bliss. This move is confirmed by *The Nevada Directory for 1868-9* that lists D. L. Bliss as the foreman of a meat market.[19] The new position must have included a lot of outside work, as the Bancroft interview stressed that Bliss's health required such a change. We also know that he had discontinued his duties as a trustee for the Yellow Jacket Mine sometime after October 1868, when his name disappeared from the official Yellow Jacket meeting records.[20]

Even though Bliss may have resigned his position at the bank for a couple of years, he obviously remained at the beck-and-call of Bill Sharon and Bill Ralston if the right opportunity arose. Rights-of-way for the V&T's trackage

73

would have to be identified and purchased or leased, an important task. Ralston biographer Lyman wrote, "Bliss was dependable. He was delegated to procure these rights. He knew every one in the Can[y]on. He could manage men and lead them."[21] Bliss accepted the offer, and set about his challenging new task.

One interesting story of Bliss's efforts to purchase or lease the railroad rights-of-way is related in Bliss's Bancroft interview. A widow had a small house near the proposed route of the tracks. She was afraid the railroad might bypass her property, so she went to see Bliss. She told him she would sell the property for $800 if they would allow her to take down and move her small house. The two agreed on the deal. When it was time to have the papers signed, Bliss visited the widow. However, she had conveniently forgotten her earlier agreement, and now insisted on $5,000 for the property, which was three or four times what it was worth. Bliss refused to pay it. Eventually, railroad workers cut off one corner of the widow's house—all the space they needed for the tracks—but she still insisted on receiving $5,000. Bliss had local authorities condemn the property, and the widow had to appear before them to plead her case. She told her story in a pitiful manner, saying she didn't recall ever offering to sell for $800. She was finally granted $2,000 for the entire property, including what was left of her house.

In addition to securing rights-of-way for Gold Hill, Virginia City, Silver City and American City, Bliss was also initially appointed as superintendent of construction at the Virginia City end of the line, while H. M. Yerington was hired as superintendent of construction at the Carson City end.[22]

The Bank of California men also had Bliss in mind for another task. His daughter Hope wrote in her biographical sketch that during the late 1860s, ". . . he [Bliss] was sent to New York on business for the Virginia & Truckee Railroad, by Mr. William Sharon . . . ." Just such an eastern trip is verified by a small news item that appeared in the *Pittsfield* (MA) *Sun* in early 1869: "Duane Bliss, formerly of Savoy, arrived in North Adams [MA] last Wednesday, overland from California, after a rapid passage of only 14 days, having rode 600 miles by stage. Mr. Bliss is connected with the United States mint at San Francisco."[23] Given this information, it's likely that Bliss took the newly completed transcontinental railroad to Council Bluffs, Iowa, the Chicago and Northwestern Railroad on to Chicago, and the Michigan Central Railroad to Detroit, where he then boarded a stagecoach to Massachusetts.

Chapter 7. The Virginia & Truckee Railroad

William Bliss, Duane's father, had moved to North Adams by this time. The assignment Bliss was carrying out for Bill Sharon was undoubtedly the main reason for his journey back East, and the visit to his father in Massachusetts was simply a side trip.

The newspaper's statement that Bliss was connected with the U.S. Mint was obviously an error. He was not.[24] Bliss's assignment for Sharon, however, could also have involved the Bank of California's interest in the San Francisco Mint, or the U.S. Mint in Carson City that would begin striking silver dollars in 1870. Also, new and more restrictive legislation on both mint operations and U.S. coinage were fomenting in Washington and New York, and Bliss's trip for the Bank of California could have involved those issues as well as the V&T Railroad. Any of these topics could explain the newspaper's reference to Bliss's association with the mint.

It was around this time that Adolph Sutro was badgering Congress to subsidize his tunnel project, and Ralston and Sharon were working against this cause, which could have been another reason for Bliss's eastern trip. One can only speculate on the true purpose of his assignment, but it must have been vitally important, as coast-to-coast journeys were not undertaken on a whim in the 1860s.

Once Bliss traveled east, H. M. Yerington was appointed general superintendent of the entire V&T line, the position he would hold for the next forty-one years. When Bliss returned from his trip, he was appointed paymaster of the operation. An interesting sidelight on these two men was their financial participation in the V&T Railroad. Yerington initially purchased one hundred shares in the corporation, a modest investment, and added a like amount three months later. Bliss, on the other hand, chose to purchase no stock at all, although he was given one share—the minimum required—when he was added to the board, perhaps indicating a lack of confidence in the financial viability of the venture.[25]

Henry Marvin Yerington was a Canadian by birth, born in 1829. He came to Nevada in 1863, and purchased and operated a quartz mill on the Carson River near Empire. However, his was one of the mills the Bank Ring wanted, and he was forced into selling it to them in 1868 for $40,000, the exact amount he had originally invested.[26] When he was approached to join the V&T, he realized it was best to let bygones be bygones, and he readily accepted the offer.

From very early in the planning of the railroad, Bill Sharon had envisioned more than just a Virginia City-to-Carson City road. He knew it would be foolish not to proceed all the way to Reno, where the tracks of the Central Pacific Railroad had recently passed through on the way to Utah Territory. Tying the Comstock into the western leg of the transcontinental railroad would open up the area to the rest of the nation, and that was an opportunity Sharon couldn't resist.

In early 1869, three months before Isaac James had even completed his surveying work, the V&T had begun setting up workers' camps for the first leg of the project from Carson City to Virginia City. In all, thirty-eight camps were established, rudimentary, unpleasant places where a gentleman would never deign to venture. The vast majority of workers were Chinese nationals, and this caused some consternation among the local folks, particularly the miners. The *Territorial Enterprise* remarked, " . . . as long as there is to every gang of these laborers a white man sitting above on the bank doing nothing but 'bossing,' we don't see any need to find fault."[27] The Chinese would eventually play an important role in Bliss's vast lumbering business.

The work went forward with vigor and enthusiasm. During the construction phase, Yerington was in charge, and Bliss was his unofficial second-in-command, stepping in whenever Yerington was unavailable. On September 28, 1869, the first milestone was reached. "At half-past seven o'clock this morning, Superintendent Yerington drove the spike to the first rail of the Virginia & Truckee Railroad at Carson City, and at half-past ten o'clock the locomotive was running on the track," the *Gold Hill News* proudly observed. The story continued: "The first spike was of pure silver, made and presented by W. C. Bousfield, Esq., the well known assayer of Virginia City . . . . If there are no interruptions, a half mile daily will be laid, and the grading in Gold Hill will be completed in ten days—thus bringing the locomotive and train here in about thirty days." [28]

Sharon then dispatched Bliss to Carson City to handle the arrangements for devising a system for receiving and storing lumber for shipment up the mountain to the Comstock. Soon after that, a depot was built—a rather plain plank building—serving the minimum needs that existed at the time. Two years later, extensive engine houses and mechanic shops would be added in Carson City when the city was selected as the site for the railroad's headquarters and general offices. As for the lumber, Bliss arranged for a lumber storage yard about a mile south of Carson City, at the terminus of the Summit Fluming Company's four-and-one-half mile long Clear Creek V-flume. The railroad built a rail spur from the main track to the

Chapter 7. The Virginia & Truckee Railroad

wood yard.[29] The following year Bliss's assignment would lead to him and Yerington striking out on their own in the lumbering business.

It would be forty-five days after construction began that the first locomotive in service—the *Lyon*, a 2-6-0 Booth's Union Iron Works' engine—came huffing and puffing its way up the grade and into Gold Hill, to the cheers of a throng of well-wishers, including Duane and Elizabeth Bliss, the Gold Hill mayor, and other local dignitaries. Sitting high up in *Lyon's* cab, waving to the crowd, was the father of the new line, William Sharon.[30]

One of the celebrants, Alf Doten of the *Gold Hill News*, described the noise decibel level of the rowdy celebration in his journal: ". . . brass band playing—flags flying everywhere—big gun of Ft. Homestead firing, whistles all blowing, people cheering, and hell of a noise generally."[31] By this time, a meeting hall had been built on the grounds of the fort, and it had become the social center of Gold Hill.

On January 29, 1870 the entire Virginia City-to-Carson City leg was open, and passenger service was immediately inaugurated. For 25 cents a person could travel from Virginia City to Gold Hill, and for $2.00 he could ride all the way to Carson City. There were also four freight trains a day scheduled in each direction, and the costs of moving ore, lumber, and equipment immediately fell dramatically. For instance, the cost of transporting cordwood from Carson City to Virginia City dropped 23 percent, while transporting ore from Virginia City to the mills on the Carson River fell by 43 percent.[32]

The V&T was well on its way to living up to its promise. Soon the railroad was using 116 ore cars, 200 platform or flat cars, 7 boxcars, and a complement of passenger and maintenance cars. It hauled 40,000 tons of ore and freight a month. By 1873, for the first half of the year only, the amount of freight hauled by the railroad was impressive:

ITEM	*TONNAGE*
Ore	*112,044*
Tailings	*6,088*
[Cord] wood	*54,210*
Lumber	*35,457*
Coal & stone	*19,534*
Merchandise	*21,010*
Livestock	*110*
Silver Bullion	*80*
TOTAL	*248,49533*

While Bill Sharon could certainly revel in the success of his newest venture, there were still many serious problems facing him. Adolph Sutro and his proposed tunnel continued to haunt the Bank Ring, and there were problems with its portfolio of mines as well. Throughout 1869 and 1870, production in all the Comstock's mines slumped badly, and stock prices plummeted. As historian Grant Smith wrote, "Ralston and Sharon were almost panic-stricken. They had staked everything on the future of the Lode—not only their newly made fortunes, but the solvency of the Bank."[34]

In May 1870, Duane Bliss was appointed general supply agent of the V&T, and was added to the company's board of directors. There was an interesting twist in the official paperwork appointing Bliss to the board. Western frontier justice, including in its mining camps, was still unsophisticated, often demanding an eye for an eye. Thus, duels were commonplace, and often used to settle a score. It was common business practice when a man was appointed to a responsible position that he signed an affidavit pledging that he would

Henry Yerington and Duane Bliss built the fabled Virginia & Truckee (V&T) Railroad for William Sharon and the Bank of California Bank Ring in the late 1860s to alleviate the problems of transporting men, materials, and unprocessed ore up and down the steep mountainside. Here we see engine #4, the Virginia, with a load of ore cars crossing the trestle at Gold Hill. (Special Collections Department, University of Nevada, Reno Library)

Chapter 7. The Virginia & Truckee Railroad

not engage in a duel, either as a principal or a second. Bliss's appointment to the board of directors included such a sworn promise.[35]

In 1870 the 10-year U.S. Census also came out. In responding to the questionnaire in July 1870, when the census taker knocked on his door, Bliss listed himself as a "Bank Clerk" rather than as a railroad employee, reflecting the organization he worked for rather than the job he was actually performing. The census also informs that Duane and Elizabeth had had their third child, a daughter, Hope Danforth, during the prior month.[36]

Finally, the *Storey, Ormsby, Washoe and Lyon Counties Directory, 1871-72*, informs that the Bliss family had moved from their Gold Hill home. The family had relocated to a house at the corner of E and Taylor streets in Virginia City, probably a larger home to accommodate the growing family. Also, in this directory Bliss's occupation is properly identified as, "Clerk, V. & T. R.R."[37]

With early successes under its belt, the V&T marched on. The thirty-one mile Carson City-to-Reno leg began in mid-1870 with the bridging of the Truckee River, and it would be completed in August 1872. When completed, the primary track of the V&T was 52.2 miles long, plus an additional 37 miles of sidings and spur tracks that went to the various mines and mills. The final cost of building the entire 89.2-mile railroad, including rolling stock, land leases, real estate, car shops and all other expenses was $4,856,042, or $54,440 per mile.[38]

When all was said and done, Bill Sharon's vision for the railroad would be justified. What would become history's most famous, profitable and romanticized short-line railroad was just beginning an illustrious eighty-year career. And for one of its most integral participants, Duane L. Bliss, the future was equally bright.

CHAPTER 8

The Carson & Tahoe Lumber & Fluming Company

By the early 1870s, Duane Bliss had been a citizen of the West for two decades. During that entire time, with the exception of brief periods when he had prospected in California's goldfields and Nevada's Comstock Lode, he had worked for other men. He either had a penchant for selecting people from whom he could learn, or he had been plain lucky, and he had benefited a great deal from his association with Dr. R. O. Tripp, Mathias Parkhurst, Almarin Paul, Bill Sharon, Bill Ralston and Darius Mills. Bliss was an intelligent man, and he was a patient man. He did not seem to be in a big rush to be the boss, to answer only to himself. He knew his time would come, and he just wanted to prepare himself for the moment when it arrived.

He had also gained wisdom from tragedy. Losing a wife and two children would have defeated a lesser man, but seems to have only made Bliss stronger and even more determined to succeed. He had started a new family, and had found happiness with his wife Elizabeth and their children. When he had taken a hiatus from the Bank of California to work in the livestock and provisions business, it has given him a chance to think clearly about his future. Even that act—leaving a promising career to spend some time on his own, improve his health, and do what he believed he needed to do—was a sign of his growing maturity.

The interviewer who spoke to Bliss for his interview in 1887—H. H. Bancroft's initials appear at the bottom of the report, so he may have actually been the man who interviewed Bliss—described his subject in the written report:

Mr. Bliss is a man of more than average height, and of strong build; his movements are quick and energetic, in fact, youthful [he would have been fifty-four when the interview was conducted] A noble head, and features strong, yet at the same time possessing an agreeable, manly expression, indicate intelligence, decision of character, firmness. A man of business, his manner is pleasant and unaffected.

*

The Carson Range is a spur of the Sierra Nevada that splits from the main mountain chain at the upper end of Hope Valley, about eighteen miles south of Lake Tahoe. It then arches northward around the eastern, or Nevada, side of the lake, while the main Sierra Nevada runs along the western, or California, side of the lake. The spur ends just above the small Nevada community of Verdi, which is a stone's throw from the Nevada/California border.

By 1870 the Bank Ring's monopoly—or combination—over the Comstock was almost total. They owned the vast majority of stock in most of the producing mines, they owned all of the successful mills, and they owned the controlling interest in water rights held by the Virginia and Gold Hill Water Company. They also controlled the transportation of material and ore to and from the Comstock via the V&T Railroad. The only link in the manufacturing and supply chain that Ralston and Sharon didn't completely control was the lumber required to build the mills, support the underground mines, and provide firewood for the mines' and mills' countless steam engines.

They did control a great deal of the lumber supply in the Carson and Washoe valleys by contractual agreement. Without being too specific, one Ralston biographer noted, ". . . corporations were organized for supplying the mines with lumber, timbers, water and fuel at reduced rates. Vast watersheds and timberlands fell into the clutches of the combine. Sawmills were erected at strategic points . . . [and] Great monarchs of the mountains . . . fell before the woodman's axe." William Sharon would also be the main defendant in an 1872 lawsuit filed by a man who claimed to have invented the V-flume that Sharon's lumbering interests had used extensively in the 1860s, but that lawsuit had failed.[1]

The meadows, ravines and hillsides of the nearby valleys were almost denuded of trees by this time, and the woodchoppers had begun to ascend the eastern slopes of the Carson Range for yet more lumber. It was only a matter of time before that area too would be barren, and the lumberjacks would have to move over the mountaintops to the heavily wooded western slopes of the Carson Range above Lake Tahoe. Trees on the western slope,

Chapter 8. The Carson & Tahoe Lumber & Fluming Company

although more difficult to move to the Comstock, were larger and produced more timbers and building material because they received more rain than those on the eastern slope. Bill Sharon realized that developing new lumber sources to feed the Comstock mines' voracious appetite would be a fulltime task, and one he did not have the time—or perhaps even the interest—in taking on himself for the Bank Ring Combine.

This was a puzzling deviation from the Bank Ring's usual way of doing business. Its history was to always hold all of the important elements of its Comstock monopoly within the family, that is, to have it all controlled by wealthy Bank Ring members. William Sharon scholar Michael Makley suggests a number of reasons why Sharon was not anxious to take on this additional project in the early 1870s. Makley wrote that in addition to running the mines, the mills and the railroad, "He [Sharon] was involved in numerous law suits, was fighting to reduce taxes on mining, was fighting attacks against the Ring and himself in the V.C. [Virginia City] and San Francisco press . . . and was running [in the election of 1872] against [John P.] Jones for the U.S. Senate."[2] Eventually, Sharon would drop out of that race. For all of these reasons, and perhaps too as a way of rewarding two of his able lieutenants for their past services to the Bank Ring's operations, Sharon turned to Duane Bliss and Henry Yerington to solve the Comstock's future lumber and cordwood problems. James A. Rigby already worked 640 acres of timberlands in the Carson Range's Summit area for the Bank Ring, so why he was not chosen to head this new business venture is not certain.[3] Rigby was in shaky financial condition personally, and perhaps this is why Sharon bypassed him. Still, later on Sharon would see that Rigby was taken care of by Bliss's and Yerington's new company. Bliss's Bancroft interview verifies all this, stating that once Sharon realized that lumbering could be a profitable business, "Sharon suggested that Yerington and Bliss take hold of the business for themselves, and they did so."[4]

Bliss and Yerington were perfectly positioned to take on the added responsibility. Yerington was already in the lumber business, having participated in a number of past lumbering ventures. In 1868 he became an absentee partner with six other men in the Summit Fluming Company, where they operated both a sawmill and a shingle mill near Spooner Summit [today, near the junction of US 50 and SR 28, above Glenbrook]. The men also owned a four-and-one-half-mile-long V-flume that began near the headwaters of Clear Creek and ran part way down Clear Creek Canyon.[5]

83

Bliss's previous assignment for Bill Sharon had been to establish a supply line of lumber from the timberlands to the railroad, set up a wood storage yard nearby, and see to building a V&T spur to the wood yard. Given the two men's backgrounds, Bliss and Yerington were well prepared to take on this new enterprise, one that would ultimately make both men very wealthy and powerful members of the Nevada and California business communities.

*

Throughout the 1860s sawmills had sprung up in the valleys below the Comstock wherever there was enough running water to make them workable. Many of them operated day and night to keep up with the steadily growing demand. In 1866, according to Myron Angel, who edited Thompson and West's *History of Nevada*, " . . . fifteen saw-mills were constantly preparing lumber [and] mining timbers for the Comstock market, while hundreds of men were cutting cord-wood for the use of the [quartz] mills."[6] This situation would change after Bill Sharon bought up or contracted with many of the independent lumbering operations for his Bank Ring monopoly. It would change again after these firms had logged out their acreage and Duane Bliss and his partners were brought in to begin lumbering the Tahoe Basin on the Carson Range's western face.

One signal development of the lumber and cordwood business in the 1860s was the use of flumes, V-shaped wooden plank boxes, butted end to end to form a smooth channel, and fed by nearby streams. The flumes rapidly and cheaply transported logs, sawn planks, or cordwood down the mountainsides using the force of gravity. Teams of oxen pulled the timber from where it was being felled to the flume in large rough-hewn wagons built on site. The wagon wheels were made of solid cross-sections of logs. The flumes were either set directly on the ground and supported by props, or held in place by trestles when crossing ravines. The purpose of the water was to ease the logs' journey down the flume, and to prevent friction fires. Reservoirs were eventually built to store the water from the winter snows on the mountaintops, and they provided a source for a strong flow of water, allowing the logs or lumber to hurtle down the mountainsides on the flumes. Historian Grant Smith put it in perspective, writing, "Massive timbers thirty-feet long were hurled down these rapids like arrows from a bow, while the flume trembled with their motion and the water was banked up before them in white curling mounds like breaking surf." So successful were these V-flumes

Chapter 8. The Carson & Tahoe Lumber & Fluming Company

that by 1880 the state's surveyor general reported that there were ten flumes totaling eighty miles in length operating in northern Nevada alone. The "king of the flumes" was twenty miles in length, built by John Mackay and James Fair at a cost of $250,000. These flumes had transported 171,000 cords of firewood and 33,300,000 board feet of lumber to the valleys below during the prior two-year period.[7]

On August 11, 1870 Duane Bliss purchased 160 acres of timberland—a quarter section—near Summit from John S. Richards, and he and Yerington entered into a partnership to provide lumber to the Bank of California's Comstock interests. In the beginning they called their firm Yerington, Bliss and Company. Titular President of the Bank of California and Bank Ring member Darius O. Mills was a third member of the partnership, providing funding for some of the early timberland purchases; but he was a silent partner.[8] For the next three years Yerington, Bliss and Company was busy buying and leasing timberlands and sawmill operations throughout the region to keep pace with the demands of the Comstock. The company acquired additional timberland in 1871, 1872 and 1873, primarily in the Clear Creek area on the eastern slope of the Carson Range.[9] Clear Creek flows all the way down the mountainside and drains into the Carson River about three miles south of Carson City. The men also purchased two sawmills from pioneer Sierra Nevada lumberman Michele Spooner near Spooner Station, another from the Elliott brothers a mile east of Glenbrook Summit, and, most importantly, a large sawmill operation from A. W. Pray at Glenbrook, on the eastern shore of Lake Tahoe in Nevada.[10]

With timberlands and mills on Spooner Summit now under their control, Bliss and Yerington needed a way to get the milled lumber down the mountain to Carson City. They turned their attention to the Summit Fluming Company, of which Yerington was already a minor stakeholder. In 1872 they purchased the company's four-and-one-half mile long V-flume that ran down Clear Creek Canyon toward Carson City. They rebuilt and extended the flume to twelve miles so its terminus reached the lumber storage yard and V&T Railroad spur a mile south of Carson City, and they immediately commenced fluming cut timbers down the mountainside.[11]

On October 15, 1873 Bliss, Mills, Yerington and James Rigby, who by now had come aboard as a minority partner, filed incorporation papers in Ormsby County as the Carson and Tahoe Lumber and Fluming Company (C&TL&FC). The corporation was capitalized at 260,000 shares of stock, divided into 500 blocks of 520 shares each, each block valued at $500, for a total capitalization of a quarter-million dollars.[12] Duane Bliss was president and general manager of the corporation. Rigby, who had been indebted to the Bank of California, had finally cleared his accounts, but it left him penniless. Bill Sharon asked Bliss and Yerington to take Rigby into the new corporation as a minority partner at a $10,000 stake. Where that money came from is not known, but Rigby remained with the corporation only until early in the next decade. From the beginning, however, Duane Bliss owned more stock in the firm than either Mills or Yerington, and he was the driving force behind the enterprise.[13]

The purchase of property and facilities in Glenbrook on Lake Tahoe from Captain Augustus W. Pray would turn out to be the linchpin in C&TL&FC's growing lumbering empire. Pray, a sea captain from Maine, had arrived at Lake Bigler [Tahoe] in 1861. Soon after his arrival, he and two partners acquired some land and built a sawmill on the shoreline, calling their enterprise the Lake Bigler Lumber Company. The following year Pray bought out his partners, and increased his Glenbrook timberlands by purchasing three large adjoining tracts from the original squatters on the land. The mill was initially water powered—it would be converted to steam power in 1864—and its two circular saws, edger and lathing machinery were able to turn out 20,000 board feet of lumber a day. A few years later Pray built a second mill nearby.[14]

This was lush land, bordered on the west by the clear, sparkling waters of the lake and on the other three sides by dense forests. A meadow, one of the most pristine spots on the entire lake, had a stream bisecting it, leading the original settlers to call the property "Glen Brook."[15]

The C&TL&FC's purchases in Glenbrook included five-and-one-half acres of lakeshore and meadowland property, in addition to Pray's large sawmill operation. They would later add adjoining timberlands to their property. At this time the firm already owned or controlled 7,000 acres of Tahoe Basin timberland.[16]

The magnificent, crystal-clear alpine lake, at an elevation of 6,225 feet, had suffered through a litany of names following its discovery—"rediscovery," the indigenous Washoe Indians would say, with justification—by Kit Carson and John Fremont in 1844. White men had variously called it Lake Bonplands, Mountain Lake, Fremont's Lake, and finally Lake Bigler, after a popular California governor. In the early 1860s it took on the name Lake Tahoe, not an altogether popular choice. Mark Twain, working at the *Territorial Enterprise* at the time, called the new name, "flat, insipid and

Chapter 8. The Carson & Tahoe Lumber & Fluming Company

Lumber Mill #1 of the Carson & Tahoe Lumber & Fluming Company at Glenbrook on Lake Tahoe was the hub of Duane Bliss and his partners' vast timbering operation, launched in 1870. For more than a quarter-century the company's loggers downed vast stands of timber in the Tahoe Basin on more than 50,000 company-owned acres of land. (Special Collections Department, University of Nevada, Reno Library)

spooney," and later wrote that the name Tahoe, ". . . suggests no crystal waters, no picturesque shores, no sublimity . . . . It means grasshopper soup. It is Indian, and suggestive of Indians."[17] The names "Bigler" and "Tahoe" would be used interchangeably, depending upon one's line of thinking, until the beginning of the twentieth century. The matter would not be officially settled until 1945 when the California legislature formally approved the name "Lake Tahoe."

By the time C&TL&FC made its purchase from Captain Pray in Glenbrook—the name by now having been shortened to one word—a bustling village had grown up in the meadow, facilitated by the completion of the King's Canyon, or Lake Bigler, toll road. Other mills had sprung up, and a small local tourist trade had developed. The settlement's first hotel, the Glenbrook House, had opened in 1863, and Captain Pray launched the second one, the Lake Shore House, later that same year. Taking advantage of this tourism, Pray built a small steamer, the *Governor Blaisdel*, to take his guests on excursions around the lake. Glenbrook also boasted a horse livery, thirty cottages, a meat market and a large general merchandise store with a meeting hall and dance floor.[18]

San Francisco's *Alta California* newspaper, copying an article from Nevada's *Genoa Enterprise*, had informed local residents about the beauty and appeal of Lake Bigler as early as 1859, which had spurred an early trickle of tourism to the area:

> DESCRIPTION OF LAKE BIGLER—*The southeastern extremity of the lake . . . is bounded by the most beautiful shore we have ever beheld . . . . Though situated as it is, near the summit of the Sierra Nevada, at an elevation of about six thousand feet above the level of the sea, the peaks of the mountains, with which it is almost entirely surrounded, seem only as hills. The very romantic and singular position of the lake will yet make it famous the world over, and doubtless in after years it will furnish themes for the romancer; its fame will be sung by a poet, and its beauty described by the pen of a Goldsmith. . . . [The lake] is situated only about sixty miles from Placerville, by an excellent stage road, and is beyond all doubt naturally one of the most interesting and agreeable resorts for pleasure and amusement on the borders of the Pacific . . . .*[19]

An early devotee of inns and taverns, Jesus Maria Estudillo, wrote in his journal, "A Buggy Ride to Tahoe," about his visit to the Glenbrook House in 1864:

> *The [hotel] . . . is on the side of a hill with a nice brook on one side. The house has a fine view of the lake and is about a quarter mile from it. About two or three hundred yards below the house there is a nice valley or flat where some vegetables are raised. The house itself is very handsomely gotten up, furniture and rooms are of the best kind. I was astonished to meet with such good accommodations in this part of the country.*[20]

The earliest guest ledgers for the Glenbrook House indicate how popular the hostelry was with the rich and famous during its first decade. Names appearing in the ledger include Leland Stanford, Henry Comstock, William Sharon, Nevada Governors Henry Blaisdel and James Nye, Darius O. Mills, conservationist John Muir, and U.S. Secretary of State William Seward of

Chapter 8. The Carson & Tahoe Lumber & Fluming Company

"Seward's Folly" fame. Duane L. Bliss and family also appeared in the guest book for an August 8, 1868 stay.[21]

The Glenbrook House, the settlement's most popular hotel, despite its pricey reputation, had endured a number of management changes over its first six years, but in 1869 it gained stability when Bill Sharon, Bill Ralston and Charles Bonner purchased the hotel and an adjoining 200 acres of land to use as a club for Bank Ring members and other Comstock VIPs.[22] According to early Glenbrook House records, the prior year Sharon had held a party for a group of associates at the hotel, likely sizing it up for their needs. The hotel's ledger indicates that Sharon paid $280 for the event, and Henry Yerington, who accompanied him to make the arrangements, paid $40 for music for the party.[23] Two years later, when things became touch-and-go for the Bank Ring, they re-sold the hotel.

Lake Tahoe historian E. B. Scott related a story about Sharon and Ralston following their purchase of Glenbrook House. Ralston challenged Sharon to a horse race from Carson City to Glenbrook, and Sharon accepted the challenge. One of the riders was to go by way of the King's Canyon grade while the other went up and over Clear Creek. The race had a sad ending. The ever-competitive Sharon pushed his mount so hard that the hapless horse went blind from the effort, and Sharon had to forfeit the contest to Ralston.[24]

*

Having launched their lumbering enterprise, Bliss and Yerington spent the first few months getting set up, after which Bliss assumed all the operational responsibilities. Yerington would retain his position as general superintendent of the V&T Railroad until his death in 1910, and spent little time working in the lumbering business. Once the firm became successful, timberland purchases or leases—which were initially funded by Darius Mills—were financed out of the company's operating revenues.

The company was organized into three separate divisions: logging, milling and transportation. As more timberland was added to the inventory, the operation quickly grew. Hundreds of employees were hired and trained: supervisors, engineers, loggers, carpenters, mechanics, teamsters, mill hands, clerks and laborers. Thousands of tons of equipment had to be purchased, leased, or established: sawmills, wagons, draft animals, railroads, steam tugs, headquarter offices, and logging camps. It was an extremely busy time for Bliss, but he was finally the man in charge.[25]

Some historians have claimed that the C&TL&FC was a Bank Ring operation, but that is not accurate. Although C&TL&FC and the Bank Ring had forged favorable agreements to the exclusion of other companies, Bliss and Yerington still owned controlling interest, and they had never been members of the Bank Ring. Bliss did remain very close to Bill Sharon, and of course to Darius O. Mills, and he depended upon the Bank Ring's mines and mills to buy much of his product. But it was not a Bank Ring operation, like the V&T Railroad was, and both enterprises would flourish long after the Bank Ring was edged out of the Comstock.

In the early 1870s Bliss decided to move his family closer to his C&TL&FC operation, so he purchased a home on the northwest corner of Telegraph and Minnesota streets in Carson City. It was there in 1872 that Walter Danforth Bliss joined the family, the couple's fourth child. The population had grown to about 3,000 people and the small city was thriving. Before the end of the

Photographed by C. E. Peterson, Carson, Nevada.

Summit Camp, pictured here, was one of many logging camps C&TL&FC established on the western and southern sides of Lake Tahoe. The men lumbering the forest, along with a support crew of laborers, cooks, and others, lived and worked solely in these camps while they took down the trees in the region. (Special Collections Department, University of Nevada, Reno Library)

Chapter 8. The Carson & Tahoe Lumber & Fluming Company

decade it would boast a federal post office, a central plaza surrounded by government offices, stores, and hotels, a new U.S. Mint facility, the Nevada State Orphans Home, the Nevada State Prison built of stone from an on-site quarry, and the impressive Neoclassical Italianate Nevada State Capital Building. The V&T Railroad headquarters, with offices, maintenance facilities, and a huge rectangular engine house with nearly a dozen large bays for maintaining and repairing the railroad's growing stable of locomotives, also showcased the capital city.[26]

In 1872 Bliss also built a small summer home in Glenbrook for his family, a site that would be gradually expanded and enjoyed by the next three generations. Henry Yerington and James Rigby also relocated to Carson City, and all three men worked out of Carson & Tahoe Lumber & Fluming Company's offices located at the V&T Railroad headquarters. In 1874 C&TL&FC established offices in its own building just east of the V&T depot.[27]

As the decade of the 1870s progressed, the west side of Carson City, a hillside shaded by huge trees, became the city's premier residential area, and large, expensive homes were constructed by wealthy mine and mill owners and operators from Sun Mountain. In 1879 Duane Bliss built a spacious, comfortable home on the west side at 402 North Minnesota Street for his growing family. The 8,500 square foot, three-story home was the largest home in Nevada at the time, and has since become known as the Bliss Mansion. The stately home would become a social center in the state capital, boasting a large ballroom on the third floor that was also used by the Bliss children as a roller skating rink. The house was also the first in the state entirely piped for gas lighting.[28]

Despite the early success and rapid growth of Bliss's C&TL&FC, there were dark clouds over Sun Mountain, and over the Bank Ring's monopoly on the Comstock. Everything was about to change.

CHAPTER 9

Boom and Bust

While Duane Bliss was building C&TL&FC from his Carson City headquarters, the Comstock was on a wild ride. Individuals and organizations, including the Bank of California, experienced dizzying highs and depressing lows, both in the price of mining stocks and in the emotional swings of the investors who participated. Mining stocks plunged as low as a dollar a share, and skyrocketed as high as thousands of dollars a share, as savvy players manipulated the market in every way imaginable. Poor men got rich, then poor again; rich men got poor, then rich again. However, one thing was constant: nobody got bored. For Bliss and his partners, however, the demand for lumber remained strong throughout it all.

John P. Jones and his brother-in-law, Alvinza Hayward, a turncoat member of the Bank Ring, wrested control of the Crown Point mine from Bill Sharon and the Bank of California when they discovered a rich new ore deposit in the mine and kept it secret while buying up controlling interest. But Sharon engineered a swap of his Crown Point Mine stock for the stock of the neighboring Belcher mine, and everybody made money when the rich vein crossed through both mines. Four Irishmen—John Mackay, James Fair, William O'Brien and James Flood—finagled the Hale and Norcross mine away from Sharon and the Bank Ring, and they too made a fortune from their chicanery. New veins of rich ore were also discovered in the Kentuck, the Chollar-Potosi and the Yellow Jacket mines among others. Although none were spectacular, some men still got richer and some got poorer in each case. The one constant on all new ore discoveries was that they occurred at deeper depths, requiring more square-set timbering, and as a result C&TL&FC prospered.[1]

That's the way things went on the Comstock from the late 1860s through the early 1870s. Duane Bliss's daughter Hope—whose biographical sketch of her father is often questionable—said that her father lost everything, and even went into debt in late 1869 during one of the mining stock downturns.

The Comstock's voracious appetite for heavy timbers to support the mines, and firewood to feed the steam-powered mining equipment, continued to decimate the forests of the Tahoe Basin throughout the 1870s. (Library of Congress)

In this case, Hope's claim is certainly believable, although it cannot be verified. But with the C&TL&FC flourishing, Bliss, like so many others, was able to get back into the game.[2]

Everything changed in February 1873. John Mackay and his mine superintendent, colorful old-timer Captain Sam Curtis, were following a seven-foot wide seam of low-grade ore in the Consolidated Virginia Mine that Mackay and three associates had purchased for a song, because most

Chapter 9. Boom and Bust

investors considered it worthless.[3] The Consolidated Virginia was composed of four smaller mines that had joined together in 1867 with hopes of succeeding as a group at what they had failed at individually: making money.[4] Continuing to follow the seam well after most men would have given up, Mackay and Curtis were eventually rewarded when it widened and the ore began to assay richer. Spurred on, they continue to mine the vein. Nothing, however, could have prepared them for what they eventually discovered: a huge cavern of gold and silver that would become known ever after as the *Big Bonanza*.[5]

After he initially inspected the mine, Dan DeQuille of the *Territorial Enterprise* was cautious and waffling in his assessment of the Big Bonanza: "We may say that the indications are that a first-class mine is fast being developed in the Consolidated Virginia, but of course we can see into the ore deposits no further than openings have been made."[6] Judge James Walsh, a longtime miner from Grass Valley, California, was more to the point upon hearing the news of the Big Bonanza. With a twinkle in his eye, he remarked in colossal understatement, "God was good to the Irish."[7]

The Big Bonanza ended up crossing through two mines, the Consolidated Virginia and the California, both controlled by the four Irishmen. The total value of the bullion product extracted from the two mines from the discovery in early 1873 until it played out in 1880 was an astounding $104+ million dollars. A Big Bonanza indeed![8]

The real financial impact of its discovery came not from the silver itself but from the stocks of the two mines. Both stocks soared. The Consolidated Virginia had sold at $1 a share in July 1870; by January 1875 it was priced as high as $700 a share. The stock in the California mine was even wilder. It went from as low as $37 a share in September 1874—after the discovery—to $780 in January of 1876.[9] These wild fluctuations cost many speculators their paper fortunes, but the lucky ones, the ones who through skill or blind luck bought and sold at the right time, were instant millionaires. One example of the former was Philip Deidesheimer, the inventor of the square-set timbering process, who went bankrupt through mining stocks. An example of the latter was John Mackay, who achieved staggering wealth.[10]

Perhaps the best example of the wealth generated by the Big Bonanza can be found at the University of Nevada, Reno, in the W. M. Keck Museum at the Mackay School of Mines. Here are housed fifty-eight of the larger pieces from the fabulous Mackay Silver Collection, a 1,250 piece silver dinner and dessert service for twenty-four that was completed in 1878.

Shown here is a 1962 display of 58 pieces from the 1,250-piece Mackay silver service collection that was crafted by Tiffany in 1878. These pieces are now on permanent display at the Keck Mining Museum at the University of Nevada, Reno. (Special Collections Department, University of Nevada, Reno Library)

Mackay commissioned Tiffany and Company of New York to design and produce the silver service for his wife, Marie-Louise. He sent Tiffany approximately one-half ton of Comstock silver, which 200 craftsmen worked exclusively on for two years, a total of over one million man-hours of skilled craftsmanship. When the service was finished, Mackay purchased and destroyed the dies so they could never be duplicated. According to the silver service's website, "The service was delivered to the Mackays in Paris, accompanied by a silver clasped leather bound album of photographs and

Chapter 9. Boom and Bust

fitted in nine walnut and mahogany chests, each mounted with a silver plaque detailing its contents."11

The Victorian-inspired silver set is simply magnificent. It reflects the opulence and excess of the period and the Comstock Lode's place in Nevada history better than any other treasure could possibly do.

*

Bill Sharon had withdrawn from the 1872 Senate race when he realized he couldn't overtake the popular John P. Jones, but in 1874 when Senator William Stewart decided to retire, Sharon began campaigning again. One of the primary detractors in his previous campaign had been the *Territorial Enterprise*. So, in typical Sharon fashion, he bought the newspaper, installed his own man, Rollin Daggett, as editor, and went on to win the election against his arch foe, tunnel builder Adolph Sutro. Sharon appointed his friend and chief timber supplier Duane Bliss as one of the five trustees of the newspaper, and, surprisingly, his chief competitor John W. Makley as another. Alf Doten wrote that all five of the trustees were "personal and political friends" of Sharon.12

For all intents and purposes, Bill Sharon was now finished with Sun Mountain. He had amassed a huge fortune—upwards of $20 million in later years, his biographer Makely quotes from the *San Francisco Examiner*13—and was off on a new adventure. Historian Ronald James summed up Sharon's six years as a U.S. Senator: "Sharon was an extraordinarily disreputable senator. Living in San Francisco, he rarely appeared in Nevada or Washington, D.C. He presented no bills, made no speeches of record, voted in less than one percent of the roll calls, and did not participate in the critical debates about silver and the monetary system. In 1881, the [Big] Bonanza Crowd purchased Sharon's senate seat for James Fair."14

The Big Bonanza would revitalize the Comstock for the next seven years. Thousands of people, including many who had previously left when things looked bad, flocked to Sun Mountain in hopes of getting a small share of the big prize. Other mines were still producing ore, but the Bonanza Firm's mines remained head-and-shoulders over all the others combined. The combined populations of Virginia City and Gold Hill may have reached 25,000 people during this period, making it one of the larger communities west of the Mississippi.15

The Four Irishmen, Mackay, Fair, Flood and O'Brien— the "Bonanza Kings," as they became known—had watched Bill Sharon build his monopoly on the Comstock into one of the country's earliest vertically integrated business interests. Because their Bonanza Firm now held so much clout, they were no longer satisfied to be subservient to the "The King of the Comstock." They built their own mills, taking their business away from Sharon's Union Mine and Milling Company, and even before a big labor strike, they had purchased Sharon's interest in the Virginia and Gold Hill Water Company.[16] Then they delivered their coup de grâce: they capsized the Bank of California.

In San Francisco, Billy Ralston had spent bank funds lavishly, and had invested foolishly using the bank's money as his personal piggybank, putting the Bank of California in a tenuous situation. Things became much worse when the Bonanza Firm closed its accounts at Ralston's bank, said at one point to have had a balance of $1.8 million.[17] The Firm opened its own bank—the Nevada Bank of San Francisco—in mid-1875, according to a notice in the May 27, 1875 edition of the *Territorial Enterprise*: "Articles of incorporation of the Nevada Bank of San Francisco were filed on Monday in San Francisco. Object: to engage in and carry out the business of banking . . . The directors are: James C. Flood, William S. O'Brien, John W. Mackay, James G. Fair and Louis McLane. Capital stock, $5,000,000, divided into 50,000 shares of the par value of $100 each."

Only a month earlier, on April 28, an ad in the *Territorial Enterprise* had announced the Firm's opening of the Virginia Savings Bank, a new type of consumer bank designed for wage earners in the community. It was obvious that Mackay and his partners were serious about supplanting the Bank of California's monopoly on Sun Mountain.

Eight months later, when it appeared that the Bank of California was on the verge of collapse, Ralston was fired. Shortly thereafter, he was found dead in San Francisco Bay, either by suicide or as victim of accidental drowning. The Bank Ring, for all intents and purposes, was finished on the Comstock. An August 27, 1875 headline in Reno's *Nevada State Journal* said it all: "Bank of California Busted. Thousands Made Beggars."

The bank's two Comstock branches closed down immediately, and all of the stock boards, or exchanges, in San Francisco temporarily closed, the newspaper reported. A run on the other banks was feared, but it turned out to be not as serious as initially believed.[18] Later, the Bank of California would rise again like a Phoenix, thanks to the money, diligence and genius of

Chapter 9. Boom and Bust

Bill Sharon and Darius O. Mills. However, it would never again be a serious player on the Comstock.

The Bonanza Firm did continue to use the V&T Railroad rather than starting their own line to compete, so owners Bill Sharon and Darius O. Mills, who had purchased Ralston's interest in the railroad upon his death, continued to make some money from their competitors. They did have to lower their rates for the Bonanza Firm, however, when James Fair threatened to build his own railroad if cheaper rates weren't made available to them. However, the Bonanza Firm did enter the lumbering business, and like everything the Firm did, they did it in a big way, providing new competition for Bliss and Yerington and their C&TL&FC.

The Bonanza Firm named their lumbering division the Pacific Wood, Lumber and Flume Company, and purchased 12,000 acres of timberland. They expanded two sawmills in the Carson Range on Hunter Creek and Evans Creek, southwest of Reno. The Hunter Creek product was flumed down to the Evans Creek mill, and the product from both mills was then flumed fifteen miles down to the Truckee Meadows, where it met the V&T Railroad at Huffaker's in the valley south of Reno. The main flume had a daily capacity of 500 cords of wood, or a half-million board feet of lumber. At its peak, the Pacific Wood, Lumber and Flume Company's two facilities employed 800 men, all busy cutting, sawing and fluming product. Another 120 men, all Chinese, stacked the wood at Huffaker's, and loaded it onto the V&T for delivery to the Firm's mines on the Comstock.[19]

One humorous story of the Four Irishmen's fifteen-mile V-flume has come down to us. Two of the men, James Fair and James Flood, decided it would be fun to ride the flume from top to bottom. They ordered two V-shaped boats built to fit into the flume, with pointed prows in front and squared-off sterns. On a sunny September day the two Irishmen and three other men—one a reporter from the *New York Tribune*, to which we owe a debt for the story being recorded—climbed into the boats and pushed off. Down the flume they flew, blinded and drenched by the spray thrown up by the prow of the craft. They flew around hair-raising turns and across high, narrow trestles hundreds of feet above the gorges below. The entire ride lasted thirty minutes, and the five men arrived at the bottom battered and bruised, but mostly jubilant that they were still alive.[20]

Because of the voracious appetite of Mackay's mines, over the next five years they would be responsible for wiping out the extensive timber stands in the Evans and Hunter Creek areas, and be forced to close their sawmills. It has been estimated that they had used more than fifty million board feet just for the square sets for their five mines on the Comstock.[21] After the closure they again became customers of Bliss's C&TL&FC.

CHAPTER 10

Building a Lumbering Monolith

In May of 1874 Duane Leroy Bliss Jr. was born in Carson City. Duane and Elizabeth now had four boys and one girl; there would be no more children for the couple.

As a rule, Bliss was removed from the chaos that existed on the Comstock during the first half of the 1870s. Many of his mining customers were still located on Sun Mountain, but he now lived and worked in Carson City. Most of the company's initial timberlands were on the virtually untouched eastern slopes of the Tahoe Basin and in the valleys and meadows at the south end of Lake Tahoe, and that's where the majority of his time was spent. At its height—after it had cleared the eastern slope of the Sierra and moved over the mountaintop to the western slope—C&TL&FC would own between 50,000 and 80,000 acres of timberland in the Tahoe Basin. This included land in El Dorado and Placer Counties in California, and in Douglas, Ormsby and Washoe Counties in Nevada. Included in C&TL&FC's timberland inventory were miles and miles of pristine Lake Tahoe shoreline, much of which Bliss had purchased for as little as $1.25 an acre.[1]

C&TL&FC also purchased acreage from the Central Pacific Railroad in the northern and northwestern parts of the Tahoe Basin. These were alternate sections of land that the U.S. Government had granted the Central Pacific Railroad in the traditional checkerboard pattern, the government keeping each alternate section for settlement. Often C&TL&FC would purchase pieces of the government's alternate sections from preemptors, businessmen who would buy the land ostensibly for settlement, then immediately resell it to C&TL&FC and other lumber companies. C&TL&FC also purchased acreage from people who took up property under the Timber Culture Act, an 1873 law that allowed homesteaders to buy additional land if they would plant trees on a portion of it.[2]

The most common species of trees that were sought by lumbering companies were conifers. The western yellow, or Ponderosa pine (*Pinus*

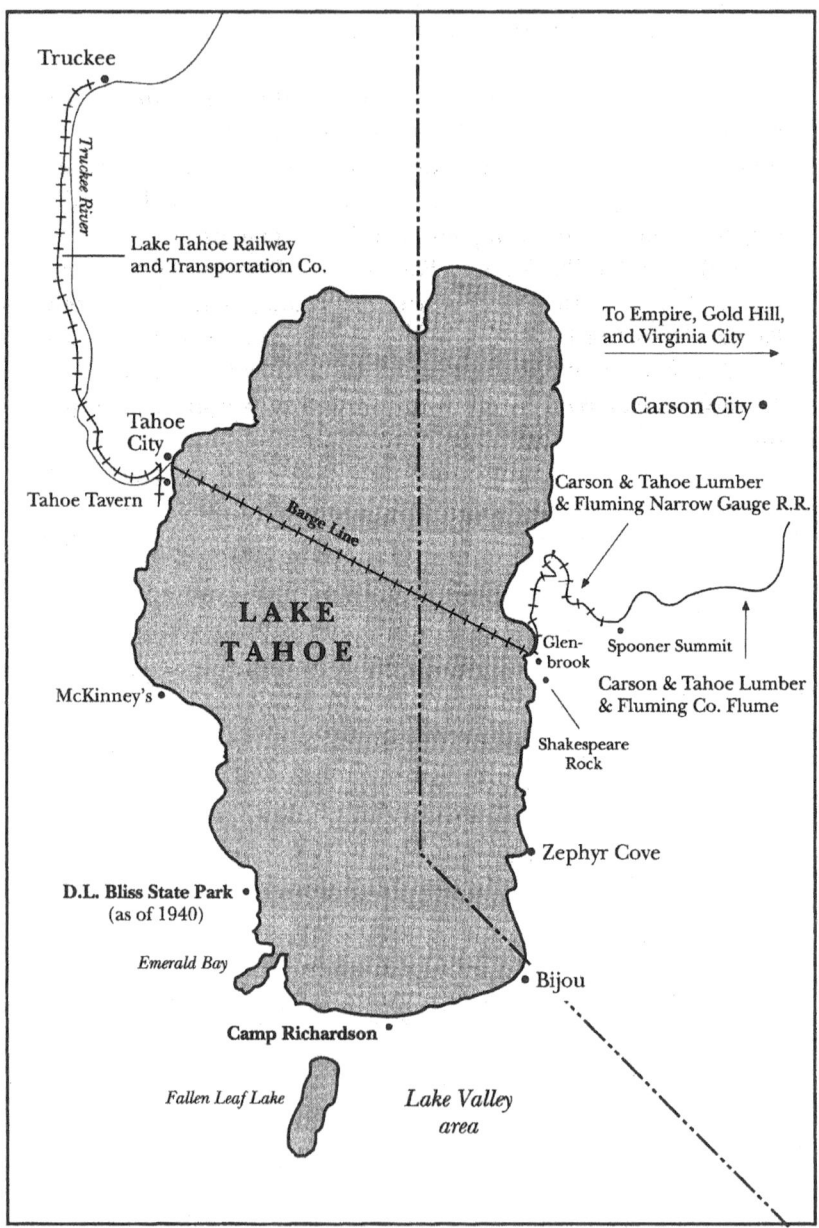

Map of Lake Tahoe shows the locations of Duane Bliss and his partners' Carson & Tahoe Lumber & Fluming Company enterprises, and his later Lake Tahoe Transportation Company enterprises (Tahoe Tavern and Lake Tahoe Railway.) Around the lake, the lumber company owned between 50,000 and 80,000 acres of timberlands. (© 1997 University of Nevada Press, from Tahoe Heritage by Sessions S. Wheeler with William W. Bliss)

Chapter 10. Building a Lumbering Monolith

ponderosa) and the closely related Jeffrey pine (*Pinus jeffreyi*) were good general purpose trees for the lumberman, and they were abundant. The sugar pine (*Pinus lambertiana*) was good lumber for building because if was clear, and the Douglas fir (*Pseudotsuga menziesii*) was prized for its strength. The incense cedar (*Calocedrus decurrens*) was used for shingles and for ground contact because it resisted decay, and the white fir (*Abies concolor*) was used for firewood, usually called cordwood. Red fir (*Abies magnifica*) typically grew in inaccessible areas at higher elevations, and was thus less popular. The existence of old growth red fir stands and the lack of stump fields suggest that it was harvested on a greatly reduced scale compared to other species.[3]

Lumber operators preferred to cut and mill their own trees, but Duane Bliss found it cost effective to occasionally use contractors to do the work. One such contract was entered into by C&TL&FC in 1875 with a man named Matthew Gardner. C&TL&FC had acquired a large timber holding of several thousand acres in 1872 at the southern end of Lake Tahoe, in Lake Valley. In May 1875 Gardner signed a contract with Bliss to handle the lumbering for C&TL&FC on the tract, a deal stating that he that would provide sixty million feet of logs. The first six million feet were to be delivered before the winter of 1875, and twelve million feet each year thereafter until the contract was fulfilled.[4]

With a contract in hand, Gardner went right to work, according to the *Gold Hill News*:

> *For the more rapid extraction of timber the Major [Gardner] has built a landing at the margin of the lake, and constructed a railroad something over a mile in length, reaching back into the forests. . . . The logs . . . are being hauled to the shore and floated across the lake a distance of 12 to 15 miles to mills near Glenbrook, where they are cut into lumber and mining timbers, hauled to the Summit and sent dashing through the company's flume to Carson City, where it is again shipped by railroad [the V&T] to Gold Hill and Virginia City.*[5]

The newspaper, reflecting the opinion of many of the people who lived on Sun Mountain and on or around Lake Tahoe, was not bashful about taking a stand against this practice:

> *It is the intention as soon as the timber is cut off to move it over a few hundred yards, and thus continue to mow down swath after swath of the great trees until the*

portion of the valley owned by the company is swept of its wealth and beauty, and is left as bleak and desolate as the mountain sides of Clear creek.

Lucky Baldwin [a wealthy and successful Comstock miner] . . . will not sell or allow a stick of the great pines to be taken from his premises, being determined that at least that much of the glory of the old forests shall remain, when the surrounding hills and mountains present only bleak sides and barren rocks.[6]

This was the very beginning of the cry of the conservationists to do something before all of the Tahoe Basin was denuded of its great forests.

C&TL&FC also contracted with Gardner to log some timberland for them on the western side of the lake at Sugar Pine Point, and also with George W. Chubbuck to cut trees on 10,000 acres of leased timberlands near Bijou, at the southeastern corner of the lake.[7]

*

It is difficult to grasp the size and scope of the Carson & Tahoe Lumber & Fluming Company during the peak years of the Comstock. Suffice it to say that it was a massive enterprise. One archaeologist doing site work on some of C&TL&FC's most important facilities summed it up nicely more than a century after the last tree had been felled:

At the height of C&TL&FC activities, company land holdings, either owned outright or leased, amounted to approximately 1/5 of the entire Lake Tahoe Basin. The works of this company were the most extensive and comprehensive of all those supplying lumber and cordwood for the Comstock. By 1873 the company had developed an impressive network that was designed to cut and move lumber out of the Lake Tahoe Basin, over the Carson Range at Spooner Summit and down to the Comstock mines. They owned and/or operated three mills at Glenbrook, a box and planing mill at Carson City, a telephone system, two steamers, booms for logs and barges for hauling, breakwaters, three logging railroads and one freighting railroad, locomotives and freight and log cars, a large lumber yard at Spooner Summit and one at Carson City, and a shop for equipment repair and maintenance. An extensive network of wood camps and flume camps and auxiliary mills were placed in strategic locales to construct and maintain an expansive system of flumes and reservoirs, a labyrinth of haul roads, skid trails and log chutes, along with wood wagons, pack mules, oxen and horses. . . . . The company held a virtual monopoly over wood and water resources in the region until 1898.[8]

Chapter 10. Building a Lumbering Monolith

On the morning of October 26, 1875 a catastrophic fire occurred on Sun Mountain. A coal oil lamp was upset in a small lodging house on A Street in Virginia City—"a drunken carouse was going on," reported the *Territorial Enterprise* the next day—and in a matter of minutes the entire house was engulfed in flames. Once the flames burned through the flimsy roof, winds carried it to nearby rooftops until the entire business quarter was a raging inferno.

Comstock historian Eliot Lord recorded the chaos that followed:

> *Bells rang out the alarm with their sharp, startling clangor, and steam-whistles blew ear piercing blasts, sounding above the crackling of the flames, the shouts of the firemen, the cries of escaping women and children, and the rattling of engines and cart-wheels. Lines of hose were quickly attached to hydrants, and engines began to throw water upon the fire; but the firemen might as well have attempted to quench a volcano..*[9]

The massive wall of flame was visible from fifteen miles away, but the city's buildings were not the only victims of the inferno. The Ophir mine reported afterwards that 1,000 cords of wood and nearly 400,000 feet of mining timber meant to shore up the mine were lost. Nor did the fire respect the property of the "Bonanza Kings" who by this time ruled the Comstock. The Consolidated Virginia mine's hoisting works and mill, and the California mine's mill were also destroyed, a reported loss of $1.3 million.[10]

One oft-repeated story of the fire came from journalist Charlie Goodwin. When the St. Mary in the Mountains Catholic Church began to burn, a devout old Irish woman ran to the Consolidated Virginia mine shaft where John Mackay and his employees were frantically trying to keep the fire from descending the shaft. She sought out Mackay himself, and implored him to help save the church. "Damn the church!" Mackay replied. "We can build another if we can keep the fire from going down these shafts."[11] The men did manage to keep the fire from going into the shaft, where it would have had the potential to jump from mine to mine and burn for weeks.

Another personal story was reported by author, historian, and mining attorney Grant H. Smith, born and raised on the Comstock, whose book is one of the finest contemporary chronicles on Comstock history. "A quick thinking uncle on Truckee Meadows, seeing the clouds of smoke, hurried up with a big hay wagon, and rescued the author's [Smith's] family," he wrote.[12]

By noon, the fire had burned itself out. When the final toll was taken, the heart of Virginia City—a half-mile square—had been completely destroyed. Over 2,000 buildings were gone, at a loss totaling $10 million, according to one estimate, and 2,000 people were left homeless. Virginia City, with the unselfish assistance of cities and towns across the West, would completely recover.

Duane Bliss and his C&TL&FC associates were kept extraordinarily busy for the next six months milling and delivering hundreds of thousands of board feet of lumber via the V&T Railroad to rebuild Virginia City. Despite the sudden boom in business, it was not the kind of situation anyone would ever hope to see repeated.

C&TL&FC had initially purchased two sawmills from Captain Pray in Glenbrook. One, Pray's first mill, was on the meadow near the southwest corner of Glenbrook Bay, while the second one was on the northern end of the same meadow. The company closed its other mills, with the exception of the Summit Mill. By the time of the Virginia City fire C&TL&FC had built another mill in Glenbrook, just south of Pray's original mill. Bliss hired French Canadian and Italian lumberjacks, long experienced in the lumbering industry, and he imported experienced mill workers from faraway Maine. Through a sub-contractor, he also hired Chinese workers—most left over from the construction of the Central Pacific and V&T Railroads—to chop and gather the massive amount of cordwood the firm sold. Cordwood was a natural adjunct to the lumber business. All mines and mills were operated by steam engines, with the exception of a very few that were located on the Carson River, which used water power. After the V&T Railroad was completed in the early 1870s, a few mills tried coal as the fuel-of-choice, but neither water nor coal ever came close to replacing wood as the Comstock's primary energy source. Many large trees, perhaps as high as eighty feet, would only produce one good saw log of twenty feet in length or less. The remaining scrap could be salvaged and chopped for cordwood. This not only provided a secondary source of income for the lumbering companies, but also kept the forest floor clear of debris that might be a fire hazard. C&TL&FC's system of flumes also made it easy to float the cordwood to market rather than having to haul it by mules or on the backs of the Chinese woodchoppers, as had been done in the earliest days of the company. In addition to providing fuel for the hundreds of steam engines, cordwood also warmed the hearths of all of Sun Mountain's homes and businesses.

Chapter 10. Building a Lumbering Monolith

In the 1860s, during the winter off-season, Chinese woodchoppers had sold firewood in Virginia City, Gold Hill and the other Sun Mountain communities. This was a chore the indigenous Paiute Indians initially handled, but the Chinese were more industrious and persistent, and eventually won out. During the especially harsh winter of 1868/69, the *Territorial Enterprise* of September 29, 1869 even gave the Chinese wood peddlers credit for saving the population of Virginia City from freezing. But when the V&T Railroad tied Virginia City into Carson City in 1870, and cordwood could be delivered to Sun Mountain at a greatly reduced rate, the Chinese were forced out of that market.[13]

Most lumbering crews worked in five-man teams. The highest paid and most experienced men on the teams were the sawyers, burly fellows who wrestled two-man crosscut saws and heavy axes through the groves of giant trees. A swamper's job followed, the man who cut the branches from the fallen tree and cleared a path for the oxen teams that would pull the tree to the flume. The chainer connected a heavy chain from the fallen tree to the yoke of the oxen teams; and the teamster led the oxen to the mouth of the flume. These men were all lodged in a series of logging camps built near the sections being cut, or, when the work was nearby, in the bunkhouses, boarding houses and cottages purchased from Captain Pray in Glenbrook.[14]

The lumber industry had its own vocabulary when it came to job titles. In addition to the ones listed above, there were river hogs, pin whackers, chickadees, deacons, top loaders and cookees. There were also whistle punks, scalers, fallers, buckers, grease monkeys, donkey punchers, pond men, flume herders and chokermen.

During the first half of the 1860s, with the Civil War raging, and in the years immediately following the war, the three interlocking industries—mining, milling and lumbering—often competed for manpower among those that had not been called or volunteered for military service. Many men were drawn to the West not only by the Comstock's promise of jobs and potential wealth, but for the safety of the area from the war's battles. Once on site, many of them discovered that the returns for harvesting timber were more stable than working in the mines, and somewhat safer, too. As lumbering historian Wilson pointed out, "Some of these were men who crossed not only a continent but an ocean as well to reach the California-Nevada border."[15]

Although it's impossible to pinpoint exactly the wages earned by Tahoe Basin lumbermen during the 1870s and 1880s, one expert puts the figure at an average of $150 a month for the higher skilled positions. Given a six-day workweek, that would come to $6 a day for lumberjacks. Usually, however, a portion of a man's salary was deducted for meals and lodging. Naturally, the lesser skilled positions would earn one dollar or so less per day.[16] By comparison, Grant Smith's study for the Nevada Bureau of Mines and Geology stated that miners were paid between $4 and $5 per day, depending upon their experience and the depth at which they worked the ore. A miner working above the 2,400-foot level was required to work a ten-hour shift to earn the same wage as a miner working below 2,400 feet earned working an eight-hour shift. Ore mill workers, on the other hand, were paid from $4 to $6 for an eight-hour shift, the higher end of the scale being reserved for those who worked with mercury and other dangerous chemicals.[17] Thus, the earnings for the three industries were similar. Since there were normally jobs available in all three industries, men would normally seek jobs based upon their experience, and the relative safety and comfort of the job being offered.

None of the foregoing, however, applied to one particular group of workers: the Chinese. Most of the earliest Chinese in Nevada worked as ditch diggers, and later moved into railroad construction, agriculture, or domestic service. As the lumbering industry grew in Nevada and California during the Comstock era, many sought low-wage, unskilled labor positions with the lumbering companies. Most worked as cordwood cutters and gatherers, flume and skid-line tenders and logging camp service employees. Those working as cordwood choppers/gatherers were paid from $2.00 to $2.25 per cord. C&TL&FC records indicate that most of the Chinese hired by the company worked at the Spooner Summit Flume, or as cooks and service employees in Glenbrook. As most logging in the Basin was not year-round work, many Chinese employees, like the other more skilled workers, returned to work for C&TL&FC year after year. Chinese workers were paid a much lower wage than others, even those non-Chinese working at the exact same job.[18]

No estimate exists for the number of people C&TL&FC employed. Sierra Nevada lumbering historian Dick Wilson wrote that the Bonanza Firm employed about 1,000 men to harvest and mill 12,000 acres of timberland (see Chapter 9) so it is safe to estimate that C&TL&FC, with between 50,000 and 80,000 acres of timberland, must have employed at least 3,000 men at any given time. Add in the employees of the Carson Box Factory, the three lumber railroads, and the personnel that operated and maintained the tugs and scows on the lake, and C&TL&FC's total employee count could have

Chapter 10. Building a Lumbering Monolith

easily averaged between 3,500 and 4,000 people during the eight-month lumbering season.

In her biographical sketch of her father, Hope Bliss stated that Bliss provided a type of medical insurance to all his permanent workers. Each employee paid 50c a month for medical services, and that was all they were ever charged; C&TL&FC picked up any additional costs. She also stated that at every Christmas, Bliss provided a cord of firewood at no charge to all widows and other in-need families who worked for the company, and it regularly hired men just out of the state prison in Carson City to give them a new start in life. None of these claims can be verified, but given Bliss's reputation as a fair and generous employer, they do have a ring of truth.[19]

There were, however, occasional problems that rose as a result of having so many employees. The *Carson City Appeal* announced on June 25, 1878 that there was a strike at Glenbrook among the mill workers. "There has been grumbling for some time past among the workingmen about low wages, but not until yesterday morning did the discontent take the shape of a positive refusal to work," the newspaper reported. It's doubtful if the strike succeeded in its aim, however, as there were always more trained men than jobs available. The story continued: "An order was immediately sent to Carson for more men, and we have no doubt that it was speedily filled, for Carson . . . has its full share of idle men ready to work when opportunity offers."

According to C&TL&FC records, James Rigby was now handling accounting chores for the company, approving and paying invoices.[20] He and a partner also leased a general merchandise store that Captain Pray had built on pilings over the lake. That building would eventually burn down, and be replaced with a similar structure built and operated by C&TL&FC.

*

Bliss's biggest challenge in the mid-1870s was to streamline the company's logging operations within the Tahoe Basin. The lumber and cordwood was efficiently moved from Spooner Summit, at the top of the mountain, down the eastern slope of the Carson Range by V-flumes, where it eventually arrived at the huge lumber storage yard and V&T Railroad spur near Carson City. An important part of that process was to secure a regular source of water to facilitate the lumber's ride. Marlette Lake, originally known as Goodwin Lake, was a man-made body of water fed by many creeks and drainages that lay in a depression about 1,800 feet above the northeastern shore of

Lake Tahoe. To insure a constant water supply, C&TL&FC purchased the small reservoir in the early 1870s. Through a series of smaller flumes, water was moved from Marlette Lake to three retaining ponds at Clear Creek. From there the water was fed to the main V-flume that carried the timber, lumber and cordwood down to the lumber storage yard. Thus, that part of C&TL&FC's operation was solid. As a matter of fact, the company even sold some water rights from Marlette Lake to the Virginia and Gold Hill Water Company to help slake the thirst on the Comstock.[21]

However, getting the milled lumber and cordwood up the much steeper western slope from the sawmills at Glenbrook to the V-flume at Spooner Summit had always been a problem. This was still being accomplished by the old fashioned method: draft animals slowly and laboriously pulling heavy wagons up the narrow roads to the top. Bliss realized that a narrow gauge railroad was the ideal solution to this transportation bottleneck. In 1874 he hired a surveyor, he and his crew began inspecting the steep grades between Glenbrook and Spooner Summit. The terrain was difficult; it was so steep in places that the surveyors had to do their work suspended by ropes. It was July before the surveying work was finished, so construction had to be postponed until the following year.

On April 19, 1875 work began. Two weeks later, Hank Monk, the legendary stagecoach driver who drove a route between Carson City and Placerville, California, passed through on his way over the summit. He told a reporter on the scene that times were lively down in Glenbrook since there was so much excitement and activity around the place. A force of 250 men was hard at work clearing the land and laying rail, and work was progressing faster than anticipated. Bliss had used his own Chinese woodchoppers to fill and grade the right-of-way, and his Glenbrook mill workers to lay ties and rails and spike them into place. All in all, he had used over half of his company men to do the work. Eleven trestles, a 487-foot tunnel, and a 6,000-foot switchback to maintain grade were required on the 8.75-mile stretch. In the end, the railroad cost the company over $300,000 to build.[23]

At the end of June the first mile of track had been spiked into place, and the first piece of rolling stock was set on the rails. It was a 2-6-0 Mogul type narrow gauge, wood-fired steam locomotive built by the Baldwin Locomotive Works of Philadelphia. Named the *Glenbrook*, it would soon be joined by the identical *Tahoe*, and eventually a third locomotive. All three were capable of hauling seventy tons of freight at ten miles per hour. A number of flat cars were also offloaded onto the tracks —there would eventually be forty-

Chapter 10. Building a Lumbering Monolith

This photo, taken at Slaughterhouse Canyon, shows the steep grade and sharp switchbacks the Lake Tahoe Railroad had to maneuver through in order carry milled lumber and cordwood up the western slope of the mountain from the mills at Glenbrook to the V-Flume at Spooner Summit. (Library of Congress)

five of them—many of which would later be fitted with heavy stakes on the sides to hold the cargo in place. All three locomotives were shipped to Carson City by rail, and together with other equipment were hauled across the mountains by trucks drawn by oxen and horses. In addition to the main track, there were two-and-a-half miles of sidings. By August 21 all the tracks had been completed.[24]

Once finished, the small railroad—simply named the Lake Tahoe Railroad—had no passenger accommodations. It was intended strictly as a lumber carrier, and was operated at a cost of $3,000 a month. However, adventurous souls were occasionally allowed to ride the train, precariously balanced atop the boards, planks and timbers stacked on the flat cars. A ride on the train, however, was not for the faint of heart. In 1877 a man was killed when he tumbled off his lofty perch.[25]

Lake Tahoe historian E. B. Scott described what a visitor to the small railroad would see:

> *[The locomotive] had balloon . . . smokestacks. An iron cowcatcher was carried well forward of each boiler on small running wheels. Above were huge square oil-burning headlights ornamented with gold scrollwork. Each engine could pull 70 tons of lumber or cordwood at a maximum speed of ten miles per hour on the upgrade, allowing an 11 to 12-ton loading per car.*[26]

The Lake Tahoe Railroad was the perfect solution to delivering milled lumber up the eastern mountainside, while the V-flume was just as efficient at carrying it down the western mountainside to Carson City. However, a third transportation problem still needed to be addressed: getting the logs that were felled in Lake Valley on the southern end of the lake, and directly across the lake at Sugar Pine Point, to the mills in Glenbrook. For this purpose, C&TL&FC used the lake itself, as announced in the *Territorial Enterprise* on April 4, 1877: "Bliss, Yerington & Co. [newspapers rarely used the C&TL&FC name, sticking instead the older name of the company] have inaugurated a new plan for running wood across the lake. During the past winter they have caused to be constructed immense scows [flat-bottomed barges] capable of carrying eighty cords of wood each."

The scows carrying the cordwood were pulled across the lake by one of the company's steamships that also pushed the massive logs that would become timbers and lumber. First, the pine logs were dragged by mules, horses or oxen teams to the water's edge, where the terrain permitted, or fed onto greased chutes, and pushed into the lake. Once in the water, the logs were gathered into log-booms—massive V-shaped rafts of logs—that were secured together by chains or cables. Then the booms and the scows were pushed and/or pulled by C&TL&FC's steamers to the Glenbrook mills.[27] The company's steam-driven tug, the iron-hulled *Meteor*, was purchased in 1876, and was said to be the fastest inland steamer in the world. She was built in Wilmington, Delaware and shipped in sections by rail to Carson City. From there she was hauled over the mountain by horses and oxen teams, and reassembled at Glenbrook. She was a powerful little boat, with an eighty-foot length and a ten-foot beam, capable of speeds up to twenty knots. Because she was built to pull heavy loads, she was outfitted with a three-blade propeller. Elizabeth Bliss had named the boat based upon its

Chapter 10. Building a Lumbering Monolith

C&TL&FC's narrow gauge Lake Tahoe Railroad alleviated the problem of hauling lumber up the western slope of the Sierra Nevada from the Glenbrook mills. Pictured is the steam driven locomotive Glenbrook pulling lumber cars across a low trestle as it approaches the switchback. Once at the top, the lumber was flumed down the eastern slope to the firm's vast Carson City lumber storage yard, and from there it was carried overland by the V&T Railroad and up Sun Mountain to the waiting mines. (Special Collections Department, University of Nevada, Reno Library)

sleek silhouette, but nobody could have known how resilient she would turn out to be. The *Meteor* would remain in service for sixty years.[28]

The *Meteor* was C&TL&FC's second steam tug. Bliss had purchased the first, the wooden-hulled *Emerald I*, in 1874 after she had been in service on the lake for five years. Smaller than the *Meteor* by twenty-five feet, she lacked durability, and was finally retired from service in 1881 and beached on the south shore of Glenbrook Bay. The *Emerald II* would see service with C&TL&FC from her launch in 1887 until 1898 when the company withdrew from the lumbering business. For the next thirty-seven years she would be used as a workboat for Duane Bliss's Tahoe City business enterprises. After many years of service, the *Emerald II* was finally sold for scrap.[29]

*

The mid-to late-1870s was a prosperous period on the Comstock. "More mines were in operation and more men employed than ever before," Comstock historian Grant Smith wrote.

In 1876, for example, 135 Comstock mines were included on the San Francisco stock exchanges. Every mine operator was convinced there were more great ore bodies lying undiscovered at deeper levels, and all of the large mines were sinking incline and vertical shafts to reach what they hoped would be the next Big Bonanza. Many of the mines would eventually reach depths exceeding 2,000 feet below ground, deeper than any mines anywhere had achieved up to that time. The deeper the shafts sunk into the earth, the more square-sets they required, and that continued to fuel the need for more lumber. Belying all the optimism, however, was the fact that the only mines paying dividends—the mark of profitability—were three of the Bonanza Firm's now twelve mines. The other mines were all levying assessments on stockholders to meet costs.[30]

Smith quotes journalist Joe Goodman who cited a typical scene on the Comstock during this raucous period:

In the flush days, the Comstock was one of the busiest and most picturesque sights ever witnessed. Immense hoisting works studded the mountain sides for miles with

The steamer *Meteor* was one of a large fleet of ships and barges Carson & Tahoe Lumber & Fluming Company owned. They would carry or push lumber from around the lake to the Glenbrook mill to be processed, before being moved up the mountain on the company's narrow gauge railroad. (Special Collections Department, University of Nevada, Reno Library)

Chapter 10. Building a Lumbering Monolith

their huge dump piles and capacious ore bins; quart mills were thundering and grinding in every available nook of the neighboring can[y]ons; a continuous line of many-muled teams hauling ore, wood, and merchandise constantly crowded the streets and outlying roads, and in the town itself were such throngs of people as one would expect to encounter only in the heart of a great metropolis. The scene was made doubly animate by the great prevalence of hope and high spirit. Everyone had money or felt rich with the ease with which money was to be acquired, and all met upon an equal footing, because one that was poor today might be rich tomorrow.[31]

Saloons and gambling houses, stores, restaurants and houses of ill fame all shared in the bounty. So too did the V&T Railroad that delivered almost everything up the mountainside and carried tons of unprocessed ore back down again. For those lumber companies serving the rapidly developing cities and towns in northern California and Nevada, the need for building materials was great. For those few companies serving that market and the Comstock mining market as well, business was booming! There were a dozen or so large lumbering firms serving the former market, but only three serving most of the needs of the latter: C&TL&FC, the Bonanza Firm's Pacific Wood, Lumber and Fluming Company, and to a lesser degree, Walter Hobart's Sierra Nevada Wood and Lumber Company, organized in 1878 and headquartered on the northeastern corner of the lake near Incline. By the late 1870s the Bonanza Firm's timberlands had been depleted, and it too had to depend upon C&TL&FC and Hobart's firm for timber and cordwood. Dan DeQuille, writing in *The Big Bonanza*, maintained that eighty million board feet of lumber and a quarter-million cords of firewood were being consumed annually on the Comstock, denuding the forests in the Tahoe Basin at an alarming rate.[32] As early as 1867 the *Gold Hill News* was decrying the cost of firewood to its residents, as most of it was being used by the mines and mills to fuel their steam engines: "This [$40 a cord] is the highest price ever paid for firewood in Nevada, or any place we have ever heard of."[33]

One of the reciprocating agreements between the C&TL&FC and the Sharon and Mills-owned V&T Railroad called for much higher freight rates to be charged to all other Tahoe Basin lumber companies. In May 1877 this arrangement was worked out between the two companies, and it permitted C&TL&FC to sell boards for $8.50 per thousand feet on the Comstock, while other lumber companies were forced to charge $20 because of their higher freight rates. The *Truckee Republican* wrote of this situation in 1880: "The infamous combinations between the managers of the V&T railroad and the Tahoe lumbermen [C&TL&FC] has kept up the price of wood and lumber in Virginia City to twice its real value. The most outrageous discrimination has been made against the Truckee lumbermen, and as a result, every shareholder in the mines of the Comstock has been assessed to pay the exorbitant prices demanded of the Tahoe ring for wood and mining timbers." In the same vein, the *Carson Morning Appeal* added, ". . . the question of reducing the price of wood, freight, etc., shall be vigorously agitated. . . . Wood costs in Virginia City more than double its value in Carson . . . ."[34]

It is likely, but unproven, that a huge fire in C&TL&FC's Carson City lumber storage yard in November 1877 was retribution for the favorable treatment the company received at the hands of the V&T. The *Territorial Enterprise* reported that over 75,000 board feet of lumber and 7,000 cords of firewood were destroyed, an estimated loss of $80,000 to $90,000 to the company. "[The] wood yard . . . caught fire or was set on fire," the newspaper said. The *Sacramento Union* reported that an additional 75 million board feet of wood was in danger, and that two fire engines had been dispatched from that city to assist in fighting the huge blaze. The following week the company offered a $5,000 reward for the arrest and conviction of the "person or persons who set [the] fire . . . ."[35] No one was ever arrested for causing the blaze.

Because of the enormous amount of business C&TL&FC was doing, Bliss was constantly on the lookout for new timberlands. In 1878, a 640-acre tract of land owned by the Central Pacific Railroad, part of their extensive government grant, was located on the west side of Lake Tahoe at a place called Meek's Bay. It was heavily forested, but a portion of the land was a grassy flatland that was perfect for grazing milk cows. Two young California brothers had helped their father graze a herd on the land years before, and they now had plans to buy the land for their own small herd of cows. They had saved $250, and although they realized it was a low figure they submitted a bid for the land to the railroad. The Murphy brothers were devastated when they learned that Duane Bliss had purchased the parcel just days before for the same $250 they had offered. Shortly afterwards the *Meteor* showed up at Meek's Bay towing a large cordwood barge, and lumberjacks hopped off the boat and began cutting sugar pine trees almost up to the rails of the Murphys' corrals. Irate, James Murphy mounted his horse and

Chapter 10. Building a Lumbering Monolith

The massive C&TL&FC lumber and wood storage yard in Carson City, shown here in 1876, was set afire the following year likely as retribution for the special pricing concessions granted to the company by the V&T Railroad. (Special Collections Department, University of Nevada, Reno Library)

headed around the lake to Glenbrook to confront Duane Bliss, getting more and more angry with every mile he covered. The startled Bliss listened to the young man's threats and his pleas. When Murphy finally sputtered to a stop, Bliss told him that his only interest was the trees, and that as soon as the land was cleared he would sell it to the Murphys for the same $250. In 1884, when the logging was finished, the Murphy brothers gave Bliss $250 in gold eagles in exchange for the deed to the now cut-over 640 acres. Duane Bliss was a man of his word.[36]

In 1879 and 1880 Nevada was honored by the visits of two extraordinary men, and Duane Bliss would have a hand in both events. In October 1879 General and former President Ulysses S. Grant stopped in Nevada on the last leg of a world tour with his wife and son. The party arrived by train at Truckee, California on Sunday morning, and was driven in carriages to Tahoe City on the northeastern shoreline of the lake. There, Duane Bliss met the party and escorted them aboard C&TL&FC's *Meteor*, the eighty-foot-long steamer tug that normally ferried newly-cut trees across the lake. The *Meteor* had also been built with passenger accommodations, and it was here that General Grant, Bliss and the rest of the party relaxed during their ride across the lake to Glenbrook. Once there, the party boarded a specially modified flatcar for a trip to Spooner Summit aboard Bliss's Lake Tahoe Railroad, generally considered to be the most breath-taking ride at the lake. Elizabeth Bliss had been selected to be one of the committee of four ladies who would welcome and attend to Mrs. Grant, so she was also part of the party.[38]

Following the train ride, the party was met by carriages and driven down to Carson City, where they were entertained until their departure for Virginia City the following day. The Carson City stop fueled a minor spat between officials of the two cities. Grant and his party spent an extra three hours in Carson City, arriving in Virginia City at 1:30 p.m. the following day instead of the previously announced 10:30 a.m. Naturally that threw a wrench in Virginia City's grand celebration plans, and officials blamed Carson City officials for the delay. "What a senseless hue and cry to raise about nothing," the *Carson Morning Appeal* wrote the next day. "Because the General gets there three hours later than they expected, is that any reason why the Storey County committee should make babies of themselves? Go and hide yourselves, you selfish creatures." The incident was good for three or four days of nasty verbal sparring between the respective city's newspapers.[39]

The second visit, on September 7 and 8, 1880, was even more noteworthy, as it was the first stopover ever in Nevada of a sitting U.S. President. President Rutherford B. Hayes was accompanied by First Lady Lucy Hayes, Civil War hero General William Tecumseh Sherman, Secretary of War Alexander Ramsey and a number of lesser dignitaries from Washington D.C. Following festivities in Reno, Virginia City and Carson City, President Hayes and his entourage were driven by famous stagecoach driver Hank Monk to Spooner Summit. From there, Duane and Elizabeth Bliss hosted the party to the same sites and scenes they had shown General Grant and his party, but in reverse: The Lake Tahoe Railroad ride from Spooner Summit down to Glenbrook, then the *Meteor* cruise across the lake to Tahoe City.[40] It would be another 120 years before the next sitting U.S. President would visit Nevada.

On both of these historic Lake Tahoe cruises, Ernest John Pomin, a member of the sea-faring Pomin family of Glenbrook, was master of the *Meteor*. When the C&TL&FC steamer was first commissioned in 1876, Pomin was appointed master, a job he held for the next twenty years. Described by

Chapter 10. Building a Lumbering Monolith

one reporter as "a nice gentleman and good sailor," Pomin took over as master of the SS *Tahoe* when she was launched in 1896. He served the Bliss family in that capacity until December 8, 1919, when he struck his head while boarding another of the steamers in the fleet and passed away. Pomin had served the Bliss family loyally for forty-five years.[41]

CHAPTER 11

The End of an Era

As the 1870s wound down, the Bliss family continued to enjoy their life in the busy state capital of Carson City. On a sunny August day in 1878, Duane was invited to attend a special social gathering being hosted by Comstock man-about-town Johnnie "Little Napoleon" Skae. It was a fish fry, but more importantly, a promotional gimmick for a stock deal Skae was contriving. The event was held at the Virginia and Gold Hill Water Company's Five-Mile Reservoir near the Ophir Grade. Skae's fortunes had fluctuated up and down since he had arrived on the Comstock in the early 1860s, but the day of the fish fry was one of his "up" periods, as he was a prominent manager of the water company. The reservoir had been stocked with thousands of trout, and as quickly as they were pulled from the water they were cleaned and thrown onto one of the many wood grills set up for the occasion. Virginia City's famed International Hotel had provided a staff of cooks and waiters in starched whites to service the affair. As Skae received his guests, it sounded like a 4th of July fireworks celebration with the constant popping of champagne corks. After hundreds of bottles of the bubbly, whiskey, gin and brandy had been consumed, many of the guests were even said to have jumped into the reservoir fully clothed, hauling out the trout by hand. Over 150 friends of Skae had been invited, a virtual Who's Who of Nevada. Duane Bliss, now the most important lumbering man in the two-state area, was joined by future governor Charlie Stevenson, engineer Philip Deidesheimer, future Chief Justice of the Nevada Supreme Court C. H. Belknap, presidents and operators of all of the important mines and mills, politicians, newspaper journalists, storekeepers, and a slew of other VIPs. One visitor, young Harry Gorham, later wrote about the party, describing it by saying, "Not a Lucillian feast—just fish and bread, and coffee and drinks galore and cigars by the hundreds . . . and an aggregation of as fine a body of representative men as one could hope to see."[1] Skae's Fish Fry was a grand party in the best tradition of the Old West.

Now, with five children, Duane and Elizabeth Bliss found they were uncomfortably crowded in the house on North Minnesota Street, and realized that they needed a larger home. Duane bought a lot at the corner of Robinson and Mountain streets—two decades later the Nevada Governor's Mansion would be built right across the street—and he hired an architect to design the house. From the beginning, Bliss realized he wanted this house to be special. For six months he gathered the best materials: clear-grained lumber cut from the best trees in his inventory, carefully crafted square nails, locally quarried sandstone for the foundation, the finest hardwood for an indoor roller skating rink, three train carloads of bricks for four massive chimneys, spectacular white and blue-gray Carrara marble from Italy, and other marble from Vermont and Georgia to be used to for five interior fireplaces.[2]

The foundation was laid in early 1877, and by November when the three-story, 8000 square-foot Victorian Italianate mansion was finished it was proclaimed the largest and grandest house in the state of Nevada. The home's twenty-one rooms included nine bedrooms, a number of bathrooms, a formal dining room, a game room, a parlor, butler's pantry, linen rooms and a splendid state-of-the-art kitchen. On the third floor was a full ballroom that was also used by the children as a skating rink. Germantown, Pennsylvania craftsmen built the stairways and delicate moldings, and many of the fittings and fixtures were made of Comstock silver. More than $12,000 was spent on incidental decorator items like glass doorknobs encasing blobs of mercury.

It was one of the first homes in the West to be piped for gas lighting and heating, and one of the first to have the new Bell telephone. A telephone relay system connected Bliss's Carson City home, his Glenbrook summer home, C&TL&FC headquarters in Carson City, the milling operation in Glenbrook, and the flume at Spooner's Summit, where the lines were partially strung on trees. The *Carson City Appeal* commented on this technological marvel, noting, "Anyone wishing to whisper at a distance will have to get on the right side of Mr. Bliss."[3]

The glory days of the Comstock passed with the year 1880. "Not only was it finished as a profitable mining region, but most of the ambitious, energetic men had departed or were soon to leave . . . ." wrote historian Grant Smith.[4] The mining magnates, the miners, the lawyers, the store keepers, the prostitutes, the mill workers, and blacksmiths all left to seek their fortunes elsewhere. Many went to Bodie, California, where a small bonanza

Chapter 11. The End of an Era

In 1877 Duane and Elizabeth Bliss built a larger home for their growing family at the corner of Robinson and Mountain streets in Carson City, known today as the Bliss Mansion. When completed it was proclaimed the largest and grandest home in Nevada. (Undated photo, courtesy of the Bliss Family)

revitalized that old mining camp. The Consolidated Virginia—home of the Big Bonanza—paid its last small dividend in 1880.

Despite the slowdown in the mining economy in 1880—or perhaps because of it—some of C&TL&FC's lumbering competitors put out a rumor that the firm had a shortage of product and would not be able to meet even the depressed demand for lumber and mining timbers. Not true, reported the *Nevada State Journal* in a March 12, 1880 article: "[C&TL&FC] have now on hand about one and a half million feet of logs, and have let logging contracts for the present year amounting to twenty million feet, and are only holding back on other contracts to await the result of developments on the Comstock. They also have on hand in their Carson yard over fifteen million feet of dry timber and lumber . . . ." C&TL&FC was obviously prepared to meet the Comstock's demand, whatever it might be.

Despite the slowdown during the decade of the 1880s, there would be a weak revival period when many mines and mills reprocessed leftover low-grade ore. As a result, C&TL&FC's Glenbrook mills still enjoyed an annual output of about 121 million board feet of lumber. The company continued producing through most of the 1880s, but at a steadily declining rate. But it just wasn't the same; it would never be the same again. From 1859 until 1882 the Comstock's mines had produced $320 million from ore and tailings. From that point through the 1890s only $80 million more would be realized. The country has never experienced another mining period like it. Experts have predicted that fifty-seven percent of the Comstock's treasure was silver, and forty-three percent was gold.[5]

Interestingly, during the same time period, C&TL&FC and the other lumbering firms had extracted lumber valued at more than $80 million from the Tahoe Basin alone, mostly used to produce the mineral wealth from the mines. When the lumber from the Washoe Valley, Carson Valley, and the eastern slope of the Carson Range is factored in, the figure would have easily reached $100 million. So when historians discuss all of the wealthy men the Comstock Lode produced, they often forget that the region's forests servicing Sun Mountain produced a few wealthy men too, men like Duane Bliss and Henry Yerington.[6]

Perhaps this is a fitting story to mark the end of the glory days of the Comstock, because it so well illustrates the vagaries of those who lived and toiled on Sun Mountain. It concerns the man who started it all, the quiet, introverted Irish prospector, Patrick McLaughlin. In the spring of 1859 McLaughlin and his partner Peter O'Riley had stuck their spades into the heavy blue-black sludge that had clogged their rockers as they were panning for gold near the head of Six Mile Canyon. They were the first to wonder if the sludge had any value. It did, and it led to the richest silver mining discovery in U.S. history. But McLaughlin, like so many other naïve immigrants, quickly sold his share of the claim for pennies, allowing others to get fabulously rich. McLaughlin bounced around from place to place for years after that, never quite figuring out where he belonged. His last job was as a cook for a party of miners in San Bernardino County, California, where

Chapter 11. The End of an Era

he fell ill in 1879 and died shortly thereafter in the county hospital. Patrick McLaughlin, the man who initiated the largest silver strike in history, did not leave enough money at his death to pay for a pauper's funeral.[7]

*

The V&T Railroad had also prospered mightily as a result of the Comstock Lode. In 1880, hoping to duplicate their earlier success, William Sharon and an extremely reluctant Darius O. Mills incorporated the Carson & Colorado Railroad. The road was to run from Mound House, adjacent to Carson City, to . . . well, that was never made clear, perhaps because the cunning Sharon was playing it by ear. His hope was that the narrow gauge railroad could tap the wealth from some of the mines that were springing up in eastern California settlements like Bodie, Candelaria and Panamint. Eventually, the line would run 293 miles to Hawley, California with a six-mile branch to Candelaria.[8]

Henry Yerington was named president and general manager of the line, and D. L. Bliss was vice president. Both men sat on the board of directors. In 1883 W. D. Tobey, Bliss's brother-in-law who had come west from Massachusetts, was added to the board. The railroad was built at minimal cost, and had none of the quality associated with the V&T. It made a little money for the first few years, but a decline in mining in eastern California caused it to lose money every year after 1885. It was said that Mills, who by now had moved to New York City, had to be reminded that he owned the majority of stock in the little railroad, as it was such an unimportant part of his large financial empire. Finally, in 1900, the railroad was sold to the Southern Pacific Company.[9]

Bliss also became involved in another company that was affiliated with the Carson & Colorado Railroad. Henry Yerington filed articles of incorporation in 1881 for the Southern Development Company of Nevada, into which he folded two earlier corporations, the Walker Lake and Bodie Toll Road Company and the Walker Lake Wood and Lumber Company. Yerington was president of the corporation, and he held most of the stock, and his son E. B. Yerington was secretary. Duane Bliss was a trustee and member of the board of directors, along with his brother-in-law Walter D. Tobey and two other men. Bliss was also a minor investor in the company. The stated purposes of the Carson City-based company, according to the incorporation papers, were to "buy and sell land, build and operate toll roads, locate and hold water rights and privileges in order to construct waterways and systems, and to acquire lands for timbering."[10]

The company also founded the town of Hawthorne, in Esmeralda County in east central Nevada, which served as the terminus of the Carson & Colorado Railroad. The company actively pursued its stated purposes until after the turn of the century when timbering declined and the Southern Pacific Railroad pulled out of Hawthorne. The corporation dissolved in 1920, but the tough little town hung on, became the county seat of Mineral County and the home to the Hawthorne Army Depot. Today Hawthorne has about 3,300 residents.[11]

In the mid-1880s Bliss would be involved in building another narrow gauge short line railroad, this one his own. By this time C&TL&FC controlled more than 10,000 acres of timberland at the southeastern end of Lake Tahoe, including Lake Valley. Some of this land was being cut under contract by Matthew Gardner, and another large parcel by George Chubbuck. To move his cut timber from Lake Valley to the lake shore at Bijou, where it would be pushed by steamers on to the Glenbrook mills, Chubbuck had purchased a miniature steam locomotive from Adolph Sutro's failed Sutro Tunnel project, and had laid a couple of miles of narrow gauge track. The engine was too heavy for the rails, and this and other problems pushed Chubbuck into bankruptcy.[12]

Walter Hobart's Sierra Nevada Wood & Lumber Company also owned timberland in Lake Valley, so Bliss quickly stepped in and took over the lease for the railroad right-of-way for C&TL&FC. Building on Chubbuck's lead, C&TL&FC constructed a thirteen-mile track. It skirted the foothills on the east and south sides of Lake Valley, and reached Yanks [now Meyers] just over the state line in California. The Lake Valley Railroad, as Bliss named it, ran from the interior of the valley to Bijou, and out onto an 1,800-foot pier that reached into Lake Tahoe. From there timber was dumped directly into the water for easy transport to Glenbrook.[13]

The Lake Valley Railroad would have special significance for Duane Bliss. His eldest son William graduated from the Massachusetts Institute of Technology in 1888 with a degree in civil engineering. He was only twenty-four years old, but his father showed confidence in him by appointing him superintendent of C&TL&FC's Lake Valley logging and transportation operations. William would be the first of Duane and Elizabeth's children to enter the business, a point of great pride for both of them. With Elizabeth's brother, Walter Tobey, now living in Carson City—Duane had named him

Chapter 11. The End of an Era

C&TL&FC's Lake Valley Railroad at Bijou, California is shown here around 1890. The train carried the fallen timbers onto an 1,800-foot pier and dumped them directly into Lake Tahoe. From there the logs were "rounded up" and pushed or pulled by steamer to the Glenbrook mill. (Special Collections Department, University of Nevada, Reno Library)

to head the Carson City end of the business—C&TL&FC had truly become a family business, just as Bliss had hoped, although D. O. Mills and Henry Yerington were still major stockholders in the firm as well.[14]

During the mid- to late-1870s, C&TL&FC had built the Carson Box Factory on a V&T rail spur in Carson City. The factory manufactured wooden fruit and packing boxes for many years, mostly using leftover lumber. "The box factory has been of inestimable benefit to Carson City, but like many other things gotten up by capitalists has never been properly appreciated," the *Nevada State Journal* noted on March 24, 1886. "It has given employment to and made partial mechanics of a number of boys [from the Carson City Prison] who but for it might be hoodlums." The article pointed out that in 1885 the box factory had operated for nine months, and paid out $15,000 in wages to between twenty and forty men and boys, in addition to a monthly payroll of $15,000 at the wood storage yard. "Truly, without the local railroad, the flume, the Glenbrook works and the box factory, Carson would be a very dead town," the article concluded.

The little village of Glenbrook had become a lively place by the late 1880s and early 1890s. Although it was still primarily a lumbering village, it had become quite popular during the spring and summer seasons with a small number of "in-the-know" tourists, mostly well-to-do folks from the San Francisco, Sacramento and Sun Mountain areas. There were now four small hotels to serve these visitors. The Jellerson Hotel and Dirigo Hotel, both built by Frank Jellerson and his sister Amanda Jane, were the newest lodgings in Glenbrook. Duane Bliss had built a spacious two-and-one-half story summer home, using the finest sugar pine lumber, replacing the modest cottage the family had enjoyed for years, and a one-room schoolhouse had been built to serve the village's permanent residents. Once his large summer house was built, Duane and Elizabeth spent most of the summer months in Glenbrook. Their Chinese servants kept the Carson City house opened year round, but they were seldom there.[15]

The Bliss summer home in Glenbrook, built in the early 1870s, would entertain three generations of the Bliss family. At one point, the family owned the entire Glenbrook area, but succeeding generations would be forced to sell off the land little by little to pay the taxes. In 1906 the house was converted to be part of the Glenbrook Inn & Ranch. This photo is from the early 1890s. (Special Collections Department, University of Nevada, Reno Library)

Chapter 11. The End of an Era

The winter of 1889/90 was one Glenbrook's small year-round population would never forget. Over fifteen feet of snow fell, and drifts of thirty-five to forty feet marooned every house and cottage in the community. People with two-story homes had to exit by second story windows, while those in one-story cottages had to tunnel out through the snow. "Coal oil lamps burned day and night," E. B. Scott wrote. "In the evenings the monotony was broken by dancing at Lake Shore House to the violin and piano of Jack Armstrong and Camille Spooner."[16] These were hearty folks, and they would not be deterred by a little bad weather.

In 1887 C&TL&FC's twelve-year old Glenbrook Mill #2 burned to the ground. Flatcars on a rail siding adjoining the mill were also destroyed, as was a barge loaded with lumber. The *Carson City Appeal* reported, "The wood barge which floated out in the Lake was burning yesterday. Attempts were made to approach it with a tug boat, but the heat was so intense a hundred yards away that the hands could not remain on deck." Mill #1 went on twenty-four hour a day service to take up the slack. Business had slowed considerably since the Comstock mines had almost stopped producing, so there seemed to be no rush to rebuild the destroyed mill.[17]

Duane Bliss became involved in another mining venture during the same year. Elko County in the extreme northeastern corner of Nevada had often sent out ripples of excitement when one of its many mines struck gold. The Found Treasure Mining Company was one of the latest in 1887, and Bliss became a director of the corporation, and likely an investor as well. The company was capitalized at $10 million, with 100,000 shares of stock at $100 each. Bliss family lore does not include any recollection of the investment, so it probably did not pan out too well.[18]

In August 1888 Bliss received word from Massachusetts that his father William had passed away at the age of eighty-two. The two men had long ago put their differences behind them, and Bliss was hit hard by the news of his father's death. The funeral was delayed so Bliss could travel east and be there for it. On August 9 services were held for William Bliss at the Baptist church in Savoy Hollow, where he had been a member for fifty-three years. Interment followed at nearby Adams. According to a newspaper report, "The church was well filled with friends and townsfolk."[19]

With the lumbering business on the wane, and the amount of standing timber in the basin severely depleted, C&TL&FC closed down all their operations in 1898. Logging areas, narrow-gauge railroads, barges and

Duane Bliss (far left) and his daughter Hope (seated) prepare to enter a mine on the Comstock, likely in the 1890s. (Courtesy of the Bliss family)

towing vessels, the box factory, and the sawmills were all shuttered. It marked the end of an important but damaging industry in the Tahoe Basin. Over its quarter-century operating lifespan the Carson & Tahoe Lumber & Fluming Company had cut about three-quarters of a billion board feet of timber, and a half-million cords of firewood.[20] The company would not de-incorporate until 1947 after it had disposed of its massive land inventory.

Two historic reminders of the company remain to this day: the *Glenbrook* and the *Tahoe*, the first two locomotives on the Lake Tahoe Railroad that hauled lumber and timber from the sawmills at Glenbrook up the mountainside to Spooner Summit. The *Tahoe* has been completely restored and is on display at the Nevada County Narrow Gauge Railroad Museum in Nevada City, California.

In 1943 the *Glenbrook* was re-purchased and donated to the Nevada State Museum in Carson City by Bliss descendants, where it sat beside the museum delighting children for years. In 1952 the historic locomotive was moved to Carson City's Nevada State Railroad Museum, a fitting choice since that institution sits on the same site the Carson and Tahoe Lumber and Fluming Company's massive wood storage yard once occupied. Two years later the museum's shop crew began restoring the

Chapter 11. The End of an Era

old steam-driven relic, and in mid-2015 the work will be completed and the *Glenbrook* will be re-introduced to proud Nevadans.

Both locomotives, the *Glenbrook* and the *Tahoe*, offer a brief but happy glimpse at days long past.

CHAPTER 12

Becoming a Conservationist

During the Comstock era, the Tahoe Basin was one of the major lumbering centers in the American West. One of the nation's leading scholars in American environmental history, Donald J. Pisani, put these activities in historical perspective: "The exploitation of Tahoe's basic resource threatened the interstate lake's scenic beauty . . . . It also touched off a long debate over whether Lake Tahoe should be used and developed by private enterprise or protected as parkland. Hence, the nineteenth-century lumber boom provides an important chapter in the history of western land use."[1]

With the end of large-scale lumbering in the Tahoe Basin in the mid-1880s—small-scale lumbering would continue for some time—the question of the environmental damage done to the area began to come into focus. There had been concerns voiced earlier, but as long as the lumber and timber had been feeding the profit engine of the Comstock, those voices were drowned out by both practical and economic realities. Now, these voices were beginning to be heard. William Wright (Dan DeQuille) voiced the concerns of many of his generation in his book, *The Big Bonanza*, published in 1876:

> This is all very well for the [lumber] company, and for the mining companies, who must have lumber and timber, but it is going to make sad work, ere long, of the picturesque hills surrounding Lake Tahoe, the most beautiful of all lakes in the Sierra Nevada Mountains. Where tall pines now shade all the shores and wave on all the mountain slope[s], naught will shortly be seen save decaying stumps and naked granite rocks. But timber and lumber are imperatively demanded, and the forests not only of these hills but of a thousand others will doubtless be sacrificed.[2]

Even Virginia City's *Territorial Enterprise*, whose very existence depended upon the success of the mines, decried what was happening to the forests in a February 12, 1874 editorial: "Fainter and fainter comes to us the echo of the

LUMBER BARON OF THE COMSTOCK LODE

Before large-scale lumbering began in the Tahoe Basin, a wandering journalist and artist painted this word portrait of the region: "Within the past two years the people of California and Washoe [later, Nevada] have begun to discover the beauties of this charming region, and its rare advantage as a place of summer resort. Situated in the bosom of the Sierra Nevada mountains, 6000 feet above the level of the sea, with an atmosphere of wonderful purity; abounding in game; convenient of access, and possessing all the attractions of retirement from the busy world, amid scenery unrivaled for its romantic beauties ... A new road (shown, at Point of Rocks) now winds along the shores of Lake Tahoe ... [that] will compare favorably with a journey along the shores of Como ... the scene is equal to any thing of the kind to be found in Europe." (Comments and illustration by J. Ross Browne, *Washoe Revisited*, 1863)

Chapter 12. Becoming a Conservationist

axe of the receding woodman, whose sturdy arm has laid bare the mountain side, and is now breaking the silence of the summit with the thunder of falling timber." The editorial admitted that there seemed to be no other option available to replace the timber used in the mining effort, but it still decried the environmental damage being done.

A more knowledgeable source, Scotsman and naturalist John Muir, who was America's leading preservationist and chief proponent of national parks, visited Lake Tahoe in 1873 and 1875. He remarked that logging "is being pushed so fervently from year to year, almost the entire basin must be stripped ere long of one of its most attractive features." Of the men who cut the trees, Muir wrote, "Any fool can destroy trees. Few that fell trees plant them, nor would planting avail much toward getting back anything like the noble primeval forests. . . . It took more than three thousand years to make some of the trees in these Western woods—trees that are still standing in perfect strength and beauty, waving and singing in the mighty forests of the Sierra."[3]

Despite the fervent voices of Muir, Wright and others like Henry David Thoreau and Frederick Law Olmsted, their concerns would go unheeded for up to a half-century, for few were listening at first.

*

There were many "lumber barons" in the United States during the nineteenth and early twentieth centuries: William B. Ogden in Wisconsin, John Henry Kirby in Texas, Wellington R. Burt in Michigan, Amos Patten in Maine, and Frederick Weyerhaeuser in Washington, to name a few. D. L. Bliss and Walter Hobart in the Sierra Nevada also belong in that group, even though the acreages they controlled paled to those who harvested the timber of the forests in the North Woods of New England, the upper Midwest, and the Great Northwest. All of these men came under fire from the growing conservation movement during their times, and most are still castigated in our day as despoilers of the nation's forest resources. Today, in our age of conservation, preservation and environmentalism, it's easy to judge. It is only in retrospect that the activities of these men and others like them can truly be assessed within the context of their time and the prevailing beliefs of their day.

When Europeans first populated our nation, it is estimated there were 950 million acres of timberland from coast to coast. But our earliest settlers considered these lands as wilderness, and they had no love for it. William Bradford, upon stepping off the *Mayflower*, described the land as "a hideous and desolate wilderness." These people celebrated the advance of civilization as a great blessing, and the conquest of the wilderness as God's plan for man. In fact, for the majority of our history, Americans have regarded the wilderness as a moral and physical wasteland fit only for conquest and the exploitation of its resources.[4]

That was still the prevailing mind-set during the nineteenth century era of western expansion, spurred by the belief in Manifest Destiny—the idea that our nation had the right, even the God-given obligation, to push our borders from coast to coast. The expansion of civilization was still believed to be good, and the wilderness bad. William Gilpin, the first governor of Colorado Territory in 1861-1862, and a leading voice for Manifest Destiny, stated that "Progress is God" and the "occupation of wild territory . . . proceeds with all the solemnity of a providential ordinance." It was the hand of God that pushed the nation westward and caused the wilderness to surrender to ax and plow. It was seen then as a natural thing, not despoliation.[5]

It was during this time, and perhaps fueled by these beliefs and the practical realities of the day, that men like D. L. Bliss, Walter Hobart and others swept away vast timberlands in the Tahoe Basin to fuel the profit engine of the Comstock. Historians estimate that the Comstock produced about $400 million in wealth from the 1860s through the 1890s. During that same period it is estimated that between 400 and 500 million board feet of lumber were taken from the Tahoe Basin, at a value of around $90 million, mostly from the Nevada side of the lake. Clearly the lumber industry produced a significant share of Nevada's wealth in the last half of the nineteenth century.[6]

A 1976 report by the U.S. Department of Agriculture Forest Service opined that about two-thirds of the nation's original forestlands still existed. However, an early warning bell was being tolled as early as 1865—the Comstock era—when a timber famine was predicted to occur within thirty years. This never happened. "Differences of opinion and conflict have marked the course of conservation throughout our nation's history," the Forest Service report noted. "The majority of the people, particularly during the country's formative years, regarded the forests as an inexhaustible resource."[7]

As the nineteenth century progressed, the voices for conservation did become louder, and the number of citizens who took up the cause increased. The U.S. Government, if not all of its citizens, had shown its concern for the

Chapter 12. Becoming a Conservationist

forests in the last years of the eighteenth century. In 1799 Congress passed the Federal Timber Purchase Act, the earliest recognition of the need to husband timber resources. By the dawning of the Comstock era in 1859, a number of federal and state laws had been passed, each designed to add to the protection of the forests and the wood crucial for the building of naval vessels. But it was not until 1876—one hundred years after the signing of the Declaration of Independence—that the real beginning of forest protection was inaugurated by the federal government. That came with the concurrent appointment of the first federal forestry agent and the introduction in Congress of a bill to insure preservation of the forests of the public domain adjacent to the sources of navigable rivers and streams.[8]

Despite this promising start, the federal government stumbled badly with the passage of two other laws, both of which were well-intentioned but poorly drafted. The 1878 Free Timber Act granted the people of the nine western states the right to cut timber at will on mineral lands for both domestic and foreign mining purposes. The Timber and Stone Act, passed the same year, authorized the first-ever sale of public timberlands on land that was unfit for farming. There was a limit of 160 acres per individual or corporation at prices as low as $2.50 an acre.

The language of both laws was convoluted, and many provisions of the laws were impractical and unenforceable. For the lumbering companies, these laws were an open door to get their hands on large tracts of timberland by taking advantage of the loopholes in the laws, or, on occasion, to even commit fraud to get the lands. These two ill-conceived laws had unwittingly opened the door to wholesale cutting and destruction of the nation's forests.[9]

Earlier, the Homestead Act of 1862 had provided another example of a well-intentioned but poorly applied piece of legislation that led to abuses. Many settlers who purchased 160-acre plots, ostensibly to settle and farm, fraudulently transferred the property to timber interests. Often the timber companies would use their own employees as "dummy" buyers to get the property, which was often prized timberland.[10]

The government's history of poorly worded legislation, plus low-level government employees who often participated in these schemes themselves, led to the very abuses of the forests they had intended to protect. Leading conservationist and author Douglas Strong made the point clearly:

Many of these laws ran counter to the interests of westerners, who resented interference from Washington and desired larger acreages than the law allowed.

> Lumberman, ranchers, miners and others devised ways to circumvent existing regulations. For example, when Congress passed the Swamp Land Act of 1850, permitting states to acquire title to marshy and swampy land, it hoped that the states would develop the land. For a small bribe, however, government land-office inspectors often rated good timberland as "swamp and overflow," and the state then sold this land to private parties.[11]

While the Federal Government often stumbled in the early years, the state of California took positive action. In 1883 newly elected Governor James Stoneman appointed the Lake Bigler [Tahoe] Forestry Commission, based upon legislators' belief that it was the state's duty to preserve California's natural scenery for the health, pleasure and recreation of state residents and tourists. It was the first such agency in the nation. By this time much of the forest on the Nevada side of the lake had been cut, while the California side was relatively unspoiled. (Ironically, today most of the California side has been heavily developed and subdivided into urban lots, while the Nevada side, much of which has remained in private hands, is again in pristine, new-growth forest state.) Eventually, however, some missteps by the California commission led to the failure of its mission, and it was dissolved in 1892.[12]

After many blunders by the U.S. Government, the forest conservation movement finally began in earnest in the last decade of the nineteenth century. In the 1890s Congress established a number of national parks—Sequoia, General Grant (later King's Canyon) and Mt. Rainier. These all joined the first one, Yellowstone National Park, which had been established back in 1872. In 1891 the Creative Act protected the nation's timber supply from over-exploitation by setting aside protected forestlands called Forest Reserves. These changes came about toward the end of the Comstock era, so they had minimal impact on the activities of the major lumber companies operating in the Tahoe Basin. In the case of the largest of these companies, Bliss's C&TL&FC, it still had adequate uncut timberlands remaining in its inventory, so there was plenty of lumber left to match the rapidly diminishing demands of the Comstock's mines.

The fight for the conservation of forest resources continued on into the early days of the twentieth century. Attitudes were changing, but it took one long, drawn-out affair to finally tip the scales in favor of the preservationists. Ironically the affair ended in a loss for forest preservation, but it was a classic

Chapter 12. Becoming a Conservationist

case of losing the battle but winning the war. It was called Hetch Hetchy, and it changed everything.

California's Hetch Hetchy is a spectacular, high-walled valley formed by ancient glaciers and carved out by the Tuolumne River. John Muir referred to it as one of nature's rarest and most precious mountain temples. In 1864, in an attempt to protect the Yosemite area, the U.S. Congress passed a bill creating the Yosemite Grant, which set a precedent for the formation of national park legislation. When Congress passed that legislation in 1890, the Hetch Hetchy Valley, on Yosemite's western flank, was formally included within the Yosemite Grant's boundaries, affording it protection along with the rest of the Yosemite area. (Yosemite would not become a national park until 1906.)

San Francisco had long been in search of a source of fresh water for its growing population. As early as 1883 city engineers had studied the feasibility of damming the narrow, lower end of Hetch Hetchy to create a reservoir for the city, located about 150 miles away. Just after the turn of the century the city applied to the federal government to create the reservoir, but as the area was part of the Yosemite Grant, the application was denied. Thus began a thirteen-year, high profile fight between advocates of the "beauty value" of nature versus advocates of the "use value" of nature. It was a battle that would ultimately overturn the earliest Pilgrims' firmly held conviction that converting the wilderness to man's use was a God-given obligation. However, there would be one more victory for the use-value side. On December 19, 1913, after years of rancor, the use-value side won and San Francisco was granted the right to build the dam. Wilderness scholar Roderick Nash summed up the battle: "The preservationists had lost the fight for the valley, but they had gained much ground in the larger war for the existence of wilderness."[13]

John Muir, founder of the Sierra Club, had participated in the struggle at every turn. Of the Hetch Hetchy affair he remarked, ". . . the conscience of the whole country has been aroused from sleep."[14] Were he still alive, Muir would no doubt be happy to learn that there is an organization, Restore Hetch Hetchy, which is to this day actively agitating to tear down O'Shaughnessy Dam and restore the Hetch Hetchy Valley to its natural state.

*

Naturalist John Muir called the Hetch Hetchy Valley one of nature's most "precious temples." This 1911 photograph was taken two years before the federal government allowed the city of San Francisco to create a reservoir in the valley. (Library of Congress)

D. L. Bliss, in accumulating between 50,000 and 80,000 acres of Sierra Nevada timberland for his C&TL&FC in the 1860s and 1870s, had participated in some of the schemes engendered by the federal government's early stumbles. In addition, he had purchased acreage from the Central Pacific Railroad in the northern and northwestern parts of the Tahoe Basin. These were alternate sections of land that the U.S. Government had granted the Central Pacific Railroad in the conventional checkerboard pattern, the government keeping each alternate section for settlement. Often C&TL&FC would purchase parcels of the government's alternate sections from preemptors, businessmen who would buy the land ostensibly for settlement, then immediately resell it to the lumber companies. Bliss also re-purchased acreage from people who took up property under the Timber Culture Act.[15]

Chapter 12. Becoming a Conservationist

Technically speaking, these practices were illegal. But the U.S. Government's flawed land use laws made these practices so widespread among the lumber companies that Bliss openly admitted he had taken advantage of the loopholes when talking with representatives of the Public Lands Commission in 1879.

Many latter-day conservation historians, while decrying the loss of the old-growth forests, still argue that critics like Muir, Wright and other early writers overstated the damage done to the Tahoe area by large-scale logging. Although considerably thinned, the forests were not "completely denuded," as many charged. Noted wildlife biologist George E. Gruell, author of *Fire in Sierra Nevada Forests: A Photographic Interpretation of Ecological Change Since 1849*, included a number of rare old photographs in his book from the logging period of 1873—1880, the heyday of the large logging companies. Some of these photographs clearly show that the mountains were not denuded, that abundant trees were left behind in most of the logging areas.[16]

This is not meant to infer that significant loss of the old-growth trees in the Tahoe Basin did not occur. It did, but it was not the complete decimation that some claimed. Approximately one-third of the Tahoe Basin was never logged. Those portions that were logged eventually regrew, but the forests were different in many ways in regards to density, species distribution, and vulnerability.

In addition to the serious thinning of the trees, there was also other damage done during the Comstock era. Logging camps, mills, flumes and railroad tracks lay abandoned. Forest roads quickly became overgrown and impassable, and former roadside inns and post offices disappeared, according to Lake Tahoe environmental historian Douglas Strong. Fires fueled by logging debris left on the forest floor became a widespread problem for years. Employment plummeted too, as thousands of jobs disappeared. [17]

Duane Bliss and C&TL&FC are due credit for addressing the forest fire issue. In 1879, in testimony before the Public Lands Commission in Carson City, Bliss said: "Until recently . . . we have only taken such timbers as would make logs, but lately we have cleaned off not only what was fit for logs but what would make wood. At first the cutting of the timber increased the chances of fire, because we left the limbs on the ground, but after we began to utilize the limbs for cord-wood it decreased the chances of fire." Some other lumber companies did not take this extra step because the sale of cordwood was not nearly as profitable as the sale of timber for use by the mines, or lumber for building, and it was time and labor intensive.

In his testimony, Bliss added: "Up at Lake Tahoe, whenever we discover fire, no matter on whose land, we go and put it out, or send help to put it out, right at the start . . . because it is our interest to prevent the spreading of such fires and save other adjoining timber."[18]

Carson & Tahoe Lumber & Fluming Company, as the largest lumbering company in the basin, was responsible for much of the impact on Tahoe's forests. However, that statement was challenged by D. L. Bliss's most ardent supporter, his daughter Hope. "He [D. L. Bliss] had an army of men . . . not only felling trees; the minimum size, cut, being over two feet in diameter; but, besides this restriction, he had them leave many large groups of the primeval growth of those pines—averaging six and seven feet in diameter—along the picturesque shores of Lake Tahoe," she wrote in 1907.[19]

In the early 1940s, Hope Bliss wrote a second biographical sketch of her father, in response to, or, as she noted, "to augment" the book, *The Desert Challenge: An Interpretation of Nevada,* by Richard Gordon Lillard, published

Chapter 12. Becoming a Conservationist

by University of Nebraska Press in 1942. She again raised the issue of her father's environmental concern for Lake Tahoe during C&TL&FC's logging years. "With Father's . . . foresight in not allowing trees under one foot to be cut [note: she indicated two feet in her earlier writings, cited above] the growth is thick all over Lake Tahoe's hillsides and particularly noticeable around Glenbrook, Nevada, of really large trees. Father had, also, many groups of the primal pines left intact on Lake Tahoe's shores, at Idlewild and other places . . . ."[20]

Hope's admiration for her father is understandable. However, in a number of cases, as cited above, she overstated the facts, and as a result many of her inaccurate claims have found a home in otherwise respectable history books. Duane Bliss's position on forest conservation is one of those issues. As pointed out earlier, forest conservation was not an area of concern during the heyday of the C&TL&FC. Any conservation concerns Bliss may have had did not surface until the early 1890s. At that time he had begun to turn his attention to creating Lake Tahoe as a first class tourist destination, and with that plan came an awareness of the necessity of protecting the forestlands around the lake. Too, the voices of the conservationists and preservationists had grown stronger due to expanded public awareness, and likely forced Bliss to rethink the beliefs he had followed during his C&TL&FC days.

Don Lane is a U.S. Forest Service wilderness ranger who is very familiar with Tahoe's forests and backcountry, as he has served there for more than forty years. Lane spoke to the lack of environmental concerns of C&TL&FC and its leading competitors, but also in defense of these same logging companies:

> *Much of the era that Duane Bliss was directing the C&TL&FC logging business in the Lake Tahoe Basin occurred at a time some historians would characterize as a time of "Manifest Destiny," in the country, when the resources (the forests, waters and native fish and wildlife) were viewed as being "endless" or "renewable." . . . there [is] no historical evidence I've ever seen indicating any Tahoe logging company (including C&TL&FC) had the foresight, the long-term vision or intention to restock logged over lands that wouldn't be economically productive for decades . . . . The mid to late 1800s around Lake Tahoe and around the American West was a time of expansion and settlement in this country . . . not preservation.*[21]

Duane Bliss's own words back up the validity of Lane's thinking that early lumbermen had little knowledge of, or interest in, conservation: "I am unable to say how long it takes for a second growth to grow up. If all the timber was off the hills, it would take a very long time before new trees would grow up. It is of very slow growth. Fifteen or twenty years will not make much of a tree. Some trees we cut are 200 or 300 years old. I think we cut one that was 1,000 years old. It was 11 feet in diameter."[22]

As to Hope Bliss's assertion that her father was protective of the forests around Glenbrook and Idlewild, there is some truth to that claim, but it was likely more self-interest than conservation concern that motivated those actions. Bliss would undoubtedly have been more selective in logging the forest around Glenbrook where he had his summer home and his milling interests. As Don Lane speculates, "[Bliss's] motivation may have lain in the aesthetic enhancement of [his] lake shore holdings and the desire to promote tourism at Glenbrook."[23]

As to Hope Bliss's assertion about her father protecting "the primal pines . . . at Idlewild," this was accurate, but once again, there were personal interests at work. Idlewild was one of the first exclusive residential areas created at Lake Tahoe in the early 1880s. It was part of the Tahoe Pines area where C&TL&FC had a great deal of logging property. Bliss's protection of the trees in that area was likely motivated by the fact that one of the principal owners and developers of Idlewild was his C&TL&FC partner, Henry Yerington.[24]

Finally, Hope Bliss's statement that it was her father's environmental concern that led him to cut no trees less than one or two feet in diameter proves nothing. Most lumber companies left trees that size standing. It had nothing to do with conservation, and was done because a tree that small was not large enough to be cost-effectively used as mine timbering, railroad ties, or even for most building purposes.

These observations in no way impugn the character of Duane L. Bliss. He was not alone; few, if any, of the lumbermen of the day were conservationists. Bliss was a brilliant businessman, and he was a man of his time. Conserving our forest resources was simply not an important issue while the Comstock era was at its peak, although by the late nineteenth century it did finally come more sharply into focus.

*

Lake Tahoe conservationists had their first big success in 1899 with the federal government's creation of the Lake Tahoe Forest Reserve. It set aside

Chapter 12. Becoming a Conservationist

136,000 acres of forestland on the west, or California, side of the Basin, in the Desolation Valley area at the crest of the Sierra Nevada, just southwest of the lake. Although a good start, the land set aside was only about half of what John Muir and his Sierra Club had been lobbying for.[25]

It is during this period that we see D. L. Bliss jump on the forest conservation bandwagon. By this time Bliss was involved in the tourism industry with his Lake Tahoe Railway & Transportation Company (discussed in upcoming chapters) and he had become one of the foremost supporters of the Lake Tahoe Forest Reserve. The C&TL&FC records contain a number of letters Bliss wrote to federal legislators early in the twentieth century attempting to get them to vote for an extension of the Lake Tahoe Forest Reserve.[26] He also wrote to naturalist John Muir, one of the nation's most virulent large-scale logging critics, setting up a meeting in San Francisco to discuss the Forest Reserve issue.[27] And finally, he traveled to Washington D.C. in March, 1904 to personally meet with Gifford Pinchot, the first Chief of the United States Forest Service and a strong advocate for the conservation of the nation's forests through planned use and renewal.[28]

During the movement to increase the size of the Lake Tahoe Forest Reserve, the Federal Government's General Land Office, or GLO, appointed Albert F. Potter as a grazing expert. In 1903, two to three decades after the heaviest timbering activities had taken place around Lake Tahoe, Potter visited the Tahoe Basin and met with a number of important California conservation organizations. He reinforced the conclusion of many other early investigators that the Tahoe Basin was recovering rapidly from the earlier logging activities. This opinion that did not sit well with many of the most ardent conservationists who wished to paint a dire picture in order to support their forest despoliation beliefs.[29]

Since Bliss's C&TL&FC still owned 20 to 25 percent of the land in the Tahoe Basin, Bliss was one of the linchpins in making or breaking the Forest Reserve extension. The problem, however, was a system called "in-lieu lands." An 1887 federal law stipulated that large private property owners like the Central Pacific Railroad and C&TL&FC would be given other public domain property outside the Forest Reserve in lieu of land they would agree to give up for incorporation into the reserve. But opponents of the plan argued that trading these companies thousands of acres of choice public lands in return for land they had already stripped of timber would be a mockery. This issue, in addition to some nasty political issues, was also the stumbling blocks in attempts to create a Lake Tahoe National Park in 1900 and again

145

in 1913. Nevada's powerful U.S. Senator William J. Stewart sponsored the 1900 legislation that failed, and Bliss—a lifelong Republican—had solidly endorsed and supported Stewart's efforts.[30]

In 1904 Bliss made an offer to Senator Stewart to sell C&TL&FC's Lake Tahoe land to the government for $4 an acre, although the cut-over land was only valued at 50c to $1 an acre. When Senator Stewart attempted to negotiate with Bliss, he would not budge on his price. Stewart retired from the Senate the following year, and that same year Congress abolished the in-lieu land legislation of 1897, putting an end to the issue.[31]

In both of these causes—the attempt to extend the size of the Forest Reserve at Lake Tahoe, and the attempt to create Lake Tahoe National Park—Bliss was ardently working on the side of the conservationists. But, as environmental historian Douglas Strong pointed out, "Bliss recognized, too, the potential economic benefit of the sale or exchange of land still held by the Carson and Tahoe Lumber and Fluming Company in the Basin."[32]

Despite the Federal Government's failure to resolve the park issue, both California and Nevada would eventually set up protected state parks in the Tahoe Basin. In 1927 California established a state park at the site of a thirteen-acre, state-owned fish hatchery near Tahoe City. The following year California successfully passed a park bond issue, and in 1929 it established a park at Rubicon Point, site of one of the lake's most magnificent vistas. The state acquired 900 acres of scenic land, including 14,840 feet of lakeshore and 3,500 feet of lakeshore on Emerald Bay, half of which was donated by the children of D. L. Bliss in their father's name. D. L. Bliss State Park has since grown to 2,149 acres, and is one of the most beautiful and popular state parks in the nation.[33] It is a fitting testament to the man who would turn Lake Tahoe into an international tourism destination.

The final word on the long-term changes in the Tahoe Basin due to timber exploitation during the Comstock era goes to Alan H. Taylor, professor at the Department of Geography, Earth and Environmental Systems Institute, Pennsylvania State University: "The structure and composition of forests that now cover the east shore of Lake Tahoe are very different from the pre-Euro-American forests. Overall, the original forest was more open, less dense, and was composed of trees that varied widely in diameter. . . . A new forest began to establish immediately after stands were logged, and forests in the Carson Range are now mostly dense 100 - 200 [year] old second growth, where trees are relatively small in diameter."[34]

Chapter 12. Becoming a Conservationist

As Sierra Nevada historian Don Lane wrote, ". . . a re-grown previously logged-over forest is ecologically not the same as a forest untouched/unmodified by human hands . . . There's more to the natural world than meets the eye."[35]

CHAPTER 13

The Grand Old Man of Lake Tahoe

The term "vertical integration" describes a style of business management control where a company expands its ownership into a number of different areas along the supply, production and distribution chain. For example, a car manufacturer that buys a tire manufacturer, a glass manufacturer, an upholstery manufacturer and a dealer network that sells the final product has adopted a form of vertical integration. The concept is said to have been introduced by Andrew Carnegie in his Carnegie Steel Company—the forerunner of U.S. Steel—in the last quarter of the nineteenth century. In Carnegie's time, it was called "a combination."[1]

The argument can be made that Bill Sharon had employed these same principles of vertical integration with the Bank of California's Comstock venture in the 1860s, a decade before Carnegie put his combination together, by owning or controlling all of the steps in the manufacturing and distribution processes. Sharon and the Bank Ring owned or controlled the bank that provided the initial funding for the operation; they owned the mines that provided the raw material, the ore; they owned the mills that processed the ore; and they owned the water that was vital to the production process. Additionally, they owned the railroad that delivered the raw materials and the finished product; they initially owned or controlled the lumbering companies that made the deep-level mining possible; and they owned the bank where the final product—the profits—ended up. This was a classic vertical integration enterprise, years before Carnegie's time.

Duane Bliss worked within this combination, and he understood the process, even though he would never have heard the term "vertical integration." He used the process effectively with C&TL&FC. He and his partners owned the timberlands where the trees stood, the ships and barges that moved the timber from the lakeshore to the mills at Glenbrook, and the sawmills where the trees were turned into timber and lumber. They also owned the railroads and the flumes that moved the timber and lumber to the storage yard (which they also owned), Marlette Lake that provided the water for the flumes, and they controlled the V&T Railroad through preferential pricing that carried his final product to the marketplace. As Bliss planned his next venture at Lake Tahoe, the principles of vertical integration would again be an important part of his plan.

In 1893, in the waning days of the lumbering industry in the Tahoe Basin, Duane Bliss had begun planning his next business undertaking. He could see that the days of the C&TL&FC were numbered, and now, nearing sixty years old, he wanted to create something anew that he and his sons could carry into the future. He had witnessed the small but growing tourism base at Glenbrook—there were now four small hotels serving a growing number of visitors—and he had watched ex-Comstock miner E. J. "Lucky" Baldwin prosper with his fancy Tallac House hotel at the south end of the lake. Bliss believed that the surface had barely been scratched as far as summer tourism at Lake Tahoe was concerned. His visionary new business enterprise would have three components. First, he would build the most luxurious ship Lake Tahoe had ever seen to move passengers, freight and mail around the lake. Second, he would build a railroad that would connect Tahoe City on the northeastern Tahoe shoreline in California with the Southern Pacific Railroad tracks in Truckee, sixteen miles distance, thus tying into the transcontinental railroad. This would open Lake Tahoe to tourists from around the nation, and perhaps from around the world. Third, he would build one or more grand resort hotels where visitors could spend endless days and nights enjoying all that the lake had to offer. It was a grand vision, a vision that would eventually earn Duane Bliss popular recognition as "The Grand Old Man of Lake Tahoe."[2]

To launch the enterprise, in November 1895 Bliss incorporated the Lake Tahoe Transportation Company, with Glenbrook as its principal place of business. All 1,000 shares of outstanding stock were owned by the Bliss family, in the following amounts: D. L. Bliss, Sr., 425 shares; Charles Tobey Bliss and Walter D. Tobey, 250 shares each; William Seth Bliss, Walter Danforth Bliss and D. L. Bliss, Jr., 25 shares each.[3]

The next step in the plan was to build a ship. At the time, the grandest ship on the lake was the *Tallac*, owned by Lucky Baldwin and his two partners. Launched in 1890, and re-launched two years later after she burned to the waterline, the ninety-foot steamer was used to carry freight, mail and tourists around the lake. In 1901 Bliss's company would purchase that ship and the owners' agreement to discontinue their

Chapter 13. The Grand Old Man of Lake Tahoe

Duane and Elizabeth Bliss would raise four sons and a daughter. The sons would all eventually join their father in his second career, developing national and international tourism at Lake Tahoe. (Special Collections Department, University of Nevada, Reno Library)

transportation and freight activities on the lake. Bliss would pay $10,000 for the ship and the non-compete agreement, and he would rename the ship the *Nevada*.[4]

The keel of the SS *Tahoe* was laid on the day after Christmas in 1895. She was built in San Francisco, and was ready for launch in mid-June 1896. She was 169 feet long, and had stabilizers to prevent roll in heavy seas. She was propelled by twin steam engines fed by a locomotive-type boiler that was eight-feet in diameter and sixteen-feet long, and she had a top speed of eighteen knots. She was designed to be unsinkable, and had a passenger capacity of 200 people. There was an exclusive ladies cabin, a gentlemen's smoking lounge, a main salon, a dining room and on-deck seating. There was also abundant cargo space and a modern system of electric lights and bells. Appointments were exquisite, including an adornment of the finest brass, mahogany and teak, Moroccan leather upholstery, and fine Belgian carpets. The Bliss family also had an elegant private stateroom on board. Bliss's ship would be recognized as the "Queen of the Lake" for many years thereafter.

On June 24, 1896 the SS *Tahoe* was launched at Glenbrook amid great ceremony. "No such gathering of people has been seen at Glenbrook for years," crowed the *Carson Morning Appeal*. "The other steamers brought people from all parts of the Lake and it was a gala day for everybody. Carson sent a large contingent of sightseers . . . . Little baby Bliss (Duane and Elizabeth's one-year old grandchild, Will M. Bliss) who was the center of every eye, smashed a bottle of Roderer [champagne] over the bow of the vessel and the men knocked out the timbers that held the craft in place . . . she will make her trial trip today."[6]

A year later, in announcing that the steamer *Tahoe* had been awarded a contract to provide daily mail service at the lake, the *San Francisco Call* noted, "The towns and villages along the shores of placid Lake Tahoe will hereafter be in daily communication with the outside world . . . a miniature post office has been fitted up on the steamer *Tahoe* with D. L. Bliss as mail agent."[7] The *Tahoe* immediately began augmenting her revenue from delivering the U.S. mail by launching freight and passenger service too. With the first phase of his plan now complete, Duane Bliss began planning for the second phase.

*

The last few years of the nineteenth century and the first few years of the twentieth century would be a busy time for the Bliss family. Early in the 1890s a new U.S. political party, the Silver Party, appeared on the scene, supporting a platform of bimetallism and Free Silver. The new party gained no traction in any state but Nevada, where it won elections for U.S. Senators and Representatives, as well as the governor's office. Governors John E. Jones, who served between 1895 and 1896, and Reinhold Sadler, who served from 1896, following Jones' death, through 1902, were both members of the Silver Party.

As the gubernatorial election of 1898 had been approaching, the Republican Party was casting about for the best man to challenge the incumbent Sadler. One of the names most frequently mentioned was Duane Bliss, who had an enviable reputation for honesty and integrity in the state. The *Sacramento Record-Union*, decrying what they viewed as the deplorable record of Nevada's Free Silver politicians, noted: "The Republicans have

Chapter 13. The Grand Old Man of Lake Tahoe

The regal steamship, the SS *Tahoe*, was launched in June 1896. Duane Bliss intended for her to be the finest ship on the lake, and she accomplished that lofty goal by any measure. She was 196 feet long and could accommodate up to 200 passengers in luxurious comfort. (Special Collections Department, University of Nevada, Reno Library)

any number of dignified and able men for the position . . . [including] D. L. Bliss of Carson, a man of the highest standing in every line of life."[8] Bliss, however, had no interest in public life. He had carefully formulated his plans for Lake Tahoe, and if the invitation to run ever came from the Republican Party, Bliss turned it down.

Duane Bliss had been mesmerized by San Francisco since that first day in 1851 when he had stepped off the *Sarah & Eliza* and viewed the bedraggled gold rush town for the first time. How much it had transformed itself in the half-century since then! The San Francisco of 1899 was a cosmopolitan city of 343,000 people, the largest city west of the Mississippi. It was the financial capital of the West, the cultural capital of the West, and the busiest port city of the West. Bliss had visited the city innumerable times in the intervening years, and he marveled at the changes each time he visited anew. He had often wanted to build a home in the city, and by 1899 he had the money and the leisure time to create such a luxury.

Walter Danforth Bliss, the fourth of Duane and Elizabeth's five children, had attended the prestigious Massachusetts Institute of Technology, or MIT (all four of the Bliss boys would eventually graduate from the school) and had then worked for five years in New York City with a prominent architectural firm. In 1898, he and MIT classmate William Faville relocated to San Francisco, where they soon opened their own architectural firm. With Walter's father's connections, the new firm secured a number of excellent commissions, and began building a fine reputation in a short period of time.[9]

One of their first commissions had been to build a home for Walter's parents at 2898 Broadway in the exclusive Pacific Heights neighborhood. It was an elaborate Dutch- Colonial manor house overlooking San Francisco Bay, and Duane and Elizabeth would spend every available weekend at it once it was finished. Over the next half-dozen years, as Bliss turned over more of the business operations to his sons, he would spend almost all of his time in San Francisco.[10]

Having accomplished the first step in his Lake Tahoe tourism plan, Duane Bliss was ready to move on. From the Carson & Tahoe Lumber & Fluming Company he purchased the tracks, rolling stock, shops, and maintenance equipment of the Lake Valley Railroad and the Lake Tahoe Railroad. He then moved it all across the lake on barges powered by *Meteor* and *Emerald #2*, which he had leased from C&TL&FC, to his new headquarters in Tahoe City. He then built a substantial maintenance and repair facility at Tahoe City for the growing fleets of ships he had planned. Ultimately, in addition to the two aforementioned, the company would also operate steamers and gasoline launches *Tallac, Wild Goose, Catalina, Annie, and Tahoe*.[11]

Three years later Bliss would augment the Tahoe City repair and maintenance facility by leasing the roundhouse, machine shop, blacksmith shop and wharfing privileges at Glenbrook from C&TL&FC. Soon thereafter, he purchased outright all of the aforementioned equipment, buildings and property from C&TL&FC and barged them to Tahoe City.[12]

In December 1898 the Bliss family incorporated the Lake Tahoe Railway and Transportation Company, acquiring all the property of the earlier Lake Tahoe Transportation Company that it replaced. Apparently there was need for a capital infusion, as two additional men were brought into the new corporation as investors and board members. The 150 shares of stock in the new company were divided like this: N. K. Masten and F. I. Kendall, both of San Francisco, thirty-seven shares each; D. L. Bliss, Sr., twenty-five shares; Walter D. Tobey and Charles Tobey Bliss, nineteen shares each; and Walter Danforth Bliss and William Seth Bliss, five shares each. Inexplicably, D. L. Bliss, Jr. was absent from the list.[13]

Chapter 13. The Grand Old Man of Lake Tahoe

Six months later all of the Bliss family stockholders signed a contract to pool their shares. This meant that the family jointly owned 76 of the 150 outstanding shares, or controlling interest in the corporation, and they agreed they would always vote their shares as a block.[14] This agreement could indicate a split between the Bliss family and the other two stockholders, who held seventy-four of the outstanding shares, or it could have just insured that no one family member could break away from the group.

Next, the Truckee and Lake Tahoe Railroad Company was incorporated, "to construct a standard-gauge railroad from Truckee, in this State [California], to a point on the northern shore of Lake Tahoe, at or near the place called Tahoe City," the *San Francisco Call* reported in February, 1897. The incorporators of the railroad were identified as D. L. Bliss, W. [Walter] D. Tobey, W.[William] S. Bliss, M. L. Requa, I. L. Requa and W. S. Wood. Capital stock was fixed at $200,000, of which, the newspaper reported, $20,000 had already been subscribed.[15] No record of individual holdings appears in the Bliss Family Records.

By December 1898, however, the plans had changed. The *Call* reported that the Lake Tahoe Railway Company had incorporated "to build a narrow-gauge road from Truckee to Lake Tahoe." Not only was the company name different, and the railroad changed from standard-gauge to a narrow-gauge, but some of the incorporators were also different. The new incorporators were D. L. Bliss, W. B. Tobey, C. [Charles] T. Tobey, N. K. Masten and F. I. Kendall.[16]

Prior to the railroad being built, transportation from Truckee, a stop on the transcontinental railroad, to the lake had been by six-horse stagecoaches that carried from twelve to fifteen passengers. During the snow season, the teams pulled large bobsleds. For many years the driver on the run—both summer and winter—had been an old fellow named Elijah "Pop" Church. Pop had developed a rapid-fire repertoire to entertain his passengers. Every landmark along the way, according to Pop, was the "Devil's this" or the "Devil's that." There was a Devil's Curve, a Devil's Bluff, a Devil's Playground, and so on. There was one exception to that rule. About three miles out of Truckee there was a large, pillar-like rock about fifteen feet high that Pop called Devil's Rock. In 1886 some bandits used the rock as a hiding place, and jumped out and robbed Pop and his passengers. From then on, the rock was called Robbers' Roost.[17]

William S. Bliss, who had been an incorporator under the company's earlier name, was no longer listed. His task had been to survey and lay out

155

LAKE TAHOE TRAIN, TRUCKEE, CALIFORNIA   2338

Duane Bliss and his sons built the Lake Tahoe Railway (not to be confused with the earlier Lake Tahoe Railroad that served C&TL&FC's lumbering business) in the late 1890s to bring national and international tourism to the lake. The train, shown here at the Truckee, California depot where it linked up with the transcontinental railroad, carried passengers all the way out onto a 1/3-mile long pier built out into the lake at Tahoe City. (Special Collections Department, University of Nevada, Reno Library)

the sixteen-mile track down the Truckee Canyon, and he had accomplished his work by the summer of 1898. He was also to supervise the laying of the track, and that was completed by the following spring.

The small railroad would be open for business by mid-July 1900, according to the *San Francisco Call:* "The railroad . . . is now running daily, trains connecting the East-bound Southern Pacific trains in the morning at Truckee . . . [and] in the evening . . . ." Initially pulling the new trains were the locomotives *Tahoe*, formerly of Glenbrook, and the *Santa Cruz* and *Engine #3* from the lumbering operations at the south end of the lake. Eventually Bliss would add an open-air observation car named *Rattler*, and a "garish parlor car" obtained from the Carson & Colorado line. Also purchased were four boxcars, two baggage cars, and a combination baggage car and smoker.[18]

Having completed his responsibilities to the railroad, Duane Bliss's son William had other career plans in mind. He had graduated with an engineering degree, and during the 1890s he had been involved in a couple

Chapter 13. The Grand Old Man of Lake Tahoe

of mining ventures in eastern Nevada. The news of a promising gold strike in tributaries of the Snake River near Nome, Alaska had captured his fancy, and he was anxious to join the gold rush. William discussed it with his father and brothers, and they all agreed that the adventure might hasten his emotional recovery from the loss of his wife, Mabel, who had passed away prematurely. Duane, Sr. particularly understood his eldest son's need to strike out on his own, since he had done the same thing himself barely half-a-century earlier. With Elizabeth and Duane still caring for their young grandson Will, there was nothing to hold William back, and in the spring of 1900 he departed.[19]

The operation of the Lake Tahoe Railway Company had been put in the hands of twenty-six year old Duane L. Bliss, Jr. as superintendent of the company. He too had graduated with an engineering degree from MIT, and he had also earned a law degree. In addition to the railroad itself, the company had also erected a telegraph line along the railway to carry on a communications business.[20] A letter from D. L. Bliss, Sr. to Nevada U.S. Senator William Stewart in 1901 thanked the senator for his assistance in obtaining a winter mail route for the train from Truckee to Tahoe City for the company.[21] Later that same year, the company would borrow a half-million dollars from the Mercantile Trust Company in San Francisco to assist in financing its many ventures.[22]

Eventually the railroad would be extended beyond Tahoe City. A spur ran south along the west side of the lake for a few miles to Ward Creek, then up Ward Creek Canyon for another two miles. A second spur ran along the north side of Squaw Valley, and a third one to what is today the skiing resort of Granlibaken. The trains on these spurs carried timber and lumber for the Truckee Lumber Company, and would account for a sizable share of the railroad's revenue. Not coincidentally, the tracks from Tahoe City to Truckee ran along a right-of-way that had been leased from the Truckee Lumber Company, so this was undoubtedly a deal struck to the advantage of both companies.[23]

In 1915, author George Wharton James was the first writer to publish a book about Lake Tahoe, *The Lake of the Sky—Lake Tahoe*. He was one of the early passengers on the Bliss train, and he wrote poetically about the experience: "This ride is itself romantic and beautiful. On the day trains observation cars are provided, and the hour is one of delightful, restful and enchanting scenes. The Truckee River is never out of sight and again and again it reminds one in its foaming speed of Joaquin Miller's expressive phrase: 'See where the cool white river runs.'"[24]

This was exactly the experience Duane Bliss had hoped to create for his customers. But this was only the beginning. At the end of the sixteen-mile train ride was the family's crown jewel, the apogee of the visitors' experience: The Tahoe Tavern.

CHAPTER 14

Innkeepers to the World

Tahoe City, on the northeastern shore, or California side, of the lake, is the oldest town on Lake Tahoe. It was founded in 1864 amidst the minor excitement that arose after a small amount of gold was discovered at nearby Squaw Valley. Once the placer gold ran out, which it quickly did, many of the residents stayed on and entered the growing lumbering trade due to the mining activity on the Comstock. In the 1880s, when the Comstock began to slow down, so did Tahoe City. Only a small fishing and tourism base kept it from becoming a ghost town. When Duane Bliss moved his activities from Glenbrook to Tahoe City, it regained its prominence, and became the chief business center on the lake.[1]

The Comstock's mines had a voracious appetite for lumber, but so did the railroad industry that required millions of board feet for railroad ties. Two members of the Big Four—the legendary Sacramento developers of the Central Pacific Railroad—had purchased large parcels of forestland in the 1860s to meet the railroad's needs. Mark Hopkins and Leland Stanford owned the Donner Lumber and Boom Company, and among their holdings were large parcels of land in and around Tahoe City. In the mid- to late-1890s Duane Bliss purchased 1,000 acres from the firm, along with an additional forty lake front acres from the Pacific Improvement Company. This latter parcel was on a knoll above the lake about a mile south of the town, and was surrounded by pine and cedar groves. This was the chosen site for the third phase of Bliss's plan, the construction of a hotel that would be the grandest on Lake Tahoe.[2]

As expected, Duane Bliss selected his son Walter, who had designed their San Francisco home, to design the hotel he would name the Tahoe Tavern. Walter Bliss began the work immediately, at the same time that the railroad was being built that would transport tourists to fill the Tahoe Tavern's finished rooms.

The wharf, or pier, on Lake Tahoe was the end of the line for the Lake Tahoe Railway. The 196-foot SS *Tahoe*—dubbed "The Queen of the Lake"—moored at the end of the pier so passengers could immediately board for a lake tour. The pier was also a popular promenade for hotel guests. (Special Collections Department, University of Nevada, Reno Library)

Before construction actually began on the hotel, a one-eighth mile long trestle pier was built out over the lake. Narrow-gauge tracks were laid down one side of the pier so the train could run out over the water. Alongside the pier, also built over the water, was a warehouse, and beyond that were docking facilities for the company's steamers, including the regal SS *Tahoe*. The train arriving from Truckee would first take a short spur to the entrance of the Tahoe Tavern to dispatch hotel guests at the front door. Then the train backed out to the main tracks, and chugged its way to the very end of the 954-foot long pier. A traveler could depart the train at the end of the pier and immediately board the *Tahoe* for a lake cruise to his final destination if he was staying somewhere else around the lake.[3]

The Tahoe Tavern opened for guests on June 12, 1902. Announcing the opening in the *San Francisco Call*, an advertisement said the hotel is, "Not better than the best, but better than the rest," adding that it is ". . . said to be the finest mountain hotel west of the Rocky Mountains." Room and board were offered for $3 a day, ". . . but you can spend more if you want to."[4]

Chapter 14. Innkeepers to the World

The Tahoe Tavern was truly spectacular for its time. It was a long rambling building, three stories high, with a number of gables breaking up the roofline along its entire frontage. The roof was steep-pitched to allow the snow to slide off easily, and the entire structure was covered in shingles, oiled to a dark brown. Climbing vines wrapped themselves around every post on the long twenty-foot wide veranda, and carefully cultivated wild flowers grew out of small earth mounds and banks around the premises. Paths and walkways surrounded the building, leading out into the groves in the back, or directly down to the wharf in front of the hotel that was always abuzz with activity. A large grass lawn fronted the building, dotted with lawn chairs, swing seats and reclining chairs, all overlooking the dazzling blue water of the lake.[5]

Early Lake Tahoe historian George Wharton James was a frequent visitor to the hotel in the years after it first opened. He wrote about the comfortable, casual environment the guests enjoyed, despite the hotel's luxurious amenities and impeccable surroundings:

> . . . let it be completely understood that it is not a fashionable resort, in the sense that every one, men and women alike, must dress in fashionable garb to be welcomed and made at home. It is a place of common sense and rational freedom. If one has taken a walk in his white flannels he is welcome to a dance at the . . . dining-room, or the social-hall. If one comes in from a hunting or fishing trip at dinner time, he is expected to enter the dining room as he is . . . . Indeed, visitors are urged to bring their old clothes . . . for mountain-climbing, iding, rowing, fishing, horseback-riding, botanizing in the woods, or any other out of door occupation.
> . . . Tahoe Tavern is . . . the most wonderful combination of primitive simplicity with twentieth century luxury.[6]

The interior of the Tahoe Tavern was equally impressive. High-beamed ceilings, elk-horn chandeliers, rustic but comfortable furniture, and a massive stone fireplace welcomed guests. Bedrooms—the hotel could accommodate 450 guests—were furnished in the same comfortable style, and the brochure boasted, "Added to the luxury of the best mattresses . . . are the delights of perfectly appointed baths, large closets, steam heat and running water."[7]

The hotel also featured a laundry, its own steam plant and water system, and a resident physician. The dining room served excellent cuisine. A guest could return from a successful fishing trip aboard one of the hotel's boats, and enjoy his catch superbly prepared that very evening. The hotel enjoyed

The Bliss family built the grand Tahoe Tavern resort in Tahoe City, California to entertain guests brought in on their railroad. The lakeside hotel was hugely successful from the beginning. (Special Collections Department, University of Nevada, Reno Library)

100 percent occupancy from the day it opened. Naturally, it was seasonable; it usually opened in mid-May and closed once the heavy snows began to fall, until later years when it would operate year-round.

In 1906 the Tavern Annex was built south of the main hotel to accommodate more guests, and the following year the Casino was built north of the main hotel, and down the slope of the hill. The Casino—it had no gambling—offered a bowling alley, a barbershop, and a large ballroom with a stage on the second floor. There, the exposed ceiling was supported by heavy timber beams, hung with colorful Chinese lanterns. The dance floor was highly polished and surrounded by expensive wicker chairs and tables. Local glee clubs and amateur theatricals were often staged for the enjoyment of hotel guests, and there were professional orchestras booked for dancing.[8]

During the early years of the Tahoe Tavern, there were innumerable visitors of every stripe: politicians, foreign dignitaries, captains of industry,

Chapter 14. Innkeepers to the World

journalists, entertainment and sports luminaries, and even many regular folks. One of the most extraordinary people ever to visit the hotel—it's doubtful she was ever a paying guest—was a Washoe Indian woman named Dat-So-La-Lee. Born in about 1830 in Eagle Valley, Nevada, her married name was Louisa Keyser.

Louisa and her husband Charley were provided with a small ramshackle house in Carson City by local merchant Abe Cohn, in return for her service as a maid in his home. But Abe had a very sharp eye, and when he first saw some of the reed baskets that Louisa had made, he saw opportunity. Around the turn of the century, Abe began bringing Dat-So-La-Lee to the lake. She would sit cross-legged by the front door of the house of an old friend of Abe's at Outlet Point, near Tahoe City, where the Truckee River runs out of the lake. There, she would weave her baskets in front of admiring tourists who happened by, and sell the few she had brought along, with a handsome commission naturally going to Abe. When the Tahoe Tavern opened, Dat-So-La-Lee would sit out on the hotel grounds, surrounded by all her basket-making paraphernalia, and stoically work her magic. Hotel guests paid $50 or occasionally even more for one of Dat-So-La-Lee's masterpieces. She cured roots and branches of willow, incense cedar, red fir and tamarack from which she made the incredible dyes that graced her work. Amazingly, she accomplished all of this magic despite being nearly blind.[9]

Today, Dat-So-La-Lee's larger baskets—when one of these masterpieces is available, which is seldom—can sell for up to one million dollars, although most are part of museum and historical society collections.

*

Although the Bliss family men owned the majority of stock in the Lake Tahoe Railway and Transportation Company, which functioned as the corporate holding company for all their Lake Tahoe tourism-based ventures, most of them had outside business interests as well. Despite that, all of them retained positions as officers and board members of the company. A company letterhead from 1901 lists the following officers: D. L. Bliss, President; W. D. Tobey, Vice President; W. D [Walter] Bliss, Treasurer; C. T. [Charles] Bliss, Secretary; D. L. Bliss, Jr., Superintendent; and W. S. [William] Bliss, Chief Engineer.[10]

However, William Bliss was in Alaska, Charles Bliss was in Hobart Mills, California, having taken over the job of general manager of the Sierra

Nevada Wood & Lumber Company at the turn of the century, and Walter Bliss ran his own successful San Francisco architectural firm. Duane, Jr. was the general manager of the Tahoe Tavern once it opened, but family records indicate that the hotel was leased to an outside operating company, so Duane Jr.'s role would have been primarily one of oversight.[11]

Alaska's winters were much too severe to allow year-round mining, so William returned to the states each year and stayed with his parents in San Francisco. The annual trip also allowed William and Will to maintain their father and son relationship.

All of the businesses were humming along nicely. The Tahoe Tavern had begun receiving national, then international, acclaim, and general tourism all over Lake Tahoe was on the increase. When the Truckee to Tahoe City railroad was built, the company had constructed and operated a telegraph line between the two towns. In 1905 they signed an agreement with the Western Union Company to open a telegraph office in the hotel, and a separate agreement to establish and maintain telegraph poles for communication to other sites around the lake.[12]

Despite the fact that everything was going very well, the Bliss family had one more desire. Their Lake Tahoe experience had begun in, and been centered around, the small settlement of Glenbrook. The summer cottage—now a two-and-a-half story house—that Duane Sr. had built for the family held fond memories for all of his children, who had grown up romping through the nearby meadows, forests and streams. The rails, rolling stock, buildings and other materials from the Lake Tahoe Railway had already been moved to Tahoe City and re-used for the Truckee-to-Tahoe City line. And in 1903 the last visible vestiges of the C&TL&FC disappeared from Glenbrook when the Truckee Lumber Company purchased the idle sawmill to replace one that had burned down.[13] Of the move, the *Carson City Appeal* noted, "The Glenbrook mill has probably turned out more lumber than any mill in Nevada, as nearly all the lumber that was used on the Comstock and in this city came from the saws that were turned there."[14] It was truly the end or an era for Lake Tahoe.

In March 1906 Walter and Duane, Jr. incorporated the Glenbrook Improvement Company. The corporation had four owners, who also served as the directors: Walter Bliss held 200 shares; Duane Bliss Jr. held 100 shares; P. J. Pomin, a member of a longtime Glenbrook and Tahoe City family, held 100 shares; and J. U. Haley held 1 share.[15] The group's plan was to turn the

Chapter 14. Innkeepers to the World

old lumbering town into a refined summer resort for middle- and upper-class families.

Once again, brother Walter was chosen to design what would eventually become the Glenbrook Inn. It would not be an easy task. Plans called for three of the town's existing buildings to be relocated and strung together into one large inn. The first, the Lake Shore House, the second hotel in Glenbrook, had been built by Captain Augustus Pray in 1863, and sat several hundred feet back from the lakefront at the foot of the meadow. It had been purchased by the Bliss brothers for $550 from its owner, D. Couillard.[16]

The second building would be the two-story general store, built over the water in the 1870s by Captain Pray, one of Glenbrook's original settlers, and rebuilt by C&TL&FC after a fire had destroyed it. It was moved directly north of the Lake Shore House, and connected to it. It would be the inn's central structure, and would serve as the lobby, dining room, kitchen and general offices. On the second floor was a dance hall. The third building was the old Jellerson Hotel, built in the 1880s. It was moved and connected to the north side of the main structure, the old general store. The two structures that had originally been hotels would provide the guest rooms. The Bliss summer home was no longer used by the family, so it was modified to provide additional space, and a number of cottages would be built around that house to accommodate yet more guests.[17]

By May 1907 some of Glenbrook Inn's rooms were ready for occupancy. The *San Francisco Call* announced, "Glenbrook Inn and Ranch. On Nevada side of Lake Tahoe for those who want [a] genuine summer outing; rates reasonable; excellent hotel accommodations or cottage life if desired. Ask Information Bureau Southern Pacific." The first guests to sign in were a foursome from Alameda, near San Francisco, and a gentleman from Carson City. As Bliss family author Sessions Wheeler wrote, "The seventy-year history of the Glenbrook Inn had begun."[18]

Lake Tahoe historian George Wharton James was a frequent visitor to the Inn:

> *The Inn, and its veranda overlooking the lake, is built with an eye to comfort and convenience. Every need for pleasure and recreation is arranged for. For those who enjoy privacy, cosy [sic] cottages are provided, around which beautiful wild flowers grow in wonderful profusion. The guests here are especially favored in that the Inn has its own ranch, dairy, poultry farm, fruit orchard and vegetable garden.*

The Glenbrook Inn & Ranch was opened in 1906 by two of Duane Bliss's four sons. The rustic property appealed to middle-class families and those who enjoyed all the outdoor activities that were provided. The Inn & Ranch remained in the Bliss family until it closed in 1976. (Special Collections Department, University of Nevada, Reno Library)

> *The table, therefore, is abundantly provided, and everything is of known quality and brought in fresh daily.*
>
> *Glenbrook Inn makes no pretense to be a fashionable resort. It especially invites those individuals and families who wish to be free from the exhausting "frivolities of fashion." Rest and recreation, amusement and recuperation are the key-notes.*[19]

Like the Tahoe Tavern, its sister hotel across the lake, the Glenbrook Inn offered its guests a long list of activities they could participate in: fishing, boating, trail hiking, horseback riding, automobile touring, and swimming for those hearty enough to test the lake's frigid water. Rates were lower than those of the Tahoe Tavern, and the Glenbrook Inn entertained more middle class tourists as a result.

The Glenbrook Inn was the final piece of the tourism puzzle for the farsighted D. L. Bliss and his family.

CHAPTER 15

A Life Well Lived

As he had handed over the reins of his responsibilities to his sons, Duane Bliss began travelling less. He now spent more time in his prestigious San Francisco home on Broadway in Pacific Heights, and he and Elizabeth spent more quiet time together. That isn't to say that Bliss had become a homebody. He loved San Francisco, and enjoyed taking advantage of everything the city had to offer. He was a member of the exclusive Pacific Union Club, the Bohemian Club, and the business-oriented Transportation Club, and he was a prominent and active Mason, having achieved the rank of Knight Templar.[1] For three consecutive years, and entirely at his own expense, Bliss had hosted the 400 members of the Transportation Club to a weekend at Lake Tahoe, serving as the perfect host to the large membership.[2] The corporate headquarters of all of his companies had been transferred to San Francisco, and he maintained an active office in the city that he visited on most days.

Bliss enjoyed living the good life. He smoked expensive Havana cigars, drank the finest brandy and wine, and boarded a fine livery of coach horses to take him wherever he wanted to go in the city. He was a regular customer at San Francisco's best haberdashers, and he was a frequent visitor to the city's financial center, where he was an active buyer and seller of stocks and securities.[3] In other words, Duane Bliss enjoyed the life that he had worked so long and hard to achieve.

In December 1907 William Bliss was in San Francisco with his parents and son, enjoying his annual hiatus from the rigors of Alaskan winters. As the eldest son, he was the heir apparent to the top management position with the Lake Tahoe Railway & Transportation Company and its wide and varied asset portfolio. He would also be expected to take charge of the family's Carson & Tahoe Lumber and Fluming Company land, which still had massive real estate holdings in the Tahoe Basin. It had

Photograph of Duane L. Bliss taken a year before he passed away. (Special Collections Department, University of Nevada, Reno Library)

been a couple of years since Duane, Sr. had discussed all of the family's complex operations with his eldest son, and he decided to do so during this holiday season. On December 18 father and son boarded a Southern Pacific train—by this time, owned by the Union Pacific Railroad—for Truckee, California, transferring in that city to Bliss's private car on the family's railroad to Tahoe City. During the ride, the two men discussed the railroad's performance, which by this time was primarily dependent on passenger service, since its freight revenue from hauling lumber had almost dwindled to nothing.[4]

At the Tahoe Tavern, Duane Jr. went over the operating reports of the hotel, which was continuing to do very well. The men had dinner at the hotel, and retired for the night. The next morning Duane Sr. and William boarded the motor launch SS *Tahoe* for a trip around the lake, stopping off at Glenbrook, a courtesy visit seeing as the two men were not involved in the

Chapter 15. A Life Well Lived

ownership of the Glenbrook Inn. Then they returned to the Tahoe Tavern for another night.

The next morning, they took the train back to Truckee. William caught the connecting Southern Pacific train back to San Francisco, while his father took the eastbound train to Reno. From there, he took the V&T to Carson City where he and Elizabeth still maintained their second home—known locally as the Bliss Mansion. Soon after arriving, he went to visit his longtime friend and business associate, Henry Yerington. Bliss told Yerington that while he was in Reno, he had taken a sudden chill, but it had passed. However, later in their conversation, Bliss was overcome with another chill. Seeing that the situation was serious, Yerington quickly took him to the nearby home of the Jellerson family, who were good friends from both Lake Tahoe and Carson City, and a doctor was immediately summoned to the house.[5]

Yerington contacted Elizabeth Bliss in San Francisco by telegram, and on Sunday night, December 22, she, daughter Hope, and sons William and Walter left the city with a nurse on a chartered train for Carson City. At 1:00 a.m. on Monday morning, December 23, Duane Bliss passed away from acute pneumonia, unfortunately two hours before the special train carrying his family reached Carson City. Bliss was seventy-four years old.[6]

Newspapers throughout the West praised Bliss for his business acumen and his sterling personal character. "Through his brilliant business ability he has made the resorts of the Lake among the most widely known in the world," said the *Carson Morning Appeal*. "His death will be a profound loss to both Nevada and California," wrote *Goodwin's Weekly* of Salt Lake City, Utah. "... he was the most lovable of men, genial, open, free–handed, considerate, most charitable in his judgments ... and overflowing with good will and general kindliness toward all," wrote the *Sacramento Union*. "Bliss was one of the most hospitable men in the state," wrote the *San Francisco Call*. "One of the best known men on the Pacific Coast," wrote the *Territorial Enterprise*.[7]

Bliss's funeral service and interment were private, with only family and intimate friends invited. His four sons served as pallbearers.

Duane Bliss's will was executed on September 20, 1909. As California was a community property state, Elizabeth Bliss owned half of all the assets. Duane left his half of the estate to his wife as well, writing, "Believing my wife to have the welfare of our children as much at heart as myself, and that she will deal as justly by them, I give and bequeath to her the total revenue of the Estate left by me, during her lifetime." He further wrote that upon Elizabeth's death, the remainder of his estate should be equally divided among his five children, or their issues.[8] There is no record of the exact size of the estate, although it was significant.

Within a few years of her husband's death, Elizabeth Bliss packed up all her belongings from the San Francisco house, had them stored, and moved back east to her old home in Wareham, Massachusetts. At some point she returned to the West, either on a visit or permanently, as she passed away in April, 1921 in Carson City. Her estate, including the remaining portion of Duane Sr.'s estate, was divided equally among the five children, who were all still living.

*

William Bliss had always admired his father. When he took over as president of the family's two corporations, it was initially 'business as usual.' In 1912 William designated one large parcel of land from the 1,000 acres his father had purchased near Tahoe City to build a residential development of summer homes. The area was divided into lots, and Tahoe Tavern Heights was born. A contract was signed with H. G. McMasters, owner of Sierra Realty Company, and the firm began marketing the property to those seeking a wonderful weekend or summer retreat from the noise and traffic of the city. Homes and cottages at Tahoe Tavern Heights are still popular today with owners and renters who flock to the lake every summer.[9]

Over the next two decades at Lake Tahoe, things would change. By the early 1920s there were scores of automobiles and trucks on the road, which had eroded the railroad's passenger business. It also became more difficult for the Truckee-to-Tahoe City narrow-gauge railroad to compete for freight business because trucks had taken much of that business away. The railroad needed to upgrade to standard gauge tracks, but that would have created a debt that could have threatened the family's solvency. William approached the Southern Pacific Company with a creative solution. He would lease the railroad to the larger company for one dollar a year if Southern Pacific would agree to upgrade the tracks to standard gauge, and upon completion of the job, would pay one additional dollar and take over ownership of the railroad. One stipulation was that the railroad had to continue the Truckee-to-Tahoe City run. By 1927 the job was completed, and the railroad was turned over to its new owners.[10]

Also during the mid 1920s, the family decided to sell the remainder of their interests on the west, or California, side of Lake Tahoe. D. M Linnard,

Chapter 15. A Life Well Lived

who was a major California hotel owner at the time, along with a group of San Francisco investors, purchased the Tahoe Tavern and its adjoining land. Linnard also owned the Fairmont and Mark Hopkins Hotels in San Francisco and the Huntington in Pasadena, among others. A separate division of the Linnard Company purchased the family's steamers, the *Tahoe*, *Meteor* and *Nevada*. The price for the hotel and steamers was reported in the newspaper to be $1,000,000 (equivalent to about $14 million today.)[11] Charles T. Bliss had replaced Duane, Jr. as the general manager of the Tahoe Tavern in 1914, and when it was sold to the Linnard interests, he retired to his home in Piedmont, California. Charles passed away in 1951. Three of his siblings continued to live in San Francisco until their deaths, Duane, Jr. in 1936, Hope in 1949, and Walter in 1956.

When the new Linnard Company that owned the steamships lost its U.S. mail contract in 1934—it had already lost most of its passenger business to automobiles—the romantic era of Lake Tahoe's steamers came to an end. The three once-proud ships were anchored at their moorings at the Tahoe Tavern, where for the next six years they accumulated rust and dirt, their paint peeled and chipped away, their gleaming brass surfaces became stained and dinghy, and they were often vandalized.

In a series of events that have become legend at Lake Tahoe, William Bliss purchased the rusting hulks of the three ships from their owners in 1939 and 1940. He pledged he would sink all three ships as a memoriam to his father, rather than allowing the federal government to purchase them for scrap. In April 1939 the sixty-three year old *Meteor*—once the fastest steamer in the world—was towed on a direct line from Tahoe City to Glenbrook, and in the middle of the lake, her sea cocks were opened and she slipped quietly into the icy waters.[12] In August 1940 the majestic SS *Tahoe*—"the *Queen of the Lake*" and the linchpin in the family's pioneer tourism business—went to the same watery grave. Her prow standing almost vertically, she slipped gracefully into the water a couple of miles from Dead Man's Point in Glenbrook. And finally, in October 1940, the *Nevada* formerly the jaunty little *Tallac*—the first passenger and mail boat on the lake—joined her fleet mates in Lake Tahoe's deep blue waters.[13]

William was so disappointed in the way things had changed at his beloved Lake Tahoe that in 1937 he vowed never to return. He made good on his pledge, and passed away in 1941.

Earlier, after their mother's death in 1921, Walter and Duane, Jr. had gifted or sold their Glenbrook Development Company to their nephew,

Will Bliss, William's son. Will, a World War I veteran and an architect, took over active management of the Glenbrook Inn in the early 1930s, when the Depression shortened his architectural career. A map of the Lake Tahoe area, produced in the mid-1930s, outlines and identifies every plat of land that was still owned by the old C&TL&FC at that time. Interestingly, this map indicates that the entire Glenbrook area, including approximately five miles of shoreline running both north and south of Glenbrook proper, was no longer part of C&TL&FC's land. That indicates that at some point in the past, Will Bliss—or possibly Walter and Duane, Jr. before him—had purchased or traded for the remaining Glenbrook land from their C&TL&FC partners, or the partners' estates. Will Bliss and his wife owned it all.[14]

Will decided to sell some of the Glenbrook land in the early 1930s to raise money for refurbishing the inn. A number of millionaires had been lured to Nevada by the promise of lower taxes, and Will's plan was to sell large parcels to wealthy individuals who could then build summer homes in Glenbrook. The plan worked. Max C. Fleischmann, the owner of Fleischmann's Yeast and a principle stockholder in General Foods, was one of the first to buy and build in Glenbrook. A noted philanthropist, Fleischmann would donate millions of dollars to charitable causes in his adopted state. Afterwards Bliss made numerous sales, including one to eccentric millionaire George Whittell. Will Bliss held on to 3,300 acres that allowed the Glenbrook Inn to retain its protected isolation. Around this same time the Glenbrook Improvement Company was reincorporated in Delaware, and the Glenbrook Inn was renamed the Glenbrook Inn and Ranch.[15]

Will remained in control of his Glenbrook properties until 1960 when he passed away during the Squaw Valley Winter Olympics. Will's only son, William "Bill" Bliss, had begun working at the Glenbrook Inn as a teenager, caddying at the nine-hole Glenbrook Golf Course that was added in the 1920s. After the death of his father, Bill took control of the Glenbrook properties. He, his mother Hatherly, and his sister, also named Hatherly, now co-owned all 3,300 acres, the inn and all the other facilities and amenities in Glenbrook. But the era of the grand old summer resorts at Lake Tahoe was passing, and the closing of the Tahoe Tavern in 1964 and the Brockway Hotel/Resort in 1967 was a sign of the times. An article in *San Francisco* magazine nostalgically summed up the changes at Lake Tahoe in the late 1960s: "Lake Tahoe certainly isn't the grand vacation spot it once was. The days of touring the waters by steam vessel, splendid dining, refined sports

Chapter 15. A Life Well Lived

The second, third and fourth generations of Bliss men, shown here in the late 1920s, carried on Duane Bliss's Glenbrook legacy. Pictured from left are Will Bliss, his son William W. "Bill" Bliss, and his father William Seth Bliss, Duane's and Elizabeth's son. (Courtesy of the Bliss family)

activities and Sunday promenades in elegant attire have long disappeared—probably never to return."[16]

Bill Bliss kept the Glenbrook Inn and Ranch open until 1976, when it finally closed its doors forever. Over the years he had been forced to sell more and more of the Glenbrook land, including 2,600 acres to the U.S. Forest Service, as property and inheritance taxes mounted. Today, Bill Bliss, the fourth generation of Bliss family members to enjoy the unique magnificence of Glenbrook, maintains a small summer cottage and a beautiful home in Glenbrook, along with a handful of acres of land.[17] The meadow remains pristine, and there are still vestiges of the "old" Glenbrook scattered about. However, the private forest that encircles the meadow is dotted today with sprawling custom homes, townhouses, and cottage homes of the well-to-do, the privacy of their enclave protected by gates and fences.

*

Duane L. Bliss also left his family with another financial legacy: The extensive cut-over timbering lands once worked by the Carson & Tahoe Lumber & Fluming Company. At some time in the past, the three original C&TL&FC stockholders—D. L. Bliss, Henry M. Yerington and Darius O. Mills, or possibly their estates following their deaths—had divided the C&TL&FC acreage among the three families. Thus the Bliss, Mills and Yerington estates (H. M. Yerington and Darius O. Mills both passed away in 1910) each owned a piece of the massive land holding, rather than all of the land being co-owned in common by the three families. It is not known exactly when this change took place; however, the three separate holdings did continue to be marketed jointly for sale.[18] Thus Bliss family members stood to reap the financial benefit as their share of these lands were sold off over the years.

C&TL&FC had aggregated between 50,000 and 80,000 acres of Tahoe Basin land at its peak. An accounting of the true amount of land in the portfolio, however, is not known because C&TL&FC, like most of the large lumbering firms, adopted the practice of buying the land, cutting off the timber, and then abandoning it in order to avoid having to pay taxes on the unproductive acreage."[19] Whatever the true acreage was, selling the land still under C&TL&FC ownership would eventually take many decades, and it would become more of a burden than a blessing to the heirs of the three families.

For the next three decades the vast acreage was marketed and sold by one firm or another, but sales were agonizingly slow. There was little appetite for land where second growth forests were just beginning to mature. The owners, however, were still required to pay taxes on the acreage every year, and absorb the other upkeep costs. The U.S. Forest Service had tried for years to increase its holdings in the Tahoe Basin, but it was difficult to purchase and administer areas that contained so many large private holdings. In 1936 the C&TL&FC cutover lands still held by the Mills and Bliss estates—the Yerington lands were not included—along with the Hobart estate lands (Sierra Nevada Wood and Lumber Company) offered the Forest Service a 40,000-acre tract of land on the northern and western sides of the lake for a reported $325,000. Sadly, no federal funds were available in the middle of the Great Depression, and the U.S. Forest Service had to pass up the offer.[20]

By 1947, virtually all of the C&TL&FC lands had finally been disposed of, with the exception of a few small parcels held by descendants of Bliss and Mills. The most prominent sale had occurred shortly after the Forest Service's rejection. Multi-millionaire California playboy George Whittell

Chapter 15. A Life Well Lived

purchased 37,545 acres of the C&TL&FC land for approximately $1.34 million. He had a grand vision for the property. He was going to build a huge hotel, an aerial tramway similar to those found in the European Alps, and a year-round resort on the land.[21] He had already built a magnificent summer retreat—the legendary, castle-like Thunderbird Lodge—on some of the land he had bought earlier. But by the time he had acquired all the other land, things had changed for Whittell. Always an eccentric, the fifty-seven year old pleasure-seeker had by then become more reclusive, and none of his grand plans were ever carried out. He lived an increasingly cloistral life on his Lake Tahoe property, surrounding himself with exotic animals, until his death in 1969. Today his distinctive home and grounds are owned and maintained by the non-profit Thunderbird Lodge Preservation Society, and are on the National Register of Historic Places.[22]

In 1947, its job finally finished, Carson & Tahoe Lumber & Fluming Company directors filed a "Certificate of Dissolution" for the corporation.[23]

Like its founder, Duane Leroy Bliss, the Carson & Tahoe Lumber & Fluming Company had made it into its seventh decade. Its storied history is now kept alive through the many books and journal articles that relate the exciting times in which it flourished.

Afterword

"Virginia City, NV (August 9, 2012)—Comstock Mining, Inc. . . . announced that it has begun hauling ore from the Lucerne mine to its process area in America Flat. This marks the commencement of full mining activity and the highly anticipated return of mining to the historic Comstock Lode near Virginia City and Gold Hill, Nevada."[1]

With this press release, Comstock Mining, Inc., a Nevada-based gold and silver mining corporation, announced the first large-scale mining on the Comstock Lode since the mid-1890s.

The Lucerne pit mine, located between Gold Hill and Silver City, is part of 6,412 acres the company has been quietly assembling since 2003. It estimates that it has identified nearly $5 billion in gold and silver resources on the Comstock, given the then-current price for the two precious metals. It expected to be pouring gold and silver on or before September 15, 2012.[2]

The new venture has not had clear sailing, however. Residents of Sun Mountain's communities have been battling Comstock Mining, Inc., tooth-and-nail since the beginning.

Parts of Nevada's Storey and Lyon Counties, including all the communities within the Comstock, are designated as the Comstock Historic District by Nevada state law. Residents say large-scale mining will injure or destroy the historic character and integrity of the Comstock, and damage the local tourism-dependent economy. They also contend that the mining well severely damage the environment, which has been identified by the federal government as an official Superfund site, a program established to clean up the nation's uncontrolled hazardous waste.

Comstock Mining, Inc., says the environmental claims are overblown; and that rather than damaging the historic nature of the Comstock they will improve it by restoring historical mining structures.[3]

It will likely be many years before history reveals which side is correct.

Notes

Chapter 1 - A Voyage of Self Discovery [pages 1-6]

1. Ancestry.com; Miller, H. E. *History of the Town of Savoy*, 11.
2. Phinney, Jane Benedict, *Taking the High Road: A Two Hundred Year History of a Hilltown, Savoy, Massachusetts, 1797 – 1997*, 46-47, 122, 126.
3. Phinney, *Taking the High Road*, 122.
4. 05/05/2011 communication from Savoy historian Jane Phinney.
5. Bliss, William, "Business Log Book."
6. Berkshire Family History Association, "Berkshire Genealogist Quarterly," vol. 24, No. 2, 69; vol. 30, Issue 1, "Old Drury Academy," 32-34.
7. Bliss, William W., "Bliss Family Records, 1869 – 1949," Box 5, File 320, "D. L. Bliss Biographical Materials." This file contains two separate typewritten biographical sketches of Duane Bliss written by two of his children. One sketch, by son William S. Bliss, was written in 1908 following Duane Bliss's death; the second, an undated sketch by daughter Hope Bliss, likely also written soon after her father's death, states in a hand-written annotation, "A time outline of Father's oft-time repeated tales to me." A third biographical document in this file is son William's typewritten sketch mentioned above, but heavily annotated in the hand of daughter Hope, and containing some information not included in her own sketch. Will's sketch tends to be more chronological in nature; Hope's includes more personal information on their father, particularly up to his early twenties. Both sketches often exaggerate their father's good qualities and achievements. There is also biographical material contained in these sketches that more reliable primary sources contradict. Thus, factual information from the sketches is used cautiously and sparingly in this book because of its questionable accuracy. However, some personal anecdotes about Duane Bliss that have a ring of truth to them are included.
8. Phinney, *Taking the High Road*, 138.
9. Ancestry.com.

Notes

10. Bliss, Hope, biographical sketch; *Pittsfield, MA Sun*, 04/11/1844, 09/13/1849; *New York Herald Tribune*, 05/18/1897.
11. Bliss, Hope, biographical sketch.
12. Ibid. Malnati, Gwenda Gustafson, Bliss family genealogist, private correspondence with the author. This is one of those incidents, referred to in endnote #7 above, that appears in daughter Hope Bliss's biographical sketch, but for which there is no additional record of confirmation.
13. Bliss, Hope, biographical sketch.
14. Twain, Mark, *Roughing It, Vol. 1*, https://archive.org/stream/roughingit06twaigoog#page/n8/mode/2up

Chapter 2 - The Isthmus Over [pages 7-12]

1. McCullough, David, *The Path Between the Seas*, 33.
2. McGuinness, Aims, *Path of Empire*, 7.
3. Johnson, Theodore Taylor, *Sights in the Gold Region, and Scenes By the Way*, 2.
4. Although Bliss's children agreed that their father received inordinately generous help and support from a complete stranger he met on the ship from New York to Panama, Hope Bliss disagreed with her brother that the man's name was Diston. "The ficticious [sic] name of 'Diston'," she noted in her annotations on Will's sketch, "was not of interest nor connected with Father." The story of this generous stranger is not verified in any reputable source, including Duane Bliss's own Bancroft interview, so it's questionable if he existed.
5. Parker, Matthew, *Panama Fever*, 22.
6. McGuinness, *Path of Empire*, 33 – 34.
7. Johnson, *Sights in the Gold Region, and Scenes By the Way*, 19, 20.
8. Ibid., 30.
9. Brooks, Sarah Merriam, *Across the Isthmus to California in '52*, 42, 46-47, 51.
10. Marryat, Frank, *Mountains and Molehills*, 5.
11. Balf, Todd. *The Darkest Jungle*, 114-115.

Chapter 3 - Gold! The California Years [pages 13-25]

1. http://bancroft.berkeley.edu/info/history.html.
2. Bancroft, Hubert Howe. "Duane L. Bliss: Data Concerning the Virginia & Truckee Railroad." This timeline contradicts Bliss's son's and daughter's

Notes

biographical sketches that state that their father suffered an eight-month delay in leaving Panama due to a life-threatening bout with Chagras, or Panama, Fever.
3. Rasmussen, Louis J., *San Francisco Passenger Lists,* vol. 1, 92-94; vol. 2, 187-188; *Daily Alta California* newspaper, "Shipping Intelligence," 01/18/1851.
4. Johnson, *Sights in the Gold Region, and Scenes By the Way,* 105-107.
5. Benemann, William, *A Year of Mud and Gold,* 137-138.
6. Hill, Mary, *Gold: The California Story,* 55.
7. Wierzbicki, Felix Paul, *California as it is & as it May Be,* 49.
8. Bancroft, "Duane L. Bliss: Data Concerning the Virginia & Truckee Railroad."
9. California State Census, Tuolumne County, 1852. California conducted this rare state census because the 1850 Federal Census had omitted the counties of Contra Costa, San Francisco and Santa Clara.
10. Hill, *Gold: The California Story,* 63.
11. Bancroft, "Duane L. Bliss: Data Concerning the Virginia & Truckee Railroad."
12. Hoover, Mildred Brooke, and Douglas E. Kyle. *Historic Spots in California,* 30; Hill, *Gold: The California Story,* 94; Bancroft, "Duane L. Bliss: Data Concerning the Virginia & Truckee Railroad."
13. Regnery, Dorothy, "Parkhurst's Woodside," 3, 8, 9. For more on logging on the San Francisco Peninsula, see Stanger, Frank M., *Sawmills in the Redwoods: Logging on the San Francisco Peninsula, 1849-1967;* and Richards, Gilbert, *Crossroads: People and Events of the Redwoods of San Mateo County.*
14. Ibid., 6-8; "Aged Pioneer is Called by Death," *San Francisco Call,* 04/01/1909; Bonestell, Cutler L., *A Woodside Reminiscence,* 4.
15. Regnery, "Parkhurst's Woodside," 8; San Mateo County Historical Association, "Dr. R. O. Tripp Monograph."
16. Cloud, Roy W., *History of San Mateo County California,* vol. I, 95-96.
17. Regnery, "Parkhurst's Woodside," 7, 12, 13; *Redwood City Democrat,* 01/08/1903.
18. Bliss, John Homer, *Genealogy of the Bliss Family in America,* 601-602. This marriage, the two children that resulted from it, and the tragic death of Bliss's wife and children is not mentioned in either of the biographical sketches by his son and daughter, William and Hope. Their father's marriage to a "commoner" was apparently not the kind of image his son and daughter wished to portray of their father.
19. Regnery, "Parkhurst's Woodside," 10.
20. Maskell, Coramarie, "History of Woodside and the Woodside Library Association," 14.
21. Regnery, "Parkhurst's Woodside," 11.

NOTES

22. "Woodside Store Manuscript Collection," San Mateo County Historical Association.
23. Bliss, John Homer, *Genealogy of the Bliss Family in America*, 601-602; Maskell, "History of Woodside," 18.
24. Bliss, Hope, Biographical Sketch, "Bliss Family Records, 1869-1949."
25. Regnery, "Parkhurst's Woodside," 10; Regnery, Dorothy, *An Enduring Heritage*, 9.
26. Bliss, John Homer, *Genealogy of the Bliss Family in America*, 601 – 602; "California Mortuary and Cemetery Records, 1801 – 1932," Ancestry.com. This is likely the same child. The only citation for the child, other than the death record, is from the John Homer Bliss family genealogy book, and these types of volumes often have spelling errors or alternate variations of given names, thus "Bellzora" could have been the Bliss's child's full name.
27. Regnery, "Parkhurst's Woodside," 8, 10, 11.
28. Bliss, John Homer, *Genealogy of the Bliss Family in America*, 601-602; "California Mortuary and Cemetery Records, 1801-1932," Ancestry.com; *Sacramento Bee* newspaper, Aug. 20, 1859, Ancestry.com; Regnery, "Parkhurst's Woodside," 10, 13.
29. Regnery, "Parkhurst's Woodside," 12.
30. Bancroft, "Duane L. Bliss: Data Concerning the Virginia & Truckee Railroad."

Chapter 4 - The Comstock Lode [pages 27-43]

1. Bancroft, "Duane L. Bliss: Data Concerning the Virginia & Truckee Railroad."
2. "Pyramid Lake War," *Nevada Territorial Enterprise*, 06/02/1860; http://www.onlinenevada.org/Pyramid_Lake_War
3. "California Mortuary and Cemetery Records, 1801 – 1932," Ancestry.com.
4. Story of early mining on the Comstock, Lord, Eliot, *Comstock Mining and Miners*, 11-12, 33-38; Wright, William (writing as Dan De Quille) *A History of the Comstock Silver Lode & Mines*, 31-38; Zanjani, Sally, *Devils Will Reign: How Nevada Began*, 8.
5. James, Ronald, *The Roar and the Silence*, 19.
6. Wright, (writing as Dan De Quille) *History of the Comstock Silver Lode & Mines*, 34-35.
7. Ibid., 35.
8. Lord, *Comstock Mining and Miners*, 39-40.
9. Ibid., 54-55.
10. Wright, William (writing as Dan De Quille), *The Big Bonanza*, 32.
11. Ibid., 33.
12. Browne, J. Ross, *A Peep at Washoe and Washoe Revisited*, 64-66.

NOTES

13. Angel, Myron, *History of Nevada*, 75; Stanley, Maitland, *A Guide to Gold Hill, Nevada*, 9.
14. Mathews, M. M., *Ten Years in Nevada, or Life on the Pacific Coast*, 224.
15. *Nevada Territorial Enterprise*, 04/28/1860.
16. James, *The Roar and the Silence*, 46.
17. Irvine, Leigh H., ed. *History of the New California Its Resources and People*, vol. II, 670-672.
18. Lord, *Comstock Mining and Miners*, 85-86; Powell, John J., *Nevada: The Land of Silver*, 64-65.
19. Bancroft, "Duane L. Bliss: Data Concerning the Virginia & Truckee Railroad."
20. Lord, *Comstock Mining and Miners*, 85 – 86; DeGroot, Henry, *The Comstock Papers*, 72.
21. Bancroft, "Duane L. Bliss: Data Concerning the Virginia & Truckee Railroad."
22. Lord, *Comstock Mining and Miners*, 88.
23. Kelly, J. Wells, ed., *First Directory of Nevada Territory*, 171.
24. Storey County, NV Recorder, "Book A of Deeds," page 335.
25. Kelly, ed., *First Directory of Nevada Territory*, 171.
26. Lord, *Comstock Mining and Miners*, 404.
27. *Sacramento Daily Union*, "Killed at Washoe," 04/12/1861.
28. Angel, *History of Nevada*, 74-75.
29. Bancroft, "Duane L. Bliss: Data Concerning the Virginia & Truckee Railroad."
30. Wilson, *Sawdust Trails*, 1.
31. Angel, *History of Nevada*, 57.
32. Davis, *History of Nevada, vol. 1*, 408-409.
33. Ibid.
34. Lord, *Comstock Mining and Miners*, 89-90; Ratay, Myra Sauer, *Pioneers of the Ponderosa*, 53.
35. Wilson, *Sawdust Trails*, 2.
36. Ibid., 2.
37. Ibid., 25.

Chapter 5 - The Banker's Wife [pages 45-55]

1. Bliss, Hope, biographical sketch, "Bliss Family Records, 1869-1949"; 1860 U.S. Census for Wareham, Plymouth County, Massachusetts.
2. Duane Bliss, in his Bancroft interview, wrote that he had managed the Lindhorn & Hearst mill in Dayton. However, there is no record that such a mill ever existed. But J. Wells Kelly, editor of the 1863 *Second Directory of Nevada Territory*,

described the Landauer & Hirschman mill in Dayton, and that is likely the one Bliss intended to name.
3. Ibid.
4. Ibid., 174.
5. Browne, *A Peep at Washoe and Washoe Revisited*, 66.
6. James, *The Roar and the Silence*, 68.
7. Lord, *Comstock Mining and Miners*, 416.
8. The earliest public notice of the Almarin B. Paul Bank occurred in the *Virginia Evening Bulletin* on July 21, 1863. The bank's hours were listed along with those of other banks in a "Notice of Hours" advertisement; Stanley, *A Guide to Gold Hill, Nevada*, n.p.
9. Blauvelt, W. H., "Banking," in *History of Nevada*, Sam Davis, ed., vol. 1, 624-626.
10. *Gold Hill Daily News*, 01/02/1864 and 01/31/1865; Ansari, Mary B. *Comstock Place Names: The Names of Storey County, Nevada*, 15.
11. "Massachusetts Marriages, 1841-1915," Tobey and Pope, *Tobey (Tobie, Toby) Genealogy;* http://www.familysearch.org
12. Brown, *A Peep at Washoe and Washoe Revisited*, 178-179.
13. Wheeler and Bliss, *Tahoe Heritage*, 10-13. This letter from the new Mrs. Duane Bliss to her aunt in Massachusetts is cited in the above book as being owned by the Bliss family. It was copied and typed for preservation purposes in 1949. The current whereabouts of the original letter is unknown.
14. James, Ronald, and C. Elizabeth Raymond, Eds., *Comstock Women*, 304; Collins, Charles, ed., *Mercantile Guide and Directory for Virginia City, Gold Hill, Silver City and American City, 1864-65*.
15. Doten, Alfred. *The Journals of Alfred Doten, 1849-1903*, vol. 1, 717.
16. Wheeler and Bliss, *Tahoe Heritage*, 10-13.
17. Ibid.
18. James and Raymond, eds., *Comstock Women*, "The Advantages of Ladies' Society," 180-181.
19. *Gold Hill Daily News*, 10/13/1863.
20. James and Raymond, eds., *Comstock Women*, "The Advantages of Ladies' Society," 179-180; Stanley, *Guide to Gold Hill*, n.p.
21. Smith, Grant H., *History of the Comstock Lode, 1850-1920*, 232.
22. Tobey, Rufus Babcock, and Charles Henry Pope, *Tobey Genealogy*, 209.
23. Doten, Alf, *The Journals of Alfred Doten, 1849-1903*, 812, 813.
24. Davis, *History of Nevada*, vol. 2, 675.

NOTES

Chapter 6 - The Bank Ring [pages 57-66]

1. Doten, Alf, *The Journals of Alfred Doten, 1849-1903*, 830.
2. *Gold Hill Daily News*, "Funeral Obsequies," 04/17/1865.
3. Lyman, George D. *Ralston's Ring: California Plunders the Comstock Lode*, 17-18.
4. Makley, Michael J. *The Infamous King of the Comstock: William Sharon and the Gilded Age in the West*, 12-13; Drury, Wells, *An Editor on the Comstock*, 35.
5. Makley, *Infamous King of the Comstock*, 15.
6. Lyman, *Ralston's Ring*, 17-18; Marye, George Thomas, *From '49 to '83 in California and Nevada*, 87; Makley, *Infamous King of the Comstock*, 214 fn. 17; Tilton, Cecil G., *William Chapman Ralston, Courageous Builder*, 141.
7. Goodwin, C. C. *As I Remember Them*, 127.
8. Ibid.
9. Lord, *Comstock Mining and Miners*, 244-245; Blauvelt, "Banking," in *History of Nevada*, Sam Davis, ed., vol. 1, 628-630; Kroninger, Robert H., *Sarah and the Senator*, 17; Marye, *From '49 to '83 in California and Nevada*, 84.
10. Blauvelt, "Banking," in *History of Nevada*, Sam Davis, ed., vol. 1, 630.
11. *Gold Hill Daily News*, 05/01/1865.
12. Ibid.
13. Ibid.; Blauvelt, "Banking," in *History of Nevada*, Sam Davis, ed., vol. 1, 630.
14. Bancroft, "Duane L. Bliss: Data Concerning the Virginia & Truckee Railroad."
15. Storey County, NV Recorder, "Book Y of Deeds," page 110; "Book S of Deeds," page 458; "Book V of Deeds," page 665.
16. Ibid., "Book Z of Deeds," pages 284, 393.
17. Lavender, David. *Nothing Seemed Impossible: William C. Ralston and Early San Francisco*, 168.
18. Lyman, *Ralston's Ring*, 3.
19. Lord, *Comstock Mining and Miners*, 416.
20. For Ralston's early life, see Lyman, *Ralston's Ring*, and Lavender, *Nothing Seemed Impossible*.
21. Lavender, *Nothing Seemed Impossible*, 178-182.
22. Ibid., 182.
23. For details on the Comstock mining recession of 1865-1869, see Dana, Julian, *The Man Who Built San Francisco: A Study of Ralston's Journey with Banners*, 205-206; Lavender, *Nothing Seemed Impossible*, 183-187; Lyman, *Ralston's Ring*, 54-56.

Notes

24. Lord, *Comstock Mining and Miners*, 416.
25. *San Francisco Chronicle*, 02/18/1872.
26. Davis, *History of Nevada*, vol. 1, 413.
27. Lavender, *Nothing Seemed Impossible*, 187.
28. Dana, *The Man Who Built San Francisco*, 206.
29. James, *The Roar and the Silence*, 78-79.
30. Lord, *Comstock Mining and Miners*, 246-247.

Chapter 7 - The Virginia & Truckee Railroad [pages 67-79]

1. Bridges, Hal, "The Robber Baron Concept in American History," *The Business History Review*, 1-13.
2. "Yellow Jacket Silver Mining Company Records, 1859-1906, vol. 1, "Minutes of meeting of July 9, 1866."
3. Goodwin, *As I Remember Them*, 56-60.
4. Ibid., 58.
5. Ibid., 103-106.
6. Ibid., 126-131.
7. Goodwin, *Goodwin's Weekly*, "Death of D. L. Bliss," 12/28/1907, 4.
8. Tobey, Rufus Babcock, and Charles Henry Pope, *Tobey Genealogy*, 209; Storey County, NV Recorder, "Book 27 of Deeds," page 316.
9. Mathews, *Ten Years in Nevada*, 198.
10. James, *The Roar and the Silence*, 79 – 80; Myrick, *Railroads of Nevada and Eastern California*, 42-44.
11. Lyman, *Ralston's Ring*, 84, 115.
12. Lord, *Comstock Mining and Miners*, 249-250.
13. Wurm, Ted, and Harre W. Demoro, *The Silver Short Line: A History of the Virginia & Truckee Railroad*, 34; Tilton, *William Chapman Ralston, Courageous Builder*, 149; Myrick, David F., *Railroads of Nevada and Eastern California*, vol. 1, 136-137; Drew, Stephen, V&T Railroad scholar, email to the author, 08/01/2014.
14. Ibid.; Jeffers, Jim, "Stockholders and Dividends of the Virginia & Truckee Railroad From 1969-1900," 2-6; Tilton, *William Chapman Ralston, Courageous Builder*, 153.
15. Wurm and Demoro, *The Silver Short Line*, 32; Lord, *Comstock Mining and Miners*, 251.
16. Ibid., 251, 253.
17. Drew, V&T Railroad scholar, email to the author, 08/01/2014; Lord, *Comstock Mining and Miners*, 252.

Notes

18. Bancroft, "Duane L. Bliss: Data Concerning the Virginia & Truckee Railroad."
19. Gillis, William R., ed., *The Nevada Directory for 1868-9.*
20. "Yellow Jacket Silver Mining Company Records, 1859-1906, vol.1."
21. Lyman, *Ralston's Ring,* 112.
22. Bancroft, "Duane L. Bliss: Data Concerning the Virginia & Truckee Railroad."
23. Bliss, Hope, biographical sketch, "Bliss Family Records, 1869-1949;" *Pittsfield, MA Sun,* 03/04/1869.
24. The biennial *Official Register of the United States*, published from 1816 through 1959, lists all Federal employees. The edition that covers 1869 does not include the name D. L., or Duane L., Bliss, nor is there any other discoverable information that links him to the U.S. Mint in either San Francisco or Carson City. Likewise, his name does not appear as a resident of San Francisco in the 1868 or 1869 editions of Langley's *The San Francisco Directory.*
25. Jeffers, "Stockholders and Dividends," 2-3; Bancroft, "Duane L. Bliss: Data Concerning the Virginia & Truckee Railroad;" Drew, V&T Railroad scholar, email to the author, 08/01/2014.
26. Dangberg, Grace. *Conflict on the Carson: A Study of Water Litigation in Western Nevada*, 310.
27. *Nevada Territorial Enterprise*, 06/05/1869.
28. *Gold Hill Daily News*, 09/28/1869.
29. Bancroft, "Duane L. Bliss: Data Concerning the Virginia & Truckee Railroad;" Makley, *Infamous King of the Comstock,* 52; Knowles, Constance Darrow, "A History of Lumbering in the Truckee Basin from 1856-1936," 29.
30. Beebe, Lucius, and Charles Clegg, *Steamcars to the Comstock,* 106; Lord, *Comstock Mining and Miners,* 253.
31. Doten, *The Journals of Alfred Doten, 1849-1903*, vol. 1, 1066.
32. Lord, *Comstock Mining and Miners,* 254-255.
33. Kneiss, Gilbert H., *Bonanza Railroads*, 69.
34. Smith**,** *History of the Comstock Lode, 1850-1920,* 127.
35. Lord, *Comstock Mining and Miners,* 111; original letter of Bliss's appointment to the V&T board of directors in possession of the Bliss family.
36. U.S. Bureau of Census, 1860, for Virginia City, NV. "Inhabitants."
37. County Directory Publishing Co., *Storey, Ormsby, Washoe and Lyon Counties Directory, 1871-72.*
38. Galloway, John Debo, *Early Engineering Works Contributory to the Comstock*, 55.

Notes

Chapter 8- The Carson & Tahoe Lumber & Fluming Company [pages 81-91]

1. Lyman, *Ralston's Ring,* 89; Ratay, *Pioneers of the Ponderosa,* 57.
2. Makley, Michael, personal correspondence in possession of the author.
3. Wilson, Dick, *Sawdust Trails in the Truckee Basin,* 72 (Appendix #61); Scott, E. B., *The Saga of Lake Tahoe, Vol. 1,* 294. (Note: Scott's 2-volume history of Lake Tahoe is pleasurable reading, and a real service for those who want an overview of the history of every community around the lake. However, as a reference work it must be cited cautiously because of numerous factual errors, and the author's penchant for including dialogue that he or a personal source recollected from 50+ years earlier.)
4. Bancroft, "Duane L. Bliss: Data Concerning the Virginia & Truckee Railroad."
5. Scott, *The Saga of Lake Tahoe, Vol. 1,* 294.
6. Angel, *History of Nevada,* 626.
7. Lord, *Comstock Mining and Miners,* 256-257; Angel, *History of Nevada,* 191; Smith, *History of the Comstock Lode,* 257; Wright, *The Big Bonanza,* 178.
8. Scott, *The Saga of Lake Tahoe, Vol. 1,* 491, fn. 279.
9. Ibid.
10. Wilson, *Sawdust Trails,* (Appendix #s 117, 118, 31, 96).
11. Scott, *The Saga of Lake Tahoe, Vol. 1,* 270; Galloway, *Early Engineering Works Contributory to the Comstock,* 88.
12. "Carson and Tahoe Lumber and Fluming Company Records." In January 1882 the company would be recapitalized at $2,080,000
13. Bancroft, "Duane L. Bliss: Data Concerning the Virginia & Truckee Railroad." An 1882 re-incorporation of the company showed the following outstanding stock distribution: D. L. Bliss, 34.6%; D. O. Mills, 30.8%; H. M. Yerington, 29.6%; W. D. Tobey, 5.0% (possibly the shares initially held by James Rigby.) Source: "Carson and Tahoe Lumber and Fluming Company Records," box 3, file 2/1, "Company Papers."
14. Wilson, *Sawdust Trails,* 11.
15. Scott, *The Saga of Lake Tahoe, Vol. 1,* 265.
16. Ibid., 270.
17. Twain, Mark, *Nevada Territorial Enterprise,* 02/12/1864; Twain, *The Innocents Abroad,* Ch. XX.
18. Scott, *The Saga of Lake Tahoe, Vol. 1,* 267-270.
19. *Daily Alta California* newspaper, 7/07/1859.
20. Cross, Ralph Herbert, *Early Inns of California, 1844-1869,* 237.

Notes

21. Glenbrook House Guest Ledgers, vols. 1, 2.
22. Makley, *Infamous King of the Comstock*, 66.
23. "Glenbrook House Records, 1868-1869," 07/19/1868, 7.
24. Scott, *The Saga of Lake Tahoe, Vol. 1*, 269.
25. Wheeler and Bliss, *Tahoe Heritage*, 26-27; "Carson and Tahoe Lumber and Fluming Company Records," box 3, file 2/1, "Company Papers."
26. Ibid., 14; "V&T Railroad Directory of 1873;" Moreno, Richard, *A Short History of Carson City*, chs. 1, 2.
27. Uhlhorn, John F. *The Virginia and Truckee Railroad Directory, 1873-74,* Hathi Trust Digital Library, http://babel.hathitrust.org/cgi/pt?id= njp.32101078165972;view=1up;seq=63, pps. 12, 345, 356; Wheeler and Bliss, *Tahoe Heritage,* 14; Drew, V&T Railroad scholar, email to the author, 08/01/2014.
28. Frady, Steve, "Duane Bliss and his Lake Tahoe Railroad," *Las Vegas Review-Journal,* "Nevadan" magazine, 05/29/1977; Wheeler and Bliss, *Tahoe Heritage,* 47.

Chapter 9 - Bust and Boom [pages 93-100]

1. James, *The Roar and the Silence*, 102-106.
2. Bliss, Hope, Biographical Sketch, "Bliss Family Records, 1869-1949."
3. Two of the most respected sources on Comstock history disagree on how and who actually discovered the Big Bonanza. Lord, *Comstock Mining and Miners*, 309, wrote that the Big Bonanza began when James Fair began following a "thin seam of ore" in the Consolidated Virginia mine. Smith, *History of the Comstock Lode, 1850-1920*, 148, 150, 152, disputes Lord's version. He wrote that it was "a vein or fissure seven feet wide," not a thin seam. Smith contends that the "thin seam" story came directly from Fair, who claimed he had followed the seam "like a bloodhound." However, Smith contends that Fair was not even working in the mine until *after* the Big Bonanza discovery. Lord's version came from an interview he had with Fair later in Fair's life; and the man often referred to as "Slippery Jim" was not above trying to steal the limelight. Thus, Smith's version, taken from contemporary newspaper accounts and used in this book, is more reliable.
4. Lord, *Comstock Mining and Miners,* 308-309.
5. Smith, *History of the Comstock Lode, 1850-1920*, 148-152.
6. *Nevada Territorial Enterprise,* 10/22/1873.
7. Smith, *History of the Comstock Lode, 1850-1920*, 155.
8. Lord, *Comstock Mining and Miners,* 315.

NOTES

9. Ibid., 319-320.
10. Ibid., 316.
11. "Mackay Silver Collection," University of Nevada, Reno http://www.unr.edu/keck/mackay-silver-collection
12. Makley, *Infamous King of the Comstock*, 93; Doten, *The Journals of Alfred Doten, 1849-1903*, vol. 1, 1218.
13. Makley, *Infamous King of the Comstock*, 141.
14. James, Ronald M. "Online Nevada Encyclopedia," http://onlinenevada.org/william_sharon.
15. James, *The Roar and the Silence*, 109.
16. Smith, *History of the Comstock Lode, 1850-1920*, 159-160; James, *The Roar and the Silence*, 110.
17. Lyman, *Ralston's Ring*, 250.
18. *Nevada State Journal*, 08/27/1875.
19. Wilson, *Sawdust Trails*, 19-20, 74.
20. Stollery, David J., *More Tales of Tahoe: Lake Tahoe History, Legend and Description*, 7-8.
21. Wilson, *Sawdust Trails*, 48.

Chapter 10 - Building a Lumbering Monolith [pages 101-119]

1. Strong, Douglas H. *Tahoe, An Environmental History*, 25; Wilson, *Sawdust Trails*, 49. Many sources say C&TL&FC eventually accumulated 50,000 acres of timberlands, but a few, such as Truckee Meadows lumbering expert Dick Wilson, put that figure at 80,000 acres.
2. Ibid., 26.
3. Lindstrom, Susan G., "Archaeological Survey of 1,830 Acres," 25.
4. Scott, *The Saga of Lake Tahoe, Vol. 1*, 171.
5. *Gold Hill Daily News*, 08/05/1875.
6. Ibid.; Smith, Grant, "The Miscellaneous Documents of the House of Representatives for the First Session of the Forty-Seventh Congress, 1881—'82," Vol. 16, No. 51, page 351, Washington DC: Government Printing Office, 1882.
7. Scott, *The Saga of Lake Tahoe, Vol. 1*, 213; Strong, *Tahoe, An Environmental History*, 29.
8. Lindstrom, "Archaeological Survey of 1,830 Acres," 32-33.
9. Lord, *Comstock Mining and Miners*, 325.
10. Ibid., 326-328.
11. Goodwin, *As I remember Them*, 161.
12. Smith, *History of the Comstock Lode, 1850-1920*, 193, fn 32.

Notes

13. Hill, Leslie Kibler, "Historical Archaeology of Ethnic Woodcutters in the Carson Range," (Master's thesis, University of Nevada, Reno, 1987), 22.
14. Wheeler and Bliss, *Tahoe Heritage*, 29; Scott, *The Saga of Lake Tahoe, Vol. 1*, 274.
15. Wilson, *Sawdust Trails*, 6.
16. Lane, Don, U.S. Forest Service, private communication to the author, April 2012.
17. Smith, *History of the Comstock Lode*, 96, 387.
18. Solury, Theresa E., "Everlasting Remembrance: The Archaeology of 19th Century Chinese Labor in the Western Lumber Industry," (Master's thesis, University of Nevada, Reno, 2004), 17, 23; Galloway, *Early Engineering Works Contributory to the Comstock*, 100.
19. Bliss, Hope, "The Career of Duane L. Bliss," 2A.
20. "Carson and Tahoe Lumber and Fluming Company Records, 1864-1946," box 7, file 6, "Vouchers, 1875."
21. Scott, *The Saga of Lake Tahoe, Vol. 1*, 300-301.
22. Myrick, *Railroads of Nevada and Eastern California*, 422.
23. Ibid., Scott, *The Saga of Lake Tahoe, Vol. 1*, 273; Bancroft, "Duane L. Bliss: Data Concerning the Virginia & Truckee Railroad."
24. Myrick, *Railroads of Nevada and Eastern California*, 422; Galloway, *Early Engineering Works Contributory to the Comstock*, 96-97.
25. Ibid.
26. Scott, *The Saga of Lake Tahoe, Vol. 1*, 273.
27. Wilson, *Sawdust Trails*, 39, 41.
28. Scott, *The Saga of Lake Tahoe, Vol. 1*, 403, 405; Wheeler and Bliss, *Tahoe Heritage*. 29-30.
29. Scott, *The Saga of Lake Tahoe, Vol. 1*, 391, 393, 416-417.
30. Smith, *History of the Comstock Lode, 1850-1920*, 197, 199.
31. Ibid., 198.
32. Wright, (writing as Dan De Quille) *History the Comstock Silver Lode & Mines*, 174.
33. *Gold Hill Daily News*, 03/01/1867.
34. Knowles, "A History of Lumbering in the Truckee Basin from 1856-1936;" Pisani, Donald J., "Lost Parkland: Lumbering & Park Proposals in the Tahoe-Truckee Basin," *Journal of Forest History*, vol. 21, No. 1, Jan. 1977, 9; Wilson, *Sawdust Trails*, 49; *Carson Morning Appeal*, 10/12/1880.
35. *Nevada Territorial Enterprise*, 11/03/1877, 11/04/1877, 11/13/1877; *Sacramento Daily Union*, 11/03/1877.
36. Scott, *The Saga of Lake Tahoe, Vol. 1*, 109, 111.

Notes

37. *Carson Morning Appeal*, 10/25/1879; Rocha, Guy, "Myth #79 – Nineteenth Century Presidential Visits to Lake Tahoe and Nevada," http://nsla.nevadaculture.org/index.php?option= com_content&task=view&id=751&Itemid=418.
38. *Carson Morning Appeal*, 10/26/1879.
39. Ibid., 10/27/1879.
40. Rocha, "Myth #79 – Nineteenth Century Presidential Visits to Lake Tahoe and Nevada," http://nsla.nevadaculture.org/index.php?option= com_content&task=view&id=751&Itemid=418.
41. Scott, *The Saga of Lake Tahoe, Vol. 1,* 405; Scott, *The Saga of Lake Tahoe, Vol. II,* 181.

Chapter 11 - The End of an Era [pages 121-131]

1. Gorham, Harry M., *My Memories of the Comstock*, 36-40
2. Wheeler and Bliss, *Tahoe Heritage,* 47; Frady, Steve. "Duane Bliss and his Lake Tahoe Railroad," *Nevadan* magazine, 3; Moreno, *A Short History of Carson City*, 61 – 62; Farley, Cory, "KNBR Reveals Historic Mansions," *Reno Gazette-Journal*, 01/27/2005.
3. "Bliss Family Records, 1869-1949," box 2, files 75 and 88, *Carson City Appeal*, 03/10/1878.
4. Smith, *History of the Comstock Lode, 1850-1920,* 229.
5. Ibid., 230; Edwards, Jerome, "Comstock Lode," Online Nevada Encyclopedia, Nevada Humanities, http://onlinenevada.org/comstock_lode.
6. Strong, *Tahoe, An Environmental History,* 30.
7. Lord, *Comstock Mining and Miners,* 413.
8. Ferrell, Mallory Hope. "Slim Princess," 1-5.
9. Ibid.
10. "Southern Development Company of Nevada, Guide to the Records," Box 2, files 2/1, 3/1, 4/4.
11. Ibid.
12. Strong, *Tahoe, An Environmental History,* 29.
13. Galloway, *Early Engineering Works Contributory to the Comstock,* 93.
14. Wheeler and Bliss, *Tahoe Heritage,* 39; "Carson and Tahoe Lumber and Fluming Company Records, 1864-1946," box 3, file 2/7.
15. Wheeler and Bliss, *Tahoe Heritage,* 48; Scott, *The Saga of Lake Tahoe, Vol. 1,* 285; Bliss, Hope, "The Career of Duane L. Bliss," 10.
16. Scott, *The Saga of Lake Tahoe, Vol. 1,* 287.
17. Ibid., 284-285; *Carson City Appeal,* 10/12/1887.
18. *Daily Alta California* newspaper, 06/10/1887.

NOTES

19. *Springfield, MA, Republican,* 08/11/1888.
20. Wilson, *Sawdust Trails,* 49.

Chapter 12 - Becoming a Conservationist [pages 133-147]

1. Pisani, Donald J, "Lost Parkland: Lumbering & Park Proposals in the Tahoe-Truckee Basin," *Journal of Forest History*, vol. 21, No. 1, January 1977, 6.
2. Wright, (writing as Dan De Quille), *The Big Bonanza*, 177.
3. Strong, Douglas H., quoting Muir in "Preservation Efforts at Lake Tahoe, 1880-1980," *Journal of Forest History,* vol. 25, April 1981, 78; Muir, John, *Wilderness World of John Muir*, 231.
4. Nash, Roderick, *Wilderness and the American Mind*, vii, 23-24.
5. Gilpin, William. *Mission of the North American People, Geographical, Social and Political*, 99.
6. Pisani, "Lost Parkland," *Journal of Forest History*, vol. 21, No. 1, January 1977, 9.
7. U.S. Department of Agriculture, Forest Service, "Highlights in the History of Forest Conservation," 1.
8. Ibid., 7-16.
9. Ibid., 13-14.
10. Strong, Douglas H., *Dreamers and Defenders: American Conservationists*, 3.
11. Ibid.
12. Pisani, "Lost Parkland," *Journal of Forest History*, vol. 21, No. 1, January 1977, 80.
13. Nash, *Wilderness and the American Mind*, 161-180.
14. Ibid., 180.
15. Wilson, *Sawdust Trails,* 72 (Appendix #61); Scott, E. B., *The Saga of Lake Tahoe, Vol. 1,* 294.
16. Gruell, George E., *Fire in Sierra Nevada Forests: A Photographic Interpretation of Ecological Change Since 1849.*
17. Strong, *Tahoe, An Environmental History,* 30; Lane, Don, personal correspondence to the author, December 2011.
18. United States Public Lands Commission, *Report of the Public Lands Commission*, 605-606, 617.
19. Bliss, Hope, biographical sketch, "Bliss Family Records, 1869-1949."
20. Bliss, Hope. "The Career of Duane L. Bliss in Nevada."
21. Lane, personal correspondence to the author, December 2011.
22. United States Public Lands Commission, *Report of the Public Lands Commission*, 616.
23. Lane, personal correspondence to the author, December 2011.

Notes

24. Scott, *The Saga of Lake Tahoe, Vol. 1*, 64-65.
25. Pisani, "Lost Parkland," *Journal of Forest History*, vol. 21, No. 1, January 1977, 14. (Note: Two of the most comprehensive sources on the issues of conservation and creating parkland in the Tahoe Basin are Douglas H. Strong's "Preservation Efforts at Lake Tahoe, 1880-1980." *Journal of Forest History*, vol. 25, April 1981, cited in note 21; and Donald J. Pisani's article, cited here.)
26. "Carson and Tahoe Lumber and Fluming Company Records, 1864-1946," Box 4, file 61; Box 7, files 57, 72, 95; Box 8, file 16; Box 12, file 26; Box 13.
27. D. L. Bliss, letter to John Muir, "John Muir Correspondence, Holt-Atherton Digital Collections, http://digitalcollections.pacific.edu/cdm/compoundobject/collection/muirletters/id/ 2247/ rec/1.
28. "Carson and Tahoe Lumber and Fluming Company Records, 1864-1946," Book 4, #874-75.
29. Strong, "Preservation Efforts at Lake Tahoe, 1880 – 1980." *Journal of Forest History*, vol. 25, April 1981, 88.
30. Pisani, "Lost Parkland," *Journal of Forest History*, vol. 21, No. 1, January 1977, 14, 14-15.
31. Ibid., 16.
32. Strong, "Preservation Efforts at Lake Tahoe, 1880 – 1980," *Journal of Forest History*, 85.
33. Ibid., 92-93.
34. Taylor, Alan H. "Forest Changes Since Euro-American Settlement and Ecosystem Restoration in the Lake Tahoe Basin, USA," 14-15.
35. Lane, Don, private correspondence to the author.

Chapter 13 - The Grand Old Man of Lake Tahoe [pages 149-158]

1. "Bio: True Story" website, A&E Television Networks, http://www.biography.com/ people/andrew-carnegie-9238756
2. Wheeler and Bliss, *Tahoe Heritage*, 48.
3. "Bliss Family Records, 1869-1949," box 6, file 351.
4. Ibid., box 2, files 75 and 88.
5. Earl, Phillip, "The Last of the Old Tahoe Fleet," 30; Scott, *The Saga of Lake Tahoe, Vol. 1*, 429-433; Strong, *Tahoe, An Environmental History*, 34.
6. *Carson Morning Appeal*, 06/25/1896.
7. *San Francisco Call*, 06/19/1896.
8. *Sacramento Record-Union*, 08/23/1898.

NOTES

9. *Encyclopedia of San Francisco*, "Bliss, Walter Danforth," http://sfhistoryencyclopedia.com/articles/b/blissWalter.html.
10. Ibid.
11. Wheeler and Bliss, *Tahoe Heritage*, 52-53; Scott, *The Saga of Lake Tahoe, Vol. 1*, 436-437.
12. "Bliss Family Records, 1869-1949," box 1, file 52; box 2, file 83.
13. Ibid., box 1, file 22; box 2, file 93.
14. Ibid., box 2, file 72.
15. *San Francisco Call*, 02/27/1897.
16. Ibid., 12/13/1898.
17. McKeon, Owen F., *The Railroads and Steamers of Lake Tahoe*, 9.
18. *San Francisco Call*, 06/12/1900; Scott, *The Saga of Lake Tahoe, Vol. 1*, 41.
19. Wheeler and Bliss, *Tahoe Heritage*, 60-61.
20. Ibid., 61; *Sacramento Record-Union*, 02/26/1897.
21. "Bliss Family Records, 1869-1949," box 6, file 17.
22. *San Francisco Call*, 11/20/1901.
23. Scott, *The Saga of Lake Tahoe, Vol. 1*, 42; Strong, *Tahoe, An Environmental History*, 34-35; Wheeler and Bliss, *Tahoe Heritage*, 54.
24. James, George Wharton, *The Lake of the Sky—Lake Tahoe*, 118.

Chapter 14 -Innkeepers to the World [pages 159-166]

1. James, *The Lake of the Sky—Lake Tahoe*, 199-200.
2. Scott, *The Saga of Lake Tahoe, Vol. 1*, 289.
3. Ibid., 51; Wheeler and Bliss, *Tahoe Heritage*, 56.
4. *San Francisco Call*, adv., 05/18/1902.
5. "Tahoe Tavern, Lake Tahoe, Cal., 1904" brochure; James, *The Lake of the Sky—Lake Tahoe*, 143-144.
6. Ibid., 143.
7. "Tahoe Tavern, Lake Tahoe, Cal., 1904" brochure.
8. Scott, *The Saga of Lake Tahoe, Vol. 1*, 51.
9. Vogel, Ed, "Remembering a basket weaver's magic;" *Las Vegas Review-Journal*; Scott, *The Saga of Lake Tahoe, Vol. 1*, 54-55.
10. "Bliss Family Records, 1869-1949," box 6, file 17.
11. Ibid., box 1, file 66; Wilson, *Sawdust Trails*, 64.
12. "Bliss Family Records, 1869-1949," box 1, file 2, box 2, file 78.
13. Knowles, "A History of Lumbering in the Truckee Basin from 1856-1936," 36.
14. *Carson City Appeal*, 11/08/1903.

Notes

15. "Bliss Family Records, 1869-1949," box 4, file 281. (Note: The Glenbrook Improvement Company incorporation records indicate that P. J. Pomin was one of the investors. A man named E. J. (Ernest John) Pomin was the captain of the *Tahoe*, and had worked for the Bliss family for more than four decades. It is probable that the papers contained a typographical error, and that it was Captain E. J. Pomin, not P. J., who was one of the investors in the corporation.)
16. Scott, *The Saga of Lake Tahoe, Vol. 1*, 267; Wheeler and Bliss, *Tahoe Heritage*, 80.
17. Ibid.
18. *San Francisco Call*, 05/23/1907; Wheeler and Bliss, *Tahoe Heritage*, 81.
19. James, *The Lake of the Sky—Lake Tahoe*, 255.

Chapter 15. - A Life Well Lived [pages 167-175]

1. *San Francisco Chronicle*, 12/26/1907.
2. *San Francisco Call*, 12/24/1907.
3. "Bliss Family Records, 1869 – 1949," box 21, file 440.
4. All details about Duane Sr. and William's visit to the family properties, and the events that occurred during the trip, from Wheeler and Bliss, *Tahoe Heritage*, 81-84, and from the many newspaper obituaries that followed Duane Sr.'s death.
5. *Carson Morning Appeal*, 01/23/1907.
6. *San Francisco Examiner*, 12/24/1907.
7. *Carson Morning Appeal*, 02/24/1907; *Goodwin's Weekly*, "Death of D. L. Bliss," 12/28/1907, 4; *Sacramento Union*, "Sudden Death," 02/24/1907; *San Francisco Call*, 12/24/1907; *Nevada Territorial Enterprise*, "Death of D. L Bliss," 12/25/1907
8. "Bliss Family Records, 1869-1949," box 2, file 122.
9. Ibid., box 1, file 17.
10. Bliss, Hope, "Career of Duane L. Bliss in Nevada," 7-8; Wheeler and Bliss, *Tahoe Heritage*, 98-99.
11. *Nevada State Journal*, 04/18/1925.
12. *Reno Evening Gazette*, 11/21/1938, 04/22/1939.
13. Scott, *The Saga of Lake Tahoe, Vol. 1*, 434, 425.
14. "Bliss Family Records, 1869-1949," box 2, file 7.
15. Wheeler and Bliss, *Tahoe Heritage*, 105.
16. Ibid., 130 – 134, as quoted from *San Francisco* magazine, June 1967.
17. Ibid., 134-135; personal interview with Bill Bliss.
18. Bliss, William W. "William W. Bliss Manuscript, Maps and Drawings Collection, 1861 – 1955," Folder 3, "Section Map showing lands purchased by George Whittell." Following the deaths of D. L. Bliss, Sr. in 1907, and his wife Elizabeth

in 1921 who had inherited his half of all community property, the next three generations of the Bliss family abandoned, sold, traded, bartered and gifted various pieces of their C&TL&FC land to the extend that it makes a complete and accurate accounting of all the cut-over timberlands they inherited virtually impossible. Thus the remarks about the land on succeeding pages is the author's best attempt at a full and accurate account.

19. United States Public Lands Commission, *Report of the Public Lands Commission*, 605-606.
20. Strong, "Preservation Efforts at Lake Tahoe, 1880-1980," 91.
21. *Reno Evening Gazette*, 11/03/1937; 12/15/1937; Thunderbird Lodge Records, obtained from Bill Watson, Chief Executive Officer & Curator.
22. Ibid.
23. Carson and Tahoe Lumber and Fluming Company Records," "Certificate of Dissolution," box 3, series 2, "Company Papers."

Afterword [page 177]

1. Press Release, Comstock Mining Inc., 08/09/2012 http://www.comstockmining.com/news/press-releases?start=66
2, DeLong, Jeff, "Comstock Dig Begins," *Reno Gazette-Journal*, 08/09/2012, 1, 7.
3. Ibid.

BIBLIOGRAPHY

Primary Sources

MANUSCRIPTS, JOURNALS, DIARIES, RECORDS, DEEDS, AND CONTEMPORARY HISTORICAL ACCOUNTS

Angel, Myron, ed. *History of Nevada: with Illustrations and Biographical Sketches of its Prominent Men and Pioneers.* Oakland, CA: Thompson and West, 1881.

Bancroft, Hubert Howe. "Duane L. Bliss: Data Concerning the Virginia & Truckee Railroad, and Those Who Planned and Carried Out That Work." 1887. Mss. P-G 38, Bancroft Collection of Western and Latin Americana. Bancroft Library, University of California, Berkeley.

Benemann, William, ed. *A Year of Mud and Gold: San Francisco in Letters and Diaries, 1849-1850.* Lincoln: University of Nebraska Press, 1999.

Bliss Company Business Ledger, 1928-1937. In private hands.

Bliss, D. L. Letter to John Muir. "John Muir Correspondence: Letter from D. L. Bliss to John Muir, Aug. 29, 1899." Holt-Atherton Special Collections, Digital Collections, University of the Pacific, Stockton, CA.

"Bliss Family Records, 1869-1949." Collection 96-53. Special Collections Department, Mathewson-IGT Knowledge Center, University of Nevada, Reno.

Bliss, Hope. "The Career of Duane L. Bliss in Nevada." San Francisco: California Historical Society, early 1940s.

Bliss, John Homer. *Genealogy of the Bliss Family in America From About the Year 1550 to 1880.* Boston: J.H. Bliss (private printing) 1881. Ancestry.com.

Bliss, William. "William Bliss Business Log Book, 1831." Private communication, copy to author from Jane Benedict Phinney, Savoy, MA historian.

Bliss, William W. "William W. Bliss Manuscript, Maps and Drawings Collection, 1861-1955. Collection 97-24. Special Collections Department, Mathewson-IGT Knowledge Center, University of Nevada, Reno.

Bonstell, Cutler L. *A Woodside Reminiscence: As Told by "Grizzly" Ryder.* San Francisco: Paul Elder & Company, 1920.

BIBLIOGRAPHY

Brooks, Sarah Merriam. *Across the Isthmus to California in '52.* San Francisco: C. A. Murdock, 1894.

Browne, J. Ross. *A Peep at Washoe and Washoe Revisited.* 1864. Rep., Balboa Island, CA: Paisano Press, 1959.

"California Mortuary and Cemetery Records, 1801-1932." Ancestry.com.

"California State Census, Tuolumne County, CA, 1852." Ancestry.com.

Carr, John. *Pioneer Days in California: Historical and Personal Sketches.* Eureka, CA: Times, Publishing Co., 1891.

"Carson and Tahoe Lumber and Fluming Company Records." Nevada State Archives, Carson City, NV.

"Carson and Tahoe Lumber and Fluming Company Records, 1864 – 1946." Collection NC-72, Special Collections Department, Mathewson-IGT Knowledge Center, University of Nevada, Reno.

Child, Hamilton. *Gazetteer of Berkshire County, Mass., 1725-1885, Part First.* Syracuse, NY: *Syracuse Journal,* 1885.

Clapp, Louise Amelia Knapp. *The Shirley Letters from the California Mines, 1851-1852.* (Reprinted from the *Marysville, CA Herald.*) New York: Alfred A. Knopf, 1949.

Collins, Charles, ed. *Mercantile Guide and Directory for Virginia City, Gold Hill, Silver City and American City, 1864- 65.* Virginia City, NV: Agnew & Deffenbach, 1865.

County Directory Publishing Co. *Storey, Ormsby, Washoe & Lyon Counties Directory, 1871-72.* Sacramento: H. S. Crocker & Co., 1871.

Dayton, Elinor Bliss, and Arthur Bliss Dayton. *Bliss and Holmes Descendants: Genealogical Data and Biographical Sketches of the Descendants of Ephriam Bliss of Savoy, Mass. and Israel Holmes of Waterbury, Conn and Related Families.* New Haven, CT: New Haven Colony Historical Society, 1961.

Doten, Alfred. *The Journals of Alfred Doten, 1849 – 1903.* Vol. 1-3. Walter Van Tilburg Clark, ed. Reno: University of Nevada Press, 1973.

Gillis, William R., ed. *The Nevada Directory for 1868-9.* San Francisco: M. D. Carr, 1868.

Gilpin, William. *Mission of the North American People, Geographical, Social and Political.* Philadelphia, J.B. Lippincott, 1873.

Glenbrook House Guest Ledgers. Vols. 1 & 2. In private hands.

"Glenbrook House Records, 1868-1869." Collection NC1190, Special Collections Department, Mathewson-IGT Knowledge Center, University of Nevada, Reno.

Jeffers, Jim Jr. "Stockholders and Dividends of the Virginia & Truckee Railroad From 1869-1900." Collection 95-25, Special Collections Department, Mathewson-IGT Knowledge Center, University of Nevada, Reno.

BIBLIOGRAPHY

Johnson, Theodore Taylor. *Sights in the Gold Region, and Scenes by the Way*. New York: Baker, 1849.

Kelly, J. Wells, ed. *First Directory of Nevada Territory*. 1862. Rep., Los Gatos, CA: Talisman Press, 1962.

---. *Second Directory of Nevada Territory*. 1863. San Francisco: Valentine & Co., 1863.

Knowles, Constance Darrow. "A History of Lumbering in the Truckee Basin from 1856-1936." Unpublished Report from WPA Official Project #9512373 for the California Forest & Range Experiment Station. 1942. Nevada Historical Society, Reno.

Langley, Henry G. *The San Francisco Directory for the Year 1868*. San Francisco: S. D. Valentine & Sons, 1868.

---. *The San Francisco Directory for the Year 1869*. San Francisco: S. D. Valentine & Sons, 1869.

Lord, Eliot. *Comstock Mining and Miners*. Unites States Geological Survey. Washington DC: Government Printing Office, 1883.

Mathews, M. M. *Ten Years in Nevada, or Life on the Pacific Coast*. 1880. Rep., Lincoln: University of Nebraska Press, 1985.

"Massachusetts Marriages, 1841-1915, Wareham, MA." Salt Lake City: Church of Jesus Christ of Latter-day Saints, http://www.familysearch.org

Miller, H. E. *History of the Town of Savoy*. West Cummington, MA: Self Published, 1879.

Powell, John J. *Nevada: The Land of Silver*. San Francisco: Bacon & Co., 1876.

San Mateo County Historical Association. "Woodside Store Manuscript Collection." Redwood City, CA.

"Southern Development Company of Nevada, Guide to the Records." Collection NC74, Special Collections Department, Mathewson-IGT Knowledge Center, University of Nevada, Reno.

Storey County, NV Recorders Office. "Grantee Deeds." Virginia City, NV.

"Tahoe Tavern, Lake Tahoe, Cal., 1904." Lake Tahoe Pamphlets, 1895-1935. Collection 91-17 to 27. Special Collections Department, Mathewson-IGT Knowledge Center, University of Nevada, Reno.

Taylor, Alan H. "Forest Changes Since Euro-American Settlement and Ecosystem Restoration in the Lake Tahoe Basin, USA." Research paper in "Restoring Fire-adapted Ecosystems: Proceedings of the 2005 National Silviculture Workshop." US Forest Service, Washington DC. http://www.treesearch.fs.fed.us/pubs/25888

Thunderbird Lodge Records. Thunderbird Lodge Preservation Society, Incline Village, NV.

Bibliography

Tobey, Rufus Babcock, and Charles Henry Pope. *Tobey (Tobie, Toby) Genealogy: Thomas, of Sandwich and James, of Kittery and Their Descendants.* Boston: Charles H. Pope, 1905.

Twain, Mark. *The Innocents Abroad.* eBook, Project Gutenberg, 2006. http://www.gutenberg.org/files/3176/3176-h/3176-h.htm

---. *Roughing It.* Hartford, CT: American Publishing, 1873. Open Library.org.

Uhlhorn, John F. *The Virginia and Truckee Railroad Directory, 1873-74.* Hathi Trust Digital Library.

United States Bureau of the Census. 1870, for Virginia City, Nevada. Ancestry.com.

United States Civil Service Commission. *Official Register of the United States.* Washington D.C.: U.S. Government Printing Office, 1869.

United States Public Lands Commission. *Report of the Public Lands Commission Created by the Act of March 3, 1879, Relating to Public Lands in the Western Portion of the United States and to the Operation of Existing Land Laws.* 1880. Rep., New York: Arno Press, 1972.

Wheeler, Sessions S. "The Records of Sessions S. 'Buck' Wheeler." Collection 99-01, Special Collections Department, Mathewson-IGT Knowledge Center, University of Nevada, Reno.

Wierzbicki, Felix Paul. *California as it is & as it May Be: or, A Guide to the Gold Region.* 1849. Rep., San Francisco: Grabhorn Press, 1933.

Wright, William (writing as Dan De Quille). *The Big Bonanza, an Authentic Account of the Discovery, History, and Working of the World-Renowned Comstock Lode of Nevada.* 1876. Rep., New York: Alfred A. Knopf, 1947.

Wright, William (writing as Dan De Quille). *A History the Comstock Silver Lode & Mines.* 1876. Rep. New York: Arno Press, 1973.

"Yellow Jacket Silver Mining Company Records, 1859-1906, vol.1." Collection NC-61, Special Collections Department, Mathewson-IGT Knowledge Center, University of Nevada, Reno.

Newspapers

Carson Morning Appeal, Carson City, NV. Microfilm #N0041, Mathewson-IGT Knowledge Center, University of Nevada, Reno.

Daily Alta California newspaper. San Francisco, CA. Microfilm #N0032, Mathewson-IGT Knowledge Center, University of Nevada, Reno.

Farley, Cory, "KNPB Reveals Historic Mansions." *Reno Gazette Journal*, 01/27/2005.

Bibliography

Gold Hill Daily News. Gold Hill, NV. Microfilm #0007. Mathewson-IGT Knowledge Center, University of Nevada, Reno; Nevada Historical Society, Reno.

Goodwin's Weekly. Utah: Salt Lake City. Library of Congress, "Chronicling America: Historic American Newspapers." http://chroniclingamerica.loc.gov/lccn/2010218519 1907-12-28/ ed-1/seq-4/

Nevada State Journal. Reno, NV. Microfilm #0006, Mathewson-IGT Knowledge Center, University of Nevada, Reno.

Nevada Territorial Enterprise. Virginia City, NV. Microfilm #0506, Mathewson-IGT Knowledge Center, University of Nevada, Reno.

New York Herald Tribune. http//www.Genealogybank.com

Pittsfield Sun. Pittsfield, MA. http//www.Genealogybank.com

Redwood City Democrat. Redwood City, CA. California State Library, Sacramento, CA. California History Room, microfilm collection.

Reno Evening Gazette. Reno, Nevada. Microfilm #0009, Mathewson-IGT Knowledge Center, University of Nevada, Reno.

Sacramento Bee. http:://www.Ancestry.com

Sacramento Daily Union & Sacramento Record-Union. California Digital Newspaper Collection, Http://cdnc.ucr.edu/cdnc.

San Francisco Call. California Digital Newspaper Collection. http://cdnc.ucr.edu/cdnc.

San Francisco Chronicle. Microfilm #N0001, Mathewson-IGT Knowledge Center, University of Nevada, Reno.

San Mateo County Gazette, Redwood City, CA. SFgenealogy.com, http://www.sfgenealogy.com/sanmateo/history/smhist.htm

San Mateo County Times-Gazette, Redwood City, CA: San Mateo County Historical Association.

Springfield Republican. Springfield, MA. Http//www.Genealogybank.com

Trinity Times, (1854 – 1855); *Trinity Journal*, (1856-1860), Weaverville CA.

Microfilm

California State Library, Sacramento CA.

Virginia Evening Bulletin. Virginia City, NV. Microfilm #N0473, Mathewson-IGT Knowledge Center, University of Nevada, Reno.

Bibliography

Secondary Sources

Ansari, Mary B. *Comstock Place Names: The Names of Storey County, Nevada.* Reno: Camp Nevada, 1986.

Balf, Todd. *The Darkest Jungle: The True Story of the Darién Expedition and America's Ill-Fated Race to Connect the Seas.* New York: Crown Publishers, 2003.

Beebe, Lucius, and Charles Clegg. *Steamcars to the Comstock.* Berkeley: Howell-North, 1957.

- - -. *Virginia & Truckee: A Story of Virginia City and Comstock Times.* 1949. Rep. Berkeley: Howell-North, 1963.

Berkshire Family History Association. "Berkshire Genealogist Quarterly." Pittsfield, MA: The Association, Spring 2003.

Biltz, Norman Henry. *Memoirs of "The Duke of Nevada:" Developments of Lake Tahoe, California, and Nevada; Reminiscences of Nevada Political and Financial Life.* Reno, NV: Oral History Project, Center for Western North American Studies, University of Nevada System, 1960.

Bridges, Hal. "The Robber Baron Concept in American History," *The Business History Review,* vol. 32, no. 1, Spring 1958. Cambridge, MA: The President and Fellows of Harvard College, Harvard University.

Clemings, Russell. *Mirage: The False Promise of Desert Agriculture.* San Francisco: Sierra Books, 1996.

Cloud, Roy W. *History of San Mateo County California, Vol. I.* Chicago: S. J. Clark Publishing, 1928.

Cross, Ralph Herbert. *The Early Inns of California, 1844-1869.* San Francisco: Cross & Brandt, 1954.

Dana, Julian. *The Man Who Built San Francisco: A Study of Ralston's Journey with Banners.* New York: Macmillan, 1936.

Dangberg, Grace. *Conflict on the Carson: A Study of Water Litigation in Western Nevada.* Minden NV: Carson Valley Historical Society, 1975.

Davis, Samuel P. *History of Nevada, vol. 1.* 1913. Rep., Las Vegas: Nevada Publishers, 1984.

DeGroot, Henry. *The Comstock Papers.* Donald Dickerson, ed. Dangberg Historical Series, Reno, NV: Grace Dangberg Foundation, 1985.

"Dr. R. O. Tripp Monograph." Redwood City, CA: San Mateo County, CA Historical Association.

Drury, Wells, and Ella Bishop Drury. *An Editor on the Comstock.* New York: Farrar & Rinehart, 1936.

Earl, Phillip I. "The Last of the Old Tahoe Fleet." *Nevada in the West* magazine, vol. 2, no. 1, Spring 2011.

Bibliography

Edwards, Jerome. "Comstock Lode." Nevada Humanities, Online Nevada Encyclopedia, http://onlinenevada.org/comstock_lode.

"Encyclopedia of San Francisco." Online. San Francisco Historical Society. http://sfhistoryencyclopedia.com/

Ferrell, Mallory Hope. "Slim Princess." Reprinted on Owens Valley History website. http://www.owensvalleyhistory.com/stories2/slim_princess.pdf

Frady, Steve. "Duane Bliss and his Lake Tahoe Railroad," *Nevadan* magazine. *Las Vegas Review-Journal*, 05/29/1977.

Galloway, John Debo. *Early Engineering Works Contributory to the Comstock*. University of Nevada Bulletin, vol. XLI, no. 5, June 1947, "Geology and Mining Series No. 45." Reno: Nevada State Bureau of Mines and the Mackay School of Mines.

Goodwin, C. C. *As I Remember Them*. Salt Lake City: Salt Lake Commercial Club, 1913.

Gorham, Harry M. *My Memories of the Comstock*. Los Angeles: Suttonhouse Publishing, 1939.

Hill, Leslie Kibler. "The Historical Archaeology of Ethnic Woodcutters in the Carson Range." Master of Arts Thesis, University of Nevada, Reno, 1987.

Hill, Mary. *Gold: The California Story*. Berkeley: University of California Press, 1999.

Hoover, Mildred Brooke, and Douglas E. Kyle. *Historic Spots in California*. Palo Alto: Stanford University Press, 1990.

Irvine, Leigh H., ed. *History of the New California, Its Resources and People*. Vol. II. New York: Lewis Publishing Co., 1905.

Jackson, Joseph Henry. *Anybody's Gold: The Story of California's Mining Towns*. New York: D. Appleton Co., 1941.

James, George Wharton. *The Lake of the Sky, Lake Tahoe, in the High Sierras of California and Nevada; its History, Indians, Discovery by Fremont*. 1915. Rep., *Lake of the Sky: Lake Tahoe*. Chicago: Charles T. Powner Co., 1956.

James, Ronald M. *Castle in the Sky: George Whittell, Jr. and the Thunderbird Lodge*. Lake Tahoe, NV: Thunderbird Lodge Preservation Society, 2005.

---. "Online Nevada Encyclopedia." Nevada Humanities, The State of Nevada Department of Education, Carson City, NV.

---. *Roar and the Silence: A History of Virginia City and the Comstock Lode*. Wilbur S. Shepperson Series in History and Humanities. Reno: University of Nevada Press, 1998.

James, Ronald M., and C. Elizabeth Raymond, eds. *Comstock Women*. Wilbur S. Shepperson Series in History and Humanities. Reno: University of Nevada Press, 1998.

Kneiss, Gilbert H. *Bonanza Railroads*. Palo Alto: Stanford University Press, 1943.

BIBLIOGRAPHY

Kroninger, Robert H. *Sarah and the Senator.* Berkeley: Howell – North, 1964.

Lavender, David. *Nothing Seemed Impossible: William C. Ralston and Early San Francisco.* Palo Alto: American West Publishing, 1975.

Lillard, Richard G. *Desert Challenge: An Interpretation of Nevada.* New York: Alfred Knopf, 1942.

Lindstrom, Susan G. "Archaeological Survey of 1830 Acres Between Spooner Summit and Marlette Lake, Lake Tahoe Nevada State Park." Vol. I. Davis, CA: Far Western Anthropological Group, 2001.

Lyman, George D. *Ralston's Ring: California Plunders the Comstock Lode.* New York: Charles Scribner's Sons, 1937.

Makley, Michael J. *The Infamous King of the Comstock: William Sharon and the Gilded Age in the West.* Wilbur S. Shepperson Series in Nevada History. Reno: University of Nevada Press, 2006.

---. *A Short History of Lake Tahoe.* Reno: University of Nevada Press, 2011.

Malnati, Gwenda Gustafson. Bliss family genealogist, Athens, GA.

Marryat, Frank, *Mountains and Molehills: or Recollections of a Burnt Journal.* Philadelphia: Lippincott, 1962.

Maskell, Coramarie. "History of Woodside and the Woodside Library Association." Monograph # 447, 1942. San Mateo County, CA Historical Museum archives, Redwood City CA.

Marye, George Thomas. *From '49 to '83 in California and Nevada: Chapters from the Life of George Thomas Marye, A Pioneer of '49.* San Francisco: A. M. Robertson, 1923.

McCullough, David. *The Path Between the Seas: The Creation of the Panama Canal, 1870-1914.* New York: Simon and Schuster, 1977.

McGuinness, Aims. *Path of Empire: Panama and the California Gold Rush.* "United States in the World" series. Ithaca, NY: Cornell University Press, 2008.

McKeon, Owen F. *The Railroads and Steamers of Lake Tahoe.* San Mateo, CA: The Western Railroader, 1946.

Moreno, Richard. *A Short History of Carson City.* Reno: University of Nevada Press, 2011.

Muir, John. *The Wilderness World of John Muir.* Boston: Houghton Mifflin, 1954.

Myrick, David. F. *Railroads of Nevada and Eastern California.* Vol. 1. Berkeley: Howell-North Books, 1962-63.

Nash, Roderick. *Wilderness and the American Mind.* New Haven: Yale University Press, 1967.

Nevada State Bureau of Mines. *Individual Histories of the Mines of the Comstock.* Reno NV: Nevada State Bureau of Mines and W.P.A. Nevada State Writer's Project, 1942.

BIBLIOGRAPHY

Oliver, Gordon E. *The History of Early Banking in Nevada, 1859-1900*. MBA Thesis. Reno: University of Nevada, 1983.

Parker, Matthew. *Panama Fever: The Epic Story of One of the Greatest Achievements of All Time—the Building of the Panama Canal*. New York: Doubleday, 2007.

Phinney, Jane Benedict. *Taking the High Road: A Two Hundred Year History of a Hilltown, Savoy, Massachusetts, 1797-1997*. Savoy, MA: Self Published, 1997.

Pisani, Donald J. "Lost Parkland: Lumbering & Park Proposals in the Tahoe-Truckee Basin."*Journal of Forest History*, vol. 21, no. 1, January 1977. Forest History Society, Durham, NC.

"Pyramid Lake War." Online Nevada Encyclopedia, Department of Humanities, State of Nevada, Carson City NV. http://www.onlinenevada.org

Rasmussen, Louis J. *San Francisco Passenger Lists*, vol. 1. Colma, CA: "San Francisco Historic Record & Genealogy Bulletin," 1965.

Ratay, Myra Sauer. *Pioneers of the Ponderosa: How Washoe Valley Rescued the Comstock*. Sparks, NV: Western Printing, 1973.

Regnery, Dorothy F. *An Enduring Heritage: Historic Buildings of the San Francisco Peninsula*. Palo Alto: Stanford University Press, 1976.

---. "Parkhurst's Woodside," *La Peninsula*, Journal of the San Mateo County Historical Association, vol. XXIV, no. 1, June 1987. Redwood City, CA.

Richards, Gilbert. *Crossroads: People and Events of the Redwoods of San Mateo County*. Woodside, CA: Gilbert Richards Publications, 1973.

Robinson, Judith. *The Hearsts: An American Dynasty*. Newark DE: University of Delaware Press, 1991.

Rocha, Guy. "Myth #79 – Nineteenth-Century Presidential Visits to Lake Tahoe and Nevada." "Historical Myth a Month" series. Nevada State Library and Archives, Carson City, NV.
http://nsla.nevadaculture.org/index.php?option=com_content&view=article&id=683&   Itemid=510.

Scott, Edward B. *The Saga of Lake Tahoe. Vol. 1*. 1957. Rep. Pebble Beach, CA: Sierra-Tahoe Publishing Co., 1994.

---. *The Saga of Lake Tahoe, Vol. 2*. Crystal Bay, NV: Sierra-Tahoe Publishing, 1985.

Smith, Grant H. *History of The Comstock Lode, 1850-1920*. Reno: Nevada Bureau of Mines and Geology, 1943.

Solury, Theresa E. "Everlasting Remembrance: The Archaeology of 19th Century Chinese Labor in the Western Lumber Industry." Master's thesis, University of Nevada, Reno, 2004.

Stanger, Frank M. *Sawmills in the Redwoods: Logging on the San Francisco Peninsula, 1849-1967*. Redwood City, CA: San Mateo County Historical Association, 1967.

BIBLIOGRAPHY

Stanley, Maitland. *A Guide to Gold Hill, Nevada.* Virginia City, NV: Susy & Livy Publications, 2009.

State of Nevada Division of Water Resources. "Truckee River Chronology," Parts II and III.
http://water.nv.gov/mapping/chronologies/truckee/part2.cfm.

Stollery, David J., Jr. *More Tales of Tahoe: Lake Tahoe History, Legend and Description.* Encino, CA: Self Published, 1988.

Strong, Douglas H. *Dreamers and Defenders: American Conservationists.* Lincoln: University of Nebraska Press, 1988.

---. "Preservation Efforts at Lake Tahoe, 1880 – 1980." *Journal of Forest History,* vol. 25, April 1981. Forest History Society, Durham, NC.

---. *Tahoe, An Environmental History.* Lincoln: University of Nebraska Press, 1984.

Tilton, Cecil G. *William Chapman Ralston, Courageous Builder.* Boston: Christopher Publishing, 1935.

Tobey, Rufus Babcock, and Charles Henry Pope. *Tobey (Tobie, Toby) Genealogy: Thomas, of Sandwich and James, of Kittery and Their Descendants.* Boston: Charles H. Pope, 1905.

Townley, John M. *Turn This Water Into Gold: The Story of the Newlands Project.* Reno: Nevada Historical Society, 1977.

United States Department of Agriculture, Forest Service. "Highlights in the History of Forest Conservation." Agriculture Information Bulletin no. 83, March 1976. Washington, D.C.: U.S. Government Printing Office, 1976.

United States Department of the Interior, National Park Service. "National Register of Historic Places Inventory—Nomination Form." Virginia City Historic District, 1966.

Vogel, Ed. "Remembering a basket weaver's magic." *Las Vegas Review-Journal,* 08/27/2001. Las Vegas, NV.

Wheeler, Sessions S., and William W. Bliss. *Tahoe Heritage: The Bliss Family of Glenbrook, Nevada.* Reno NV: University of Nevada Press, 1992.

Wilson, Dick. *Sawdust Trails in the Truckee Basin: A History of Lumbering Operations.* Nevada City, CA: Nevada County Historical Society, 1992.

Wurm, Ted, and Harre W. Demoro. *The Silver Short Line: A History of the Virginia & Truckee Railroad.* Glendale, CA: Trans-Anglo Books, 1983.

Zanjani, Sally. *Devils Will Reign: How Nevada Began.* Reno, NV: University of Nevada Press, 2006.

Index

A

Alford Company, 38
The Alta California, 14, 32, 88
Angel, Myron, 84
Annie (ship), 154
Armstrong, Jack, 129
Arnold & Blauvelt, 60
Atwood, Melville, 32

B

Baker, William H., 38-39, 47, 60-61
Baldwin Locomotive Works of Philadelphia, 110
Baldwin, Alexander, 72
Baldwin, E.J. "Lucky", 104, 150
Bancroft Library, 13
Bancroft, Hubert Howe, 13-14, 18, 24, 27, 37, 73-74, 81, 83
Bank of California, 58-65, 67-68, 70, 73-75, 81, 85-86, 93, 98, 149
The Bank Ring, 57, 62-68, 70, 72-73, 75, 78, 82-85, 89-91, 93, 98, 149
Barnes Hotel, 61
Barney, Deborah, 4
Barron, William E., 72
Bates, Dexter B., 4

Belcher Mine, 93
Belknap, C.H., 121
Bell, Thomas, 72
Blaisdel, Henry, 88
Blauvelt, W.H., 60-61, 67
Bliss Mansion, 91, 169
Bliss, Belle Matilda, 23, 29
Bliss, Charles Tobey, 69, 150, 154, 163, 171
Bliss, Duane Leroy Sr.
  as bank cashier, 61
  as banker, 47, 61, 67
  birth of, 1
  birth of daughter(s), 22-23, 79
  birth of son(s), 69, 90, 101
  as cabin boy, 5
  as conservationist, 133, 135-136, 143-145
  death of, 169
  death of father, 129
  death of mother, 4
  death of oldest daughter, 28
  death of second daughter, 23
  death of first wife, 23
  education of, 3
  engagement to Elizabeth Thatcher Tobey, 45
  estate of, 169
  as foreman of meat market, 73

INDEX

as Freemason, 167
as general supply agent (V&T), 78-79
as gold miner, 17-18, 27
journey to California, 8, 10-12
Lake Tahoe Railway and Transportation Company, incorporates, 154
Lake Tahoe Transportation Company, incorporates, 150
as lumberman, 77, 84, 89
marriage to first wife, 20
marriage to second wife, 48
as mill manager, 45
as mill superintendent, 38-39
moves to Utah Territory, 27
parent(s) of, 1, 3-4, 6, 8, 20, 39, 75, 129
as paymaster, 75
as schoolteacher, 3, 6, 8
as store clerk, 20, 22-23
Tahoe Tavern Resort – opens, 160
Truckee and Lake Tahoe Railroad Company, incorporates, 155
as trustee of newspaper, 97
as Vice President of Carson & Colorado Railroad, 125
visit to Massachusetts, 45, 75
Bliss, Duane Leroy Jr., 101, 150, 154, 157, 163-164, 168, 171-172
Bliss, Eliza S. (Bates), 4
Bliss, Elizabeth Thatcher (Tobey), 45, 48-52, 54, 57, 69, 77, 79, 81, 101, 112, 118, 122, 126, 128, 152-154, 157, 167, 169-170
Bliss, Hatherly, 172
Bliss, Hope Danforth, 3-4, 6, 8, 67, 74, 79, 93, 109, 142-144, 169, 171
Bliss, Lucia Mary, 22, 24, 27-29

Bliss, Lucia Mary (Barney), 1, 3-4
Bliss, Mabel, 157
Bliss, Mary Elizabeth (Healy), 20, 22-23
Bliss, Newell, 4-5
Bliss, Thomas, 1
Bliss, Walter Danforth, 90, 150, 153-154, 159, 163-164, 169, 171-172
Bliss, Will M., 152, 164, 172
Bliss, William, 1, 3-4, 6, 8, 20, 39, 75, 129
Bliss, William "Bill", 172-173
Bliss, William Seth, 69, 126, 150, 154-157, 163-164, 167-172
Bliss, Yerington & Co. *See* Yerington, Bliss & Co.
Bodie Toll Road Company, 125
Bohemian Club, 167
The Bonanza Firm, 97-99, 108, 114-115
Bonner, Charles, 72, 89
Bousfield, W.C., 76
Bowker Hotel, 2
Bradford, William, 136
Bridges, Hal, 67
Brockway Hotel/Resort, 172
Brooks, Sarah Merrian, 11
Browne, J. Ross, 33, 46, 48, 50
  Washoe Revisited, 48
Burt, Wellington R., 135
Business History Review - Harvard Business School, 67
Butterfield, John, 7

C

California
  Alameda, 165
  Bijou, 104, 126
  Bodie, 122, 125

INDEX

Calaveras County, 17-18
Candelaria, 125
Colma, 24
Coloma, 7
Columbia, 17
Grass Valley, 95
Hawley, 125
Hobart Mills, 163
Meyers (formerly Yanks), 126
Mokelumne Hill, 18
Nevada City, 32, 40, 130
Panamint, 125
Pasadena, 171
Piedmont, 171
Placerville, 88, 110
Redwood City, 18-21, 24
Sacramento, 23, 29, 60-62, 72, 128, 159
San Andreas Valley, 18
San Bernardino County, 124
San Francisco, 6, 8, 12-20, 23-24, 28-29, 32-33, 37-38, 46, 49, 52, 58-59, 61-63, 68, 70, 74, 83, 88, 97-98, 114, 128, 139, 145, 151-154, 157, 159, 164-165, 167, 169-171
San Jose, 18-19
San Mateo County, 19
Santa Clara, 19
Searsville, 24
Tahoe City, 113, 117-118, 146, 150, 154-155, 157, 159, 163-164, 168, 170-171
Truckee, 117, 150, 155-157, 160, 168-169
Tuolumne County, 17-18
Woodside, 18-25
California Mine, 95, 105
California State Census (1852), 17

Carnegie Steel Company, 149
Carnegie, Andrew, 149
Carson & Colorado Railroad, 125-126
Carson and Tahoe Lumber and Fluming Company (C&TL&FC), 85-87, 90-91, 93-94, 99-101, 103-104, 106, 108-110, 112-113, 115-118, 122-124, 126-127, 129-130, 138, 140, 142-146, 149-150, 154, 164-165, 172, 174-175
Carson Box Factory, 108, 127
The Carson City Appeal, 129, 164
Carson City Prison, 127
Carson Morning Appeal, 116, 118, 152, 169
Carson Range, 40, 42, 82-85, 99, 104, 109, 124, 146
Carson River, 29, 45, 48, 70-73, 75, 77, 85, 106
Carson, Christopher Houston "Kit", 86
Catalina (ship), 154
Central Pacific Railroad, 42-43, 72, 76, 101, 116, 140, 145, 159
Chollar-Potosi Mine, 65, 93
Chubbuck, George W., 104, 126
Church, Elijah, 155
Civil War, 39, 54, 57, 67, 107, 118
Clear Creek, 76, 83, 85, 89, 110
Clear Creek Canyon, 83, 85
Clemens, Orion, 6
Clemens, Samuel (Mark Twain), 6, 59, 86
Cohn, Abe, 163
Comstock Historic District, 177
Comstock Lode, 24, 27-29, 31-34, 36-43, 46-48, 51-52, 54-55, 57-65, 67-68, 70-71, 73, 76, 78, 81-85, 90-91, 93, 97-108, 110, 114-116, 121-122,

211

INDEX

124-125, 129, 133, 136-138, 142, 144, 146, 159, 164, 177
Comstock Mining, Inc., 177
Comstock, Henry, 32, 40, 88
Consolidated Virginia Mine, 94-95, 105, 123
Couillard, D., 165
Creative Act of 1891, 138
Crescent City (ship), 8
Crown Point Mine, 93
Curtis, Sam, 94-95

D

D.L. Bliss State Park, 146
Daggett, Rollin, 97
Darwin, Charles, 4
Dat-So-La-Lee, 163
Davis, Sam P., 64
Declaration of Independence, U.S., 137
Deidesheimer, Philip, 41-42, 52, 95, 121
Denney, J.J., 69
DeQuille, Dan, 59, 95, 115, 133
   The History of the Big Bonanza, 42, 46, 95, 97, 114-115, 123, 133
Dirigo Hotel, 128
Donner Lumber and Boom Company, 159
Donohoe, Ralston & Company, 62
Doten, Alf, 54, 57, 59, 77, 97
Drury Academy, 3
Drury, Nathan, 3

E

Emerald Bay, 146
Emerald I (tugboat), 113

Emerald II (tugboat), 113, 154
Estudillo, Jesus Maria, 88
Evans Creek Mill, 99

F

Fair, James, 85, 93, 97-99
Fairmont Hotel, 171
Faville, William, 154
Federal Timber Purchase Act, 137
Finney, James, 31-32
Fleischmann, Max C., 172
Flood, James, 93, 98-99
Fort Homestead, 57, 77
Found Treasure Mining Company, 129
Free Timber Act (1878), 137
Freemasons Society, 55
Fremont, John, 86
Fry, John, 72

G

Gardner, Matthew, 103, 126
General Land Office (GLO), 145
Genoa Enterprise, 88
Gilpin, William, 136
Glenbrook (locomotive), 110, 130-131
Glenbrook Development Company, 171
Glenbrook Golf Course, 172
Glenbrook House, 87-89
Glenbrook Improvement Company, 164, 172
Glenbrook Inn (and Ranch), 165-166, 169, 172-173
Gold Hill Hotel, 51
Gold Hill News, 52, 57, 60, 77, 103, 115

INDEX

Gold Rush - California, 7-8, 14, 17-19, 37
Goodman, Joe, 114
Goodwin, C.C. "Charlie", 59, 68-69, 105
Goodwin's Weekly, 169
Gorham, Harry, 121
Governor Blaisdel (ship), 88
Granlibaken, 157
Grant, Julia (Dent), 118
Grant, Ulysses S., 57, 117-118, 138
Great Depression, 172, 174
Greer, Lucas, 22
Gregory-Riddle Mill, 42
Gruell, George E., 141
   Fire in Sierra Nevada Forests: A Photographic Interpretation of Ecological Change Since 1849, 141

H

Hale Mine, 93
Haley, J.U., 164
Hawk Eye Mining Co., 61
Hawthorne Army Depot, 126
Hayes, Lucy (Webb), 118
Hayes, Rutherford B., 118
Hayward, Alvinza, 64, 72, 93
Hearst, George, 41
Henderson, Aleck, 31
Hetch Hetchy, 139
Hetch Hetchy Valley, 139
Hobart, Walter, 115, 126, 135-136, 174
Holmes & Logan Company, 38
Homestead Act of 1862, 137
Hope Valley, 82
Hopkins, Mark, 159
Humboldt, Alexander Georg von, 5
Huntington Hotel, 171

I

Imperial Mine, 52
International Hotel, 121
Isthmus Over Route, 7-8, 10

J

James, George Wharton, 157, 161, 165
   The Lake of the Sky—Lake Tahoe, 157
James, Isaac E., 73, 76
James, Ronald, 31, 46, 65, 97
James, Ronald M. & C. Elizabeth Raymond
   Comstock Women, 52
Jellerson Hotel, 128, 165
Jellerson, Amanda Jane, 128
Jellerson, Frank, 128, 169
Jewett, William Smith, 15
Jones, John E., 152
Jones, John P., 83, 93, 97

K

Kendall, F.I., 154-155
Kentuck Mine, 93
Keyser, Charley, 163
Keyser, Louisa, 163
King's Canyon National Park, 87, 89, 138
Kirby, John Henry, 135
Knox, C.W., 38

INDEX

L

Lake Bigler, 86-88
Lake Bigler Forestry Commission, 138
Lake Bigler Lumber Company, 86
Lake Shore House, 88, 129, 165
Lake Superior, 36
Lake Tahoe, 16, 24, 82, 85-87, 89, 101, 103-104, 110, 112, 116, 118, 126, 130, 133, 135, 142-144, 146, 150, 152-155, 157, 159, 161, 164-165, 167, 169, 170-172, 175
Lake Tahoe Forest Reserve, 144-145
Lake Tahoe National Park, 145-146
Lake Tahoe Railway and Transportation Company, 111-112, 118, 145, 150, 154-155, 157, 163-164, 167
Lake Tahoe Transportation Company, 150, 154
Lake Valley Railroad, 126, 154
Lane, Don, 143-144, 147
Lavender, David, 61, 65
Lee, Robert E., 57
Lillard, Richard Gordon
  The Desert Challenge: An Interpretation of Nevada, 142
Lincoln, Abraham, 54, 57
Lindauer & Hirschman, 45
Linnard Company, 171
Linnard, D.M., 170-171
Lord, Eliot, 42, 105
Lucerne Pit Mine, 177
Lyman, George, 62, 74

M

Mackay Silver Collection, 95
Mackay, John, 42, 46, 85, 93-99, 105
Mackay, Marie-Louise, 96
Makley, Michael, 58, 65, 83, 97
Manifest Destiny, 136, 143
Mark Hopkins Hotel, 171
Marlette Lake, 109-110, 150
Massachusetts
  Adams, 129
  Berkshire Hills, 1
  Boston, 11, 15-16, 20, 51
  Cape Cod, 45
  North Adams, 3, 74-75
  Pittsfield, 4-5, 74
  Savoy, 1-5, 8, 20, 39, 74
  Savoy Hollow, 1-2, 20, 129
  South Wareham, 45
  Wareham, 48, 170
  Worcester, 20
Massachusetts Institute of Technology (MIT), 126, 153-154, 157
Masten, N.K., 154-155
Mayflower (ship), 136
Maynard, H.G., 47
McCullough, David, 7
McLane, Louis, 98
McLaughlin, Patrick, 32, 40, 124-125
McMasters, H.G., 170
Meek's Bay, 116
Melville, Herman, 5
Mercantile Trust Company, 157
Meteor (tugboat), 112-113, 116-118, 154, 171
Miller, Joaquin, 158

INDEX

Mills, Darius Ogden, 17, 62, 65, 68-69, 72-73, 81, 85-86, 88-90, 99, 115, 125, 127, 174
Miners' Foundry, 38
Mokelumne River, 17-18
Monk, Hank, 110, 118
Morgan, Captain Henry, 10
Morris, Minerva, 52
Mt. Rainier National Park, 138
Muir, John, 88, 135, 139, 141, 145
Murphy, James, 116-117

N

Nevada (and Nevada Territory)
  American City, 74
  Carson City, 48, 54, 74-77, 79, 85, 89-91, 93, 101, 103-104, 107, 109-112, 116, 118, 121-122, 125-128, 130, 142, 163, 165, 169-170
  Dayton, 45
  Douglas County, 101
  Eagle Valley, 163
  El Dorado County, 101
  Elko County, 129
  Empire, 75
  Empire City, 48
  Esmeralda County, 126
  Glenbrook, 83, 85-89, 91, 103-104, 106-110, 112, 117-118, 122, 126, 128-130, 143-144, 149-150, 152, 154, 156, 159, 164-165, 168, 171-173
  Gold Hill, 27, 29, 31, 33-34, 37-39, 45-50, 52, 54-55, 57, 60-61, 63, 69-70, 74, 76-77, 79, 97, 103, 107, 177
  Hawthorne, 126
  Johntown, 31
  Lyon County, 79, 177
  Mineral County, 126
  Mound House, 125
  Ormsby County, 73, 79, 85, 101
  Placer County, 101
  Reno (Lake's Crossing), 72, 76, 79, 98, 99, 118, 169
  Silver City, 27, 33-34, 37, 49-50, 52, 54, 74, 177
  Storey County, 54, 73, 79, 118, 177
  Truckee Meadows, 29, 32-33, 99, 105
  Verdi, 82
  Virginia City, 24, 27, 29, 32-34, 37, 39, 42, 46-47, 50, 52, 54-55, 58, 60-61, 63, 69, 73-77, 79, 83, 97, 103, 105-107, 116, 118, 121, 177
  Washoe, 24, 29, 37, 39, 79, 82, 124
  Washoe County, 101
  Washoe Valley, 40
Nevada (ship), 171
Nevada Bank of San Francisco, 98
Nevada Bureau of Mines and Geology, 108
Nevada County Narrow Gauge Railroad Museum, 130
Nevada State Capital, 91
Nevada State Journal, 98, 123, 127
Nevada State Museum, 130
Nevada State Orphans Home, 91
Nevada State Prison, 91
Nevada State Railroad Museum, 130
New Orleans (ship), 62
New York
  Buffalo, 13
  New York City, 4-5, 8, 15, 125, 154
The New York Tribune, 99

215

INDEX

Norcross Mine, 93
Nye, James, 88

O

O'Brien, William, 93, 98
O'Riley, Peter, 32, 40, 124
Ogden, William B., 135
Olmsted, Frederick Law, 135
Ophir Diggings, 32
Ophir Mine, 32, 37, 40-42, 63, 105, 121
Oriental Quartz Mill, 36
Ott, J.J., 33

P

Pacific Improvement Company, 159
Pacific Union Club, 167
Pacific Wood, Lumber and Flume Company, 99
Parkhurst, Matthias Alfred, 18-24, 81
Patten, Amos, 135
Paul, Almarin B., 36-39, 45-47, 52, 60-61, 69, 81
Pennsylvania State University Department of Geography, Earth and Environmental Systems Institute, 146
Penrod, Immanuel, 32, 40
Phinney, Jane Benedict, 1, 4
Pinchot, Gifford, 145
Pisani, Donald J., 133
Pomin, Ernest John, 118-119, 164
Potter, Albert F., 145
Pray, Augustus W., 85-88, 106-107, 109, 165

Presidio, 19
Public Lands Commission, 141-142
Pyramid Lake, 27
Pyramid Lake War, 27

R

Ralston, James, 59-61
Ralston, William Chapman, 58-60, 62-63, 65, 67-70, 72-75, 78, 81-82, 89, 98-99
Ramsey, Alexander, 118
Rasmussen, Louis J.
    San Francisco Passenger Lists, 14
Rattler (locomotive), 156
Redwood City Democrat, 24
Redwood Embarcadero, 19, 21
Regnery, Dorothy, 23
Requa, I.L., 155
Requa, M.L., 155
Richards, John S., 85
Rigby, James A., 83, 85-86, 91, 109
Ryder, James "Grizzly", 19

S

The Sacramento Union, 42, 116, 152, 169
Sadler, Reinhold, 152
The Salt Lake Tribune, 59
San Francisco Bay, 98, 154
San Francisco Bulletin, 42
San Francisco Call, 42, 155-156, 160, 165, 169
San Francisco Examiner, 97
San Francisco Mining Exchange, 61
San Francisco Mint, 75

Index

San Mateo County Historical Association, 22
Sarah & Eliza (ship), 14, 153
Savoy School, 3, 6, 8
Scott, E.B., 89, 112, 129
Scott, J.F., 32
Second Voyage of HMS *Beagle*, 4
Seward, William, 88
Sharon, William, 58-61, 63-65, 67-70, 72-79, 81-84, 86, 88-90, 93, 97-99, 115, 125, 149
Sherman, William Tecumseh, 118
Sierra Club, 139, 145
Sierra Nevada, 7, 29, 31, 33-34, 40, 43, 71, 82, 85, 88, 108, 133, 135, 140, 145, 147
Sierra Nevada Wood & Lumber Company, 115, 126, 164, 174
Sierra Realty Company, 170
Silver Party, 152
Silver Vale Mining Co., 61
Skae, Johnnie "Little Napoleon", 121
Skelton, Emaline, 23
Smith, Grant H., 54, 78, 84, 105, 108, 114, 122
Snake River, 157
Southern Development Company of Nevada, 125
Southern Pacific Company, 125, 170
Southern Pacific Railroad, 126, 150
Spooner Summit, 83, 85, 104, 108-110, 118, 122, 130
Spooner Summit Flume, 108
Spooner, Camille, 129
Spooner, Michele, 85
Squaw Valley, 157, 159, 172
SS *Tahoe* (ship), 151-152, 160, 168, 171
St. John's Episcopal Church, 54
St. Mary in the Mountains Catholic Church, 105
St. Patrick's Catholic Church, 54
Stanford, Leland, 88, 159
Stateler & Arrington, 58
Stephens, John Lloyd, 4
Stevenson, Charlie, 121
Stewart, William J., 97, 146, 157
Stoneman, James, 138
Strong, Douglas, 137, 142, 146
Summit Flume Company, 76, 83, 85
Summit Mill, 106
Sun Mountain, 29-31, 33-34, 36, 40, 42, 45-47, 50, 72, 91, 97-98, 101, 103, 105-107, 124, 128, 177
Sunderland, Thomas, 72
Sutro, Adolph, 70, 75, 78, 97, 126
Sutter's Mill, 7
Swansea Mill, 64

T

Tahoe (locomotive), 110, 130-131, 156
Tahoe (tugboat), 119, 154, 171
Tahoe Basin, 84, 86, 101, 104, 109, 115, 124, 130, 133, 136, 138, 140, 142-146, 150, 167, 174
Tahoe Tavern Resort, 158-164, 166, 168-172
Tahoe Tavern Heights, 170
Tallac (ship), 150, 154, 171
Tallac House Hotel, 150
Taylor, Alan H., 146
Territorial Enterprise, 34, 59, 76, 86, 95, 97-98, 105, 107, 112, 116, 133, 169
Thoreau, Henry David, 135
Thunderbird Lodge, 175

INDEX

Thunderbird Lodge Preservation Society, 175
Tiffany & Co., 96
Timber and Stone Culture Act (1878), 137
Timber Culture Act of 1873, 101, 140
Tobey, Charles T., 155
Tobey, Curtis E., 48
Tobey, Lucinda, 45
Tobey, Seth Fish, 45, 48, 52
Tobey, Thomas, 48
Tobey, Walter Danforth, 48, 125-126, 150, 154-155, 163
Transportation Club, 167
Tripp, Robert Orville, 19-24, 81
Tritle, Frederick, 72
Truckee and Lake Tahoe Railroad Company, 155
Truckee Lumber Company, 157, 164
The Truckee Republican, 116
Truckee River, 27, 29, 79, 157, 163
Tuolumne River, 139

U

U.S. Department of Agriculture Forest Service, 136, 143, 145, 173-174
U.S. Mint, 75, 91
Union Mill and Mining Company, 65, 71
Union Mine and Milling Company, 98
Union Pacific Railroad, 168
United States Census (1860), 27
United States Census (1870), 79
United States Exploring Expedition, 5
University of California, 13
University of Nebraska Press, 143
University of Nevada, Reno, 95

V

Vesey, G.H., 51
Virginia & Truckee River Rail Road Company (V&T), 14, 67, 72-79, 82, 84-85, 89-91, 99, 103, 106-107, 109, 115-116, 125, 127, 150, 169
Virginia and Gold Hill Water Company, 82, 98, 110, 121
Virginia City & Carson River Railroad, 72
Virginia Savings Bank, 98

W

W.M. Keck Museum, 95
Walker Lake Corporation, 125
Walker Lake Wood and Lumber Company, 125
Wallers Defeat Co., 61
Walsh, James, 40, 95
Washoe Gold and Silver Mining Company, 37, 52
Washoe Quartz Mill, 38, 45
The Washoe Times, 59
Wells Fargo & Co. Express and Banking Company, 46
Western Union Company, 164
Weyerhaeuser, Frederick, 135
Wheeler, Sessions, 165
White, William A., 69
Whittell, George, 172, 174-175
Wierzbicki, Felix Paul, 17
  California as it is & as it May be A Guide to the Gold Region, 16
Wild Goose (ship), 154
Wilkes, Charles, 5

INDEX

Wilson, Dick, 42, 108
Wood, W.S., 155
Woodside Dell Temperance Society, 23
Woodside Store, 19-24
Woodside Store Museum, 25
Wright, William, 31, 133, 135, 141

Y

Yellow Jacket Mining Company, 64-65, 68, 73, 93
Yellowstone National Park, 138
Yerington, Bliss & Co., 85, 112
Yerington, E.B., 125
Yerington, Henry Marvin, 74-77, 83-86, 89-91, 99, 124-125, 127, 144, 169, 174
Yosemite Grant, 139
Yosemite National Park, 139
Yount, Jack, 31

About the Author

A native of Burlington, Vermont, Jack Harpster was raised in Memphis, Tennessee and graduated from the University of Wisconsin in 1959 with a Bachelor of Science degree in Journalism. He spent 27 years in Southern California in the newspaper business, and then moved to Las Vegas in 1986. There he spent 17 years on the business management side of the city's two newspapers. Jack retired in 2002, and began writing as a hobby. He and his wife Cathy moved to Reno in 2006.

This is Jack Harpster's eighth non-fiction book, all in the personal or institutional biography genre. He has also published dozens of essays and articles on history and biography in national and local journals and magazines.

www.ingramcontent.com/pod-product-compliance
Lightning Source LLC
Chambersburg PA
CBHW050551160426
43199CB00015B/2613